Courage and Conscience

John Swett Rock (1825–1866), abolition activist, practiced medicine, dentistry, and law in Boston, and was the first black allowed to practice before the U.S. Supreme Court. The Boston Athenæum.

Courage and Conscience

BLACK & WHITE ABOLITIONISTS IN BOSTON

Edited by Donald M. Jacobs

Published for the Boston Athenæum by
INDIANA UNIVERSITY PRESS • BLOOMINGTON • INDIANAPOLIS

The paper used in this publication meets the minimum requirements of American National Standard for Information Sciences—Permanence of Paper for Printed Library Materials, ANSI Z39.48-1984.

Manufactured in the United States of America

Library of Congress Cataloging-in-Publication Data
Courage and conscience : Black and white abolitionists in Boston /
    edited by Donald M. Jacobs.
        p.   cm.
        Includes bibliographical references and index.
        ISBN 0-253-33198-6 (cl : alk. paper). — ISBN 0-253-20793-2 (pa :
    alk. paper)
        1. Slavery—United States—Anti-slavery movements.
    2. Abolitionists—Massachusetts—Boston. 3. Boston (Mass.)—Race
    relations.   I. Jacobs, Donald M.
E449.C86   1993
973.7'114—dc20   92-31395

1 2 3 4 5 97 96 95 94 93

✧ CONTENTS

✧ FOREWORD

These essays are a welcome addition to the history of African Americans in the city of Boston as well as, indeed, to the history of the city itself and of abolitionism. As one reads them, several significant points stand out. One is that although their numbers were small, as compared with those of Philadelphia and New York, Boston's African Americans were a cohesive, compact group, sharing common aspirations, values, and institutions.

Another point is that despite their cohesiveness—or perhaps because of it—they could support those among them who assumed leadership roles. When it became clear that they had their own leaders and spokespersons, it was a rather humbling experience for others, such as William Lloyd Garrison, to discover that African Americans could be articulate, eloquent, *and* independent.

Men and women such as Maria Stewart, David Walker, Leonard Grimes, and William Cooper Nell shared an independence in their thoughts and words that revealed how far they were willing to go to secure equality and justice. Walker's *Appeal* was a dramatic call to rally against tyranny. Maria Stewart pointed the way for women, black and white alike, to speak out for their rights. William Cooper Nell, the historian of the group, reminded white Americans everywhere that they had achieved no victories without the aid of their black brothers.

A significant factor contributing to the viability and effectiveness of Boston's African American community was its institutions, religious and civic. They helped keep alive the fight for desegregated schools, the vibrant activism that did so much for the abolitionist movement, and the telling of the story of the barbarism of slavery.

These essays are a tribute to the black Bostonians of the antebellum years and an inspiration to their successors, who have their own responsibilities in the active promotion of equality of justice.

JOHN HOPE FRANKLIN

✧ PREFACE

Between 1822 and 1849, during the height of abolition activity in Boston, the Boston Athenæum occupied the former James Perkins mansion on Pearl Street, barely a quarter of a mile from William Lloyd Garrison's *Liberator* office and the headquarters of the Massachusetts Anti-Slavery Society in Cornhill, and black abolitionist David Walker's clothing store on old Brattle Street. Half a mile separated Pearl Street from the north slope of Beacon Hill, the home of much of the city's black population and the site of the African Meeting House and several stops on the Underground Railroad. The works of abolition leaders such as Lydia Maria Child, Wendell Phillips, David Walker, Theodore Weld, and John Greenleaf Whittier were no doubt much discussed in the Athenæum, and these writings joined the large numbers of contemporary books, pamphlets, and broadsides that were added to Athenæum collections during these years, collections that reflect the seriousness with which Librarian Seth Bass and his colleagues took the events of this turbulent period of Boston and the nation's history. It is clear that the struggle for emancipation, and to a somewhat lesser extent the growing conflicts relating to the status of women and other reform issues, were seen by Athenæum librarians as movements of major historical significance. The collection they amassed, both by gift and by purchase, richly documents this volatile time.

The exhibition on view in the Athenæum Gallery, "Righteousness Exalteth a Nation: Abolition in Boston from 1829 to Emancipation," and this accompanying collection of essays grew out of an earlier exhibition entitled "Black Bostonians: Two Hundred Years of Community and Culture," which was on display at the Athenæum between February and March 1988. The process of reexamining and classifying the Athenæum's collection of early material on slavery and abolition is one that continues to produce rich fruits, as will be seen in the exhibition and in this book of essays on Boston abolition that the Athenæum has commissioned to accompany it. It is both instructive and enlightening to see what a comparatively small number of blacks and whites, working together, were able to do in a remarkably short span of time to help bring down the "peculiar institution" of slavery. There is much to be learned from their experience, and the Athenæum is pleased to be part of this most recent cooperative effort to carry the process forward.

The planning phase of this project has extended over several years, and we have a great many people to thank for their help and participation. Our planning efforts were supported by a generous grant from the National Endowment for the Humanities, a Federal Agency. We are also grateful for the support of the Massachusetts Cultural Council, as administered by the Boston Arts Lottery Council, and the Boston Globe Foundation. The Museum of Afro-American History and its Executive Director, Monica A. Fairbairn, have worked with us from the beginning on virtually every aspect of the planning phase of this project; the Honorary Chairman of the Museum's Board of Trustees Henry Hampton also provided valuable advice. Commissioner Bruce P. Rossley and Deputy Director Susan Hehir from the Mayor's Office of the Arts and Humanities were consistently helpful in their desire to involve City Hall in the project, and were enthusiastic about our use of an area of City Hall for part of our exhibition. Raymond L. Flynn, Mayor of Boston, and Suffolk University President David J. Sargent provided support and encouragement.

In the early planning days of this project, we were guided by a group who, collectively and individually, aimed us in the appropriate direction: Ruth Batson, Mary Bullard, Edward Clark, Deborah Clifford, Adelaide Cromwell, Edward Gittleman, Marilyn Richardson, Byron Rushing, Joan Shurcliff, and William Vance. Former Curator of the Museum of Afro-American History Marilyn Richardson and Professor Donald Jacobs of Northeastern University served as Cochairs of the more formal Planning Committee, whose members included Robert Bellinger (Suffolk University), Joan Bragen (Boston Athenæum), Randall Burkett (The DuBois Institute), Adelaide Cromwell (Boston University), Monica Fairbairn (Museum of Afro-American History), Joyce Ferriabough, Robert E. Fox (Suffolk University), Robert Hall (Northeastern University), Deborah Hoover, Donald Kelley (Boston Athenæum), Noel Johnson, Bruce P. Rossley (Mayor's Office), Ann Wadsworth (Boston Athenæum), and Kimberley Wallace Sanders (Boston University). Professor Jacobs, of course, also served efficiently as general editor of the collection of essays.

We received welcome advice on the research phase of this project from Wilson Moses (Boston University) and John Hope Franklin (Duke University). The initial survey of the Athenæum's catalogues was begun by Vernon Williams (Rhode Island College), and was ably continued by Kimberly Wallace Sanders, doctoral candidate at Boston University, whose two years on the project gave us our most comprehensive annotated listing to date of printed works in the Athenæum's collections related to slavery and abolition. After Mrs. Wallace Sanders's departure, Holly Andrews, student intern from Northeastern University, worked enthusiastically to prepare the labels for items displayed in the exhibition. Graduate students Beth Bennett and Alan Converse helped in various ways to prepare the exhibition for the Gallery. Other valuable assistance during the research phase of the project was provided by Ruth Winn and Frances Barna. Dr. Cromwell, in preparing her demographic survey of the north slope of Beacon Hill and the accompanying map, was assisted by Robert Bellinger and Beth Bower.

At the Athenæum, Donald Kelley (Project Director), Ann Wadsworth (Project Coordinator), and Joan Bragen (Director of Development) have each done yeoman's work to bring this project to fruition. Mr. Kelley shepherded every phase of the project through the peaks and valleys of its development, and was curator for the exhibition. Ann Wadsworth, in addition to her other duties, coordinated efforts relating to the development of this collection of essays and was our liaison with Indiana University Press. Joan Bragen continually found new and creative ways to attract financial support for the project. These three have served as the Athenæum backbone for the project. Assistant Gallery Director Angela Smalley handled all of the stacks of paperwork that evolve out of a project of this nature, and efficiently dealt with photo orders to the many institutions which provided photographs used in the publication. Former Gallery Registrar Anthea Harrison cheerfully assisted Mr. Kelley and the initial planning group.

Curator of Prints and Photographs Sally Pierce worked creatively and tirelessly to find appropriate visual material from the Athenæum's collections for use in the publication and also in the exhibition. Jody C. Randazzo processed in-house photographic orders with cheer and dispatch. Head of Conservation Stanley Cushing and Anne Pelikan, Barbara Hebard, and Nancy Coda of his staff cleaned and repaired all exhibition material from the Athenæum's collections, and matted and framed appropriate items for display. Head of Acquisitions John Lannon kept the project in mind as he looked through his rare-book catalogues, and purchased several new titles specifically for the exhibition. Northeastern University intern Martin Murphy, while classifying Athenæum broadsides, watched for abolition material and put aside a number of previously unrecorded items. John Gould, another intern from Northeastern, called our attention to important holdings in our collection of patriotic covers.

Associate Director Norman P. Tucker was the liaison between the Athenæum and the various area universities that provided student interns. Frances Hovey Howe, Secretary of the Athenæum's Board of Trustees and Chair of the Events and Exhibitions Committee, kept our spirits up and provided staunch support during the project's long period of gestation.

The following institutions provided photographs for the collection of essays with extraordinary speed: the Library of Congress, the Boston Public Library, the Massachusetts Historical Society, the Daughters of the American Revolution Museum, the Society for the Preservation of New England Antiquities, the American Antiquarian Society, the Sophia Smith Collection at Smith College, the Historical Society of Pennsylvania, the Tufts Library of Weymouth, Massachusetts, the National Portrait Gallery, the Corcoran Gallery of Art, the New

York Historical Society, the Charles E. Goodspeed Collection at the Worcester Art Museum, and the Bannister Nursing Care Center.

This project was, in the richest sense of the word, a cooperative effort. I am happy to have this opportunity to thank all those who contributed, and any others I inadvertently may have failed to mention.

RODNEY ARMSTRONG
DIRECTOR AND LIBRARIAN
BOSTON ATHENÆUM

✦ EDITOR'S PREFACE

Today history is being called upon to meet many challenges, among the most significant of which are the very vocal demands being made by proponents of Afro-centrism and multiculturalism. Some see these ideologies as threats, as examples of a type of chauvinism bordering on racism, and as bitter cries of disappointment. However, a much healthier approach is to work beyond the negatives and become aware of the anger and frustration that different racial and ethnic groups have felt over the years because the history books have either ignored their contribution or made a concerted attempt to distort it.

Nowhere is this more evident than within much of the historical literature of the early twentieth century that falsely claimed to offer an accurate picture of America's blacks. Books such as Ulrich Phillips's *American Negro Slavery* (1918), William Dunning's *Reconstruction, Political and Economic, 1865–1867* (1907), Claude Bowers's *The Tragic Era* (1928), and Thomas Dixon's *The Clansman* (1906), upon which the racist silent film *Birth of a Nation* was based, were able to subvert the truth and create a story of the black experience in America woven from a coarse but durable fabric of deception based largely on distortion. These books set the tone for much that was to follow. At the same time books by blacks such as W. E. B. Du Bois, Carter Woodson, and Albert Alrutheus Taylor, although factual and objective, were largely ignored by the white scholarly community. However, by the 1940s, reacting against Hitler's cruel and insane effort to destroy those people he viewed as *untermenschen,* American history, in an effort to reinterpret the African-American experience, began making some well-meaning attempts to move Clio's pendulum toward the center in order to get at the truth.

While it is true that some of these efforts have been successful, those who judge history's contribution wonder why more has not been accomplished. Part of the answer lies in the fact that those who profess to have the noblest of motives have at times unfortunately moved that pendulum too far in the other direction, creating histories of various groups that are often self-serving or filled with guilt-ridden inaccuracies.

Perhaps nowhere has the pendulum swung more wildly than in historians' efforts over the years to offer up an objective account of antebellum abolitionism. Missing for all too long were accounts that explained fully and truthfully blacks' involvement in this struggle. Not surprisingly, based on a whole array of destructive myths regarding the Negro's past, for many years blacks were usually seen as being acted upon rather than as dynamic actors in a dramatic story they helped create. As a result, William Lloyd Garrison was usually presented as the leading if not the only American abolitionist of any significance, and Quaker Levi Coffin was offered up as virtually the sole conductor operating the Underground Railroad.

Since the 1960s, however, meaningful efforts have been made to come to a better understanding and awareness of what the level of black participation actually was in the movement for abolition. Recent research on the antebellum black experience in the North, particularly in cities such as Boston, has led to the asking of some new questions. For example, why was the level of black activism and attainment of goals more impressive in Boston than in any other comparable urban area? Furthermore, how significant a role did the unique biracial component that seemed to be such an important aspect of Boston abolition play in all of this? And, in addition, if there was a meaningful biracial component, who had an impact upon whom?

For the reality is that Boston's black community, while it never constituted more than 3 percent of that city's population during the years leading to the Civil War, was nonetheless able to do more to tear down the barriers of segregation than the much larger black populations of either New York or Philadelphia. Boston's schools became integrated earlier. Massachusetts was forced to end the practice of running "Jim Crow" cars on its railroads well in advance of other states, at the same time that the state racial intermarriage law was repealed. And while the efforts of Boston's black leadership in the end proved unsuccessful, Massachusetts very nearly became the first state to allow men of color to serve in its all-white militia companies.

There were many reasons for all of this. Blacks in Massachusetts possessed full voting rights, contrary to the situation in Pennsylvania, where blacks had been disenfranchised, and in New York, where they could cast ballots only if they satisfied a property qualification that applied solely to them. Equally important, Boston was Massachusetts' state capital, while the New York state legislature met in Albany, not New York City, and Pennsylvania's convened in Harrisburg, not Philadelphia.

Add to this the fact that a significant majority of Boston's blacks resided along the north slope of Beacon Hill, virtually within the shadow of the State House, and that the city's very vocal and receptive abolitionist network, led by William Lloyd Garrison, was headquartered close by, and the reasons for the progress made by the city's blacks in the struggle against segregation become quite clear.

Then, too, there was that very important and unique ingredient of early ante-bellum black abolitionism in Boston, David Walker. Walker's strength and spirit had an enormous impact upon Boston's black community during the brief time he resided in the city, and his powerful presence could still be felt during the years after his death. Walker's unyielding determination, which served so well to fire up black efforts at self-elevation, also affected William Lloyd Garrison as he returned to Boston in 1830 to begin the task of editing an antislavery newspaper, *The Liberator.* For Garrison quickly realized two things: that he would need black support in order to succeed, and that strategically he might best gain that support by echoing some of the concerns of the late David Walker. This he did, and during the early years of struggle it clearly helped in winning blacks to his cause. It is therefore no surprise to find Walker's powerful presence nearly as evident in the essays within this volume as Garrison's.

The goals of this collection of essays are to illustrate in broad detail the forces in Boston that the activist black community was able to seize upon in order to gain equality, to examine the role played by whites, and, perhaps most important, to observe the biracial aspect of the many significant events that were helping to shape the city. It is for this reason that these essays have been brought together within this volume.

But there is also another reason: to meet today's challenges emanating from the thrust of Afro-centrism, multiculturalism, continuing racism, and nega-tively destructive myth-making. And there is no better way to meet all of these challenges than with the truth. For that, of course, is what history is supposed to be all about. These essays move meaningfully in that direction by offering a clear picture of how a relatively small group of blacks were able, with some white support but largely on their own, to make their awesome presence felt in an important northern city. In the end, as a result of their efforts, a chapter in Boston's history would significantly and dramatically be rewritten.

I want to express my appreciation to the "team" at the Boston Athenæum who worked with such diligence to assure this volume's completion. I particu-larly want to single out Donald Kelley, Ann Wadsworth, and Joan Bragen for their major ongoing contributions, together with Sally Pierce, the Athenæum's Curator of Prints and Photographs, who was always available to take that extra step to make sure just the right illustrations were on hand to strengthen the book both visually and historically.

A special word of appreciation to Eliza McClennen, who took a whole body of ideas regarding how best to depict the antebellum black community of Bos-ton's West End, and designed a map that accurately illustrates the demographic story that we wanted to tell. I also want to thank Ellie, my wife, who was always there to provide the much-needed support that becomes so important during those times when doubt begins to overtake confidence.

And finally, my most heartfelt thanks go to the essayists whose fine work appears in this volume. It was their unmatched intellectual awareness and expertise, continuing cooperation, and willingness to listen to even my most eccentric suggestions that helped convince me that we were all in this together, trying to make a meaningful contribution to human understanding as it relates to the black experience in America.

DONALD M. JACOBS
NORTHEASTERN UNIVERSITY

Courage and Conscience

CHAPTER ONE

Donald M. Jacobs

David Walker and William Lloyd Garrison

Racial Cooperation and the Shaping of Boston Abolition

Most *would probably agree that the distinctiveness of antebellum Boston abolitionism was largely the result of the dominating influence of William Lloyd Garrison, the no-holds-barred editor of* The Liberator. *But for all too long Garrison was also historically perceived as the leading figure of the national abolition movement, creating and shaping it in his own image. However, while a new generation of scholars has pretty much burst this historical bubble, Garrison nonetheless deservedly retains his preeminent role as the guiding force of the Boston antislavery struggle.*

Garrison also provided a significant support system for Boston's activist black community, particularly through the columns of The Liberator. *But this clearly worked both ways, given Garrison's own grateful admission that his newspaper, especially during its early years, could not have survived without its black subscribers. A staunch champion of black equality and black freedom, Garrison zealously espoused a number of causes successfully fought for by Boston's black community. And while the struggle for equality in Boston was predominantly a black struggle, the biracial cast of Boston abolitionism certainly helped shape it.*

But the significance of black activism cannot be underestimated. Not only can a strong case be made that blacks helped shape the abolition cause in colonial Massachusetts, but they also did so during the early 1830s, when William Lloyd Garrison was just beginning to try to establish himself and The Liberator *in Boston. For Garrison's strategy for gaining black acceptance was significantly influenced by David Walker, the North Carolina–born black abolitionist.*

Walker became a popular race leader in the city from 1825, when he first arrived, until his death in 1830. His Appeal, *published in three separate editions during 1829 and 1830, demanded an end to slavery by any means, including violent ones, and, observing firsthand the situation in Boston, also called for equality of opportunity for free blacks everywhere.*

Although Garrison the nonresistant pacifist could not accept Walker's seeming support of violent means to end slavery, Walker's strong anticolonization stand, his demand that the Massachusetts racial intermarriage law be repealed, and his urgent calls for black self-elevation and race unity were not lost on Garrison. For after Walker's death, Garrison appropriated these issues, making significant use of them in what became part of a successful effort to win black support for his cause. And although often viewed as stubborn, dogmatic, and intransigent, especially in his dealings with fellow white abolitionists, when it came to addressing the concerns of Boston's blacks, Garrison became the artful accommodationist, willing to compromise on key issues in order to keep their valued support.

All nations' histories are seasoned with bits and pieces of myth; it is the spice that often adds life to what might otherwise be a dull historical tale. Within the American historical experience, some of these myths are quite benign. For example, Parson Weems's famous fabrication, the tale of George Washington and the cherry tree, was an effort to illustrate how honest our nation's first president was, even in his youth. The legend that Betsy Ross sewed our nation's first flag was not made public until one hundred years after the event, and then in a talk given before the Pennsylvania Historical Society by Ross's grandson, who happened to be running the family flag business at the time.

Then, of course, there is the notion, now especially difficult to believe, that in the United States anyone can rise to the top and become president, no matter how poor and deprived the person's background. Abraham Lincoln is usually the first to come to mind as proof that it can actually happen. But given what myths represent, how should historians deal with them? Should they simply be discarded, thrown into some purist's trash heap, since they are not really accurate reflections of history? Or do they, in their proper place, serve a useful purpose?

These questions become particularly relevant in those instances where it is not easy to determine where fact begins and fancy ends. An obvious case in point is the widely accepted view of Abraham Lincoln as the "Great Emancipator." But where does this interpretation lead us? We know that during the early years of his presidency, at the beginning of the Civil War, Lincoln often expressed the belief that this war was not being fought to free the slaves; first and foremost it was a war to preserve the Union. And when pressured in 1862 by journalist-reformer Horace Greeley to follow the assumed lead of northern public opinion and do something about ending slavery, Lincoln refused, pointing out rather matter-of-factly that if he could save the Union by freeing all the slaves, or by

Flanked by soldiers from the all-black Shaw Honor Guard, the casket of Senator Charles Sumner lies in state in the Massachusetts State House, March 15, 1874. At Sumner's funeral, many recalled the significant role played in antebellum Boston by blacks and whites acting together in the struggle against slavery and for equality.
Photograph by E. F. Smith. Courtesy of the Society for the Preservation of New England Antiquities.

freeing none, or by freeing only some, the strategy that best assured keeping the Union intact was the one he would follow. When he finally did officially proclaim the slaves to be free, effective January 1, 1863, many historians have accurately argued that with one stroke of his pen Lincoln had actually freed no one, given the obviously limited nature of the emancipation document.

Indeed, a nation often revels in its myths, especially when they can be reshaped by history so that they appear to be true. For in the end it can reasonably be argued that Lincoln's Emancipation Proclamation did set the events in motion that would actually lead to the freeing of all the slaves as long as the North won the Civil War. When one adds the widely accepted view that Lincoln was probably the nation's greatest president, what enters the genie's bottle as merely a figment of one's imagination suddenly becomes magically transformed. Thus the end result: the hallowed image of Lincoln as the great leader who unlocked slavery's chains.

But then students of American history are also left with the unfortunate corollary to all of this: the notion or myth that the blacks of the United States did nothing to bring about their own freedom, that it was all done for them with little if any meaningful active participation on their part. As W. E. Woodward, a popular historian of the 1920s, bluntly stated in his 1928 biography of Ulysses S. Grant:

> The American negroes are the only people in the history of the world . . . that ever became free without any effort of their own. . . . [The Civil War] was not their business. They had not started the war nor ended it. . . . They twanged banjos around the railroad stations, sang melodious spirituals and believed that some Yankee would soon come along and give each of them forty acres of land and a mule.[1]

This is yet another of those unfortunate "myths of the Negro past" long accepted as unimpeachable truth by all too many whites. It portrayed the blacks of the United States as weak and dependent, always looking to the nation's whites for the guidance and leadership that would bring an end to slavery in the South and segregation in the North. Then one myth led to another. For if Lincoln was indeed the "Great Emancipator," wasn't Boston's William Lloyd Garrison the abolitionist who single-handedly shaped the antislavery movement? And didn't he set the stage for eventual black participation once this supposedly downtrodden race had finally been awakened to the fact that they should also be involved in the effort to bring down the institution of slavery?

And didn't William Lloyd Garrison actually rouse all America, or at least all of the North, to the truth about the evils of slavery? Or is this yet another myth that needs to be watered down with a heavy dose of reality? One obvious way to get at the truth, especially as it relates to Garrison's role, is to focus carefully on the movement against slavery, particularly as it began to take shape in Boston. In this way it will be possible to determine where the strident Garrison actually belongs within Clio's historical hierarchy, and also to see where Boston's blacks belong, especially the militant precursor of Boston abolitionism, David Walker.

During the seventeenth century, the Puritans of Massachusetts Bay began to develop a variety of notions about the rightness or wrongness of slavery. For if the Bible was God's word on the subject, as they so firmly believed, the members of this holy Commonwealth, this "city on the hill," certainly seemed to be the recipients of some very mixed messages. Included in the Massachusetts Body of Liberties of 1641, the first real attempt by the citizenry of the colony to codify the law, is a section which states, rather ambiguously, that

> there shall never be any bond slavery, villenage or captivitie amongst us unlesse it be lawfull captives taken in just warrs and such strangers as willingly sell themselves or are solde to us: And such shall have the libertyes and Christian usages which the law of God established in Israell concerning such persons doth morally require, provided this exempts none from servitude who shall be judged thereto by Authoritie.[2]

This statement, however, is aimed mainly at issues revolving around not black Africans but Indians, since the number of blacks in Massachusetts at this time was quite small. The first recorded evidence of blacks' being seen in the Bay Colony refers to several living with their master, Samuel Maverick, on Noddles Island (later East Boston) in 1638. Clearly this document left the door open for the Puritans to move in almost any direction they might choose. So by the 1640s, while two Massachusetts sailors were tried and found guilty of "manstealing" and forced to return their black cargo to Africa, Emanuel Downing could send a letter to his brother-in-law, John Winthrop, the governor of the colony, advising him of the colony's need for cheap black labor:

> I do not see how wee can thrive untill we get into a stock of slaves sufficient to doe all our business. . . . And I suppose you know verie well how wee shall maynetayne 20 Moores cheaper than one English servant.[3]

However, by the turn of the eighteenth century, some semblance of an anti-slavery attitude began to appear in Boston. The foremost proponent of this view was Judge Samuel Sewall, whose sharply worded attack upon the institution of slavery, *The Selling of Joseph* (1701), was an attempt by the renowned jurist to construct through biblical analogy a powerful case against slavery's continuance in Massachusetts. Not long after, the selectmen of the town of Boston also mounted an unsuccessful attack against slavery, recommending that it be outlawed in the colony.[4] Such expressions of antislavery feeling, however, were at best sporadic and were met with strong opposition from some of Boston's most respected leaders, including the powerful Cotton Mather, who on one occasion went so far as to express his sincere appreciation after receiving a slave as a gift.[5]

Significantly, by the end of the first decade of the eighteenth century, only thirty-three of the approximately four hundred blacks living in Boston were free. And as soon as the *Boston News-Letter*, the Massachusetts colony's first newspaper, began publishing in 1704, almost every issue contained advertisements announcing slaves for sale or describing some recent runaway and offering a reward for his or her capture.[6]

By the Revolutionary War era, however, Boston's blacks, most of whom were still enslaved, began to take matters into their own hands, uniting for the first time to petition the Massachusetts General Court for their freedom. In response, a legislative committee temporarily set their request aside.[7] Not to be put off, in 1774 "A Son of Africa" wrote a strong attack against slavery that appeared in the *Massachusetts Spy*. But then as events began to head swiftly toward rebellion against English rule, all efforts to move the whites to act against the institution came to naught, as the notion that "if we don't hang together, we will all hang separately" convinced many that it might be best, at least for the time being, to do everything possible to maintain North-South unity by ignoring the issue of freedom for the blacks.[8]

By this time in Massachusetts, the brunt of the leadership in the battle against slavery had begun to be borne by black abolitionist Prince Hall, who can quite accurately be described as the colony's first true antislavery leader. Hall had come to Boston from Barbados in 1765 when he was seventeen years old, and soon his name began to appear on antislavery petitions circulating among the colony's blacks.[9]

Hall was also heavily involved in efforts to break down the barriers of prejudice in Boston. But his unsuccessful attempt to gain black membership in the local Masonic organization eventually led to his founding of the first of many all-black Masonic lodges that would later bear his name. In 1777, well after the beginning of the Revolution, Hall, together with several fellow blacks, caring not one bit if the debate over slavery seriously divided the northern and southern states, affirmed that "every principle from which America has Acted in the cours [*sic*] of the unhappy Deficulties [*sic*] with Great Britain pleads stronger than a thousand arguments in favour of your petitioners" and their demands for freedom.[10] For if the Americans felt that they had been enslaved too long by British tyranny and must now fight to throw off their chains of bondage, how were America's blacks supposed to react to their own long, far more cruel enslavement?

Slavery finally came to an end in Massachusetts in 1783 as a result of the successful effort by the Worcester County slave Quock Walker, who was able by his arguments to convince the Massachusetts Supreme Court that it might be wise to examine more carefully the state constitution's views on slavery. This effort led Chief Justice William Cushing, after much deliberation and debate involving two separate cases dealing with Walker's situation, to come to the conclusion that

> your Constitution of Government, by which the people of this Commonwealth have solemnly bound themselves sets out with declaring that all men are born free

FIFTH ANNIVERSARY
OF THE
MASSACHUSETTS ANTI-SLAVERY SOCIETY,
WEDNESDAY, JANUARY 25, 1837.

[☞ The public meetings, during the day, will be held in the SPACIOUS LOFT, OVER THE STABLE OF THE MARLBOROUGH HOTEL, and in the evening, in the REPRESENTATIVES' HALL.]

HOURS OF THE MEETINGS.

Meeting for Delegates at 9 o'clock in the morning, at 46, Washington-Street.

First public meeting at 10 o'clock A. M., in the LOFT OVER THE STABLE OF THE MARLBOROUGH HOTEL.

Second public meeting at 1-2 past 2 o'clock, P. M. same place.

Evening meeting at 1-2 past 6 o'clock, in the REPRESENTATIVES' HALL.

☞ The Committee of Arrangements respectfully inform the ladies that ample accommodations have been prepared for them. The loft is spacious, clean, well warmed, and will accommodate, with ease and perfect safety, at least 1000 persons.

☞ AMOS DRESSER, a citizen of this State, who was 'Lynched' at Nashville, for the crime of being an Abolitionist, will be present, and during the meetings in the afternoon and evening, will give a history of that affair.

By virtue of special compact, Shylock demanded a pound of flesh, cut nearest to the heart. Those who sell mothers separately from their children, likewise claim a legal right to human flesh; and they too cut it nearest to the *heart.—L. M. Child.*

On, woman! from thy happy hearth
Extend thy gentle hand to save
The poor and perishing of earth—
The chained and stricken slave!
Oh, plead for all the suffering of thy kind—
For the crushed body and the darkened mind. *J. G. Whittier.*

Broadside advertising the fifth-anniversary meeting of the Massachusetts Anti-Slavery Society, 1837. The Boston Athenæum.

and equal. . . . This being the case, I think the idea of slavery is inconsistent with our own conduct and Constitution; and there can be no such thing as perpetual servitude of a rational creature.[11]

Thus the institution of slavery was toppled in Massachusetts and, based mainly on economic factors, eventually all across the North. But very different economic and social considerations convinced southerners that they could not follow suit; nor were the moral implications of the Cushing decision so strong as to help fan the flames of broad-based abolition. And while it is true that Massachusetts would soon begin to serve as a central staging area for a national antislavery effort, as well as related attempts to call into question patterns of segregation that had begun to make significant inroads as soon as slavery began to die out locally, these expressions of deep-seated concern would not initially emanate from the likes of William Lloyd Garrison. Instead the major opposition would come from Boston's black community, from the Massachusetts General Colored Association, and especially from an emigré to Boston who would have a major impact upon the city's blacks and even upon Garrison, David Walker.

Title page of David Walker's *Appeal* (1829). Trustees of the Public Library of the City of Boston.

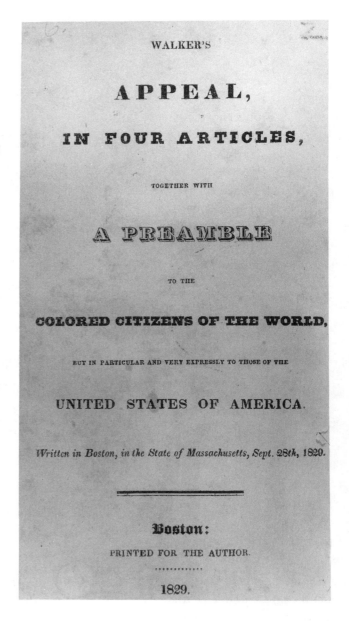

WALKER'S

APPEAL,

IN FOUR ARTICLES,

TOGETHER WITH

A PREAMBLE

TO THE

COLORED CITIZENS OF THE WORLD,

BUT IN PARTICULAR AND VERY EXPRESSLY TO THOSE OF THE

UNITED STATES OF AMERICA.

Written in Boston, in the State of Massachusetts, Sept. 28th, 1829.

Boston:

PRINTED FOR THE AUTHOR.

1829.

According to early but somewhat ambiguous sources, David Walker was born free in Wilmington, North Carolina, probably in 1785. He traveled widely in the South and may have lived in Philadelphia for a short time before settling in Boston in 1825, where he was one of approximately 350 blacks listed that year in the city directory. He appeared simply as "David Walker, clothes dealer."[12] By 1828 Walker had moved his place of business in the city from City Market to 20 Brattle Street, and then the following year to number 42, where he remained the proprietor of a new and used clothing store until his untimely death in 1830. By 1827 he had taken up residence in that part of Boston boasting the largest concentration of blacks, on Belknap Street (now Joy Street) along the north slope of Beacon Hill, close by the impressive new State House building.

By this time Walker had already become active in the Boston-based Massachusetts General Colored Association, an organization that had been established in 1826 by several of the city's leading black citizens, most notably William G. Nell, father of William Cooper Nell, who would later become Boston's leading champion of integration. Groups such as this, founded six years before William Lloyd Garrison's New England Anti-Slavery Society, served two main purposes: to protest actively against the evils of slavery and to battle against white-supported segregationist policies so that the free blacks of Massachusetts might achieve full equality. Quickly caught up in this struggle, Walker began almost immediately to make his presence felt within Boston's black community.[13]

An imposing figure, Walker was some six feet tall and strongly built, with what was described as a "slender and well-proportioned physique." Those who knew him well said that he also "possessed a noble and courageous spirit," and that he was "ardently attached to the cause of liberty."[14] In this sense Walker fit in well with the antislavery standards set by the Massachusetts General Colored Association. He was an unabashed abolitionist who, having grown up in the South, knew slavery; and knowing it, he had built up a powerful hatred of it.

William Lloyd Garrison, on the other hand, would come by his own radical brand of abolitionism somewhat later. Some might even argue that his early background did not automatically fit him for the role of heroic abolitionist that he would eventually seize, beginning in the early 1830s, just after David Walker's death. Raised in poverty, Garrison was born in Newburyport, along the northern shore of Massachusetts, in 1805. His mother was a devout, God-fearing Baptist who constantly tried to instill her own fear of the Lord into both of her sons, William, or Lloyd as he was often called, and James, who was the older of the two by four years. Much of her effort worked with young William, but not with his brother, who chose to travel in their father's wobbly footsteps, turning to drink and deserting the family in order to follow where the sea might lead, in his case to an unhappy life eventually destroyed by alcoholism.[15]

As far as we know, David Walker did not drink, nor did he ever edit a newspaper, but he did serve as one of the two Boston agents (together with the Reverend Thomas Paul of the First African Baptist Church) for the New York *Freedom's Journal,* America's first black newspaper, during the two years it published, from 1827 to 1829.[16] As a result, Walker quickly came to realize the power of the printed word in the shaping of popular opinion. Garrison during the early 1820s would edit several newspapers, initially adopting a policy favoring Federalism and, not at all surprising given his family's difficulties, temperance. He had not yet begun to see the plight of the slaves as a major concern.

When he did begin to set his journalistic sights on the sorry state of the nation's blacks, Garrison at first chose to champion the cause of colonization, a movement advocating the resettlement of blacks in Africa, a scheme very much opposed by David Walker. As Walker later would explain in his *Appeal,* which appeared in three separate editions in 1829 and 1830, as long as whites supported a policy which chose to uproot black people, they would never give any

William Lloyd Garrison at thirty. Mezzotint by John Sartain (ca. 1835). Trustees of the Public Library of the City of Boston.

thought to the possibility of turning away from segregation and accepting black demands for equality. Walker also reasoned that those who favored colonization were intent upon solidifying slavery's hold by sending troublesome free blacks out of the country.

Nor did this argument elude Garrison when, on January 1, 1831, his editorial compass having pointed the way back to Boston, he published the first of more than eighteen hundred weekly issues of *The Liberator,* never missing a single one in thirty-five years. At the outset, in an open letter to "our free colored

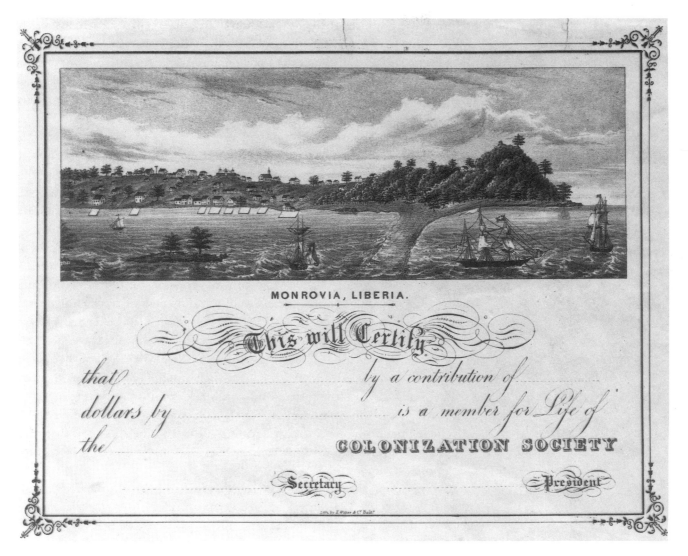

Receipt form for donations made to the Colonization Society. The illustration shows an idyllic view of Monrovia, Liberia. The Boston Athenæum.

David Claypoole Johnston. Pen and ink drawing for the first masthead of *The Liberator* (1831). Trustees of the Public Library of the City of Boston.

brethren," he promised the nation's 320,000 free blacks, particularly the nearly 160,000 that lived above the Mason-Dixon line, that "your moral and intellectual elevation, the advancement of your rights, and the defense of your character will be a leading object of our paper."[17] By now he had turned strongly against slavery, even choosing the seemingly radical path of immediatism, viewing slavery as such a grievous sin that it had to be eradicated at once.

Strategically, Garrison was beginning to realize that in order for his newspaper to survive, it must have black support. He made this quite clear in an early solicitation for subscribers when he admitted that while "we know that . . . adversity has marked you for his own; yet among 300,000 of your number, some patronage may be given. We ask, and expect, but little . . . [but] that little may save the life of the Liberator."[18]

But gaining broad-based black backing would not be easy, since in the eyes of many Negroes, Garrison up to this point had established a rather uneven track record, especially during his flirtation with colonization. So it is not surprising that he soon adopted a strategy that would not only demonstrate some degree of acceptance of certain of David Walker's ideas, but also begin to take the monkey of colonization off his back. Consequently the editor of *The Liberator* stated very emphatically that from this point on "we will strenuously oppose any scheme, under whatever pretense . . . which attempts to transport them to Africa." For Garrison knew that Boston's black community was quite concerned over efforts to build support for the colonization idea in the city. Not only did he much admire "their sagacity and spirit," but he also knew that with regard to colonization, they "entertain but one sentiment on the subject; they are opposed to emigration."[19]

Garrison now seemed to know exactly what he had to do. In the first edition of his *Appeal,* Walker had urged his people to unify in order to elevate themselves. He had complained about the fact that too many of Boston's colored were bootblacks or barbers or cleaners of white men's clothes. Not nearly enough were carpenters or mechanics, and none at all, as far as he knew, practiced a profession. All too many blacks, he charged, seemed happy to let things remain that way. For his part, Garrison also urged Boston's blacks to do everything they could to bring about their own improvement. "Our colored population can and ought to support merchants, mechanics, and masters of their own. . . . They ought to cooperate like a band of brothers, and depend upon themselves to raise their own character."[20]

Walker had also expressed concern when a young boy that he knew had told him that after nine years in Boston's segregated schools, he still knew no grammar, mainly, as the boy explained, because "the school committee forbid the colored children learning any . . . they would not allow any but the white children to study grammar."[21] It is not surprising, then, that when William Cooper Nell in 1840 began the first petition drive to integrate Boston's schools, William Lloyd Garrison lent both his support and his signature.

In response to Boston's unfair segregation patterns, David Walker wondered why blacks were not allowed to serve in any legislative capacity, or as constable, or even in the jury box, especially when one of their own was on trial. And why weren't whites and blacks allowed to intermarry in Massachusetts? Because a state law passed in 1786 (an offshoot of an older Massachusetts colonial law going all the way back to 1706) forbade such an arrangement. As far as Walker was concerned, this was just another race-inspired prohibition that helped perpetuate the subjugation of the black race to the white. Not that Walker, as he emphatically stated in his *Appeal,* "would give a pinch of snuff to be married to any white person I ever saw in all the days of my life," but it was the prohibition itself and what it really meant that rankled most.[22]

When Garrison returned to Boston and began publishing *The Liberator,* in only the second issue he leveled a strong blast at Massachusetts' forty-five-year-old racial intermarriage law, echoing the sentiments, if not the language, expressed the year before by Walker. From Garrison's perspective, this legislation, which virtually annulled all marriages in the Commonwealth between whites and blacks and in addition severely punished anyone who performed them, was "disgraceful to the state—inconsistent with every principle of justice—and utterly absurd and preposterous."[23] Throughout *The Liberator*'s early months of publication, Garrison in nearly every issue made some reference to the law in an effort to force the state legislature to take decisive action. He enticed. He goaded. He harangued. Could anyone really define what constituted white or black, he asked? Are any two people who choose to marry ever exactly the same color? And if the state's lawmakers really felt in all their wisdom that it was proper to allow racial distinctions to determine the legality or illegality of marriage, "why, then, let us have a law prohibiting tall people from marrying short ones, and fat people lean ones." To Garrison, the absurdity of it all was beyond belief.[24]

But Garrison's arguments fell on deaf ears, and the racial intermarriage law was not finally repealed until 1843. But Boston's blacks had heard Garrison, and since he had clearly turned away from colonization, his ideas began to strike a more responsive chord among Boston's black leadership. For now John Hilton, an active member of the Massachusetts General Colored Association, and also Grand Master of Boston's Prince Hall Masonic Lodge, decided to send a sizable donation to Garrison's *Liberator* and to point out, in words that must have elated Garrison, that "the descendents of Africa . . . are now convinced of the sincerity of your intentions, and are proud to claim you as their advocate."[25]

Even more enthusiastic was the highly respected James G. Barbadoes, one of the elder statesmen of Boston's black community, who was particularly grateful for the sentiments Garrison had recently expressed in a speech delivered to a large group of the city's blacks.

God bless you, Liberator! . . . In behalf of the colored people of this city . . . I would acknowledge the debt of gratitude under which we labor. . . . We congratulate you for the service you have been to the colored inhabitants of this place, and as a benefactor to the African population, generally.[26]

Would all this have pleased David Walker? Not entirely. Not only had Garrison only recently turned away from colonization, but he was also a staunch nonresistant or pacifist. From Garrison's perspective, slavery might be the gravest sin ever perpetrated upon humankind. Yet to try to bring it down by violent means was nearly as sinful. Instead Garrison felt strongly that slavery must be made to disappear by pricking the conscience of the slaveholder, thus convincing those who owned slaves how horribly wrong the institution was—no easy task, especially when one tries to square this with Garrison's support for immediatism.

Before coming back to Boston in 1830, Garrison had been in Baltimore, assisting Benjamin Lundy with the editing of Lundy's *Genius of Universal Emancipation,* when a copy of the first edition of David Walker's *Appeal* crossed his desk. Garrison was quite surprised by the language of the pamphlet, particularly by what he felt to be its violent spirit. Walker had apparently come across a story in a local Boston newspaper that had been copied from a southern journal relating how a group of slaves who were being transported by their master, probably for resale elsewhere, happened to break free. But before rushing off to freedom, they turned upon their master and were about to take their revenge when a female slave, seeing what was happening, helped the master onto his horse so that he might escape. Walker could not believe what he had read. How, he asked, could any black betray fellow slaves when

> the whites have had us under them for more than three centuries, murdering, and treating us like brutes. . . . They do not know . . . that there is an unconquerable disposition in the breasts of the blacks, which when it is fully awakened and put in motion, will be subdued, only with the destruction of the animal existence. . . . If you commence [an effort to gain your freedom], make sure work—do not trifle, for they will not trifle with you—they want us for their slaves, and think nothing of murdering us in order to subject us to that wretched condition—therefore, if there is an attempt made by us, kill or be killed. Now, I ask you, had you not rather be killed than . . . be a slave to a tyrant? . . . It is no more harm for you to kill a man, who is trying to kill you, than it is for you to take a drink of water when thirsty.[27]

Garrison was deeply troubled by the language in Walker's pamphlet. But as the controversy spread, complete with southern demands that the mayor of Boston, Harrison Gray Otis, arrest Walker for his "detestable" views, Garrison's perspective seemed to shift somewhat. While he was not at all surprised at the South's angry response to this pamphlet "written by a colored Bostonian," he was nonetheless struck by the author's "impassioned and determined effort." But while his own nonviolent views led him to "deprecate its circulation," in a more positive vein he expressed his belief that "we cannot but wonder at the bravery and intelligence of its author."[28]

Some time later, after Walker's death and just after Garrison's new venture, *The Liberator,* had made its first appearance in Boston, Garrison felt the need to comment on the contents of Walker's *Appeal* once more, noting that although "we have repeatedly expressed our disapprobation of its general spirit, nevertheless, it is not for the American people . . . to denounce it as bloody or monstrous. Mr. Walker but pays them in their own coin." And while Garrison could never bring himself to "preach rebellion," only "submission and peace," we must admit, he affirmed, "that if any people were ever justified in throwing off the yoke of their tyrants, the slaves are that people."[29]

Nor was Garrison in agreement with the charge being made in other Boston newspapers that Walker had not even written the pamphlet. Although he admitted that he had never had the opportunity to meet Walker,

> we are assured by those who intimately knew him that his "Appeal" was an exact transcription of his daily conversations. . . . Some editors have affected to doubt whether the deceased Walker wrote this pamphlet. On this point, skepticism need not stumble; the "Appeal" bears the strongest internal evidence of having emanated from his own mind. No white man could have written in language so natural and enthusiastic.[30]

Strategically having come to realize the necessity of black support in order for his newspaper, and perhaps even his cause, to survive, it is no surprise that Garrison almost immediately began to encourage Boston's black community to use *The Liberator* as a forum through which they could express their views and concerns. In the process he might have attempted to distance himself from David Walker. Or he could have just ignored him. But Garrison knew full well that Walker had been a pillar of the local black community. Not only had he been highly respected, but some of his contemporaries had also come to the conclusion that, given the South's nearly hysterical response to his *Appeal,* Walker's death in 1830 might not have been due to natural causes.

Garrison realized that he had to deal with all of these concerns. This resulted in the stance he began to adopt on colonization, racial intermarriage, black unity, and even the question of the *Appeal*'s authorship, all in spite of Walker's support of blacks' using any means necessary to gain their freedom.

Was this merely a strategy on Garrison's part? Undoubtedly to some extent. Coming down on Walker's side on certain issues could only help Garrison in his effort to disarm those black critics in Boston who still were not quite sure they could trust him. But to see Garrison here as little more than a calculating opportunist is to lose sight of several important realities.

Toward the end of 1834, in one of the last issues of *The Liberator* published that year, Garrison proudly proclaimed that some three-quarters of the subscribers to his newspaper were black. According to Garrison, they also paid their bills more promptly than the white subscribers. If all this be true, it appears that the editor of *The Liberator* had been largely successful in his effort to build black support for his newspaper. And while Garrison was constantly in need of more subscribers, without his black readership the paper would have failed.[31]

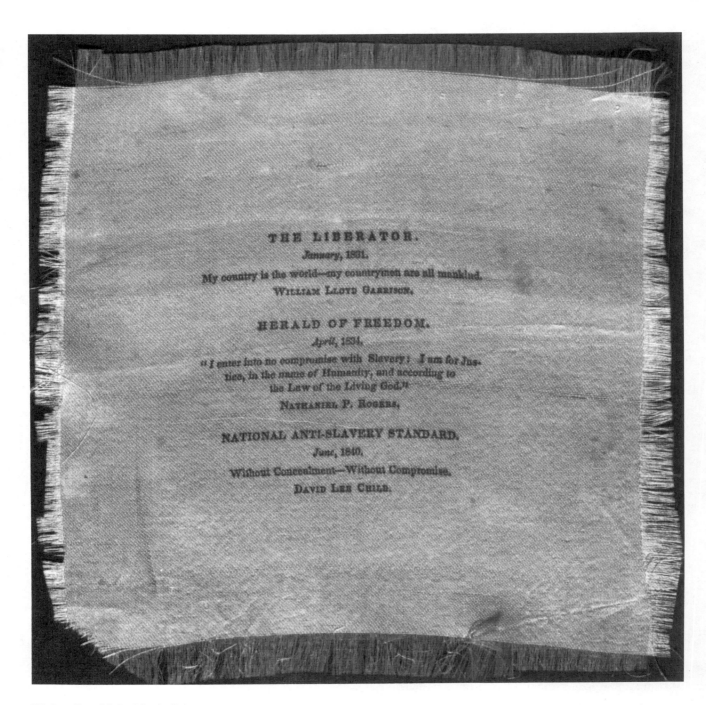

Silk handkerchief with abolition slogans. Typical of items sold at antislavery fairs to support abolition causes. From about 1840. Private collection.

Equally important is the impact black attitudes on other key issues would eventually have on Garrison, for over the coming years he would often bend over backwards to support black causes that were obviously in conflict with his philosophies. One such example is the question of voting rights for blacks (for Garrison saw all government and all trappings of government as evil, and this included casting a ballot). Yet Garrison often listed in *The Liberator* places where blacks could obtain ballots, and even suggested candidates for whom they should vote.[32]

This willingness on Garrison's part to soften his usual beliefs if they in any way served as a detriment to the black struggle for freedom can also be seen in the manner in which he responded to blacks' demands that they be allowed to serve in the all-white militia companies of Massachusetts. Although a radical nonresistant, Garrison began to support such black demands as early as 1839, even though he himself remained a pacifist who could not accept violence of any kind. Eventually even he came to accept the inevitability of violence when he realized just prior to the Civil War that slavery would be brought to an end only as the result of a bloody sectional conflict.[33]

By this time Garrison's memories of David Walker had probably grown quite dim. In an early issue of *The Liberator*, Garrison had promised that he would soon publish and offer an analysis of Walker's *Appeal*. But instead, toward the end of April 1831, he gave this responsibility over to one of his white readers whose critical abilities he clearly respected. In response Garrison chose to make only a few brief editorial comments that were of little consequence. And after the last of the three commentaries had appeared in May,[34] the name of David Walker virtually disappeared from the pages of *The Liberator*. Perhaps Garrison felt that he had by now gained the full confidence of Boston's blacks, and that there was no longer any need to recall in his newspaper the memory of this fiery black abolitionist.

But truth be told, while David Walker had played many of the first notes, in the end William Lloyd Garrison had completed the musical piece to a tune not totally different from what might have resulted had Walker been the lone composer. The point is clear. When the New England Anti-Slavery Society came into being on a snowy evening in early January 1832, at a meeting including both blacks and whites that took place, quite significantly, in the First African Baptist Church on Belknap Street, William Lloyd Garrison had already begun to set the direction that abolition would take in Boston, across Massachusetts, and in much of New England and beyond over the coming years.

But he had taken some very important early cues from Boston's black community. And some of the most important of these cues had come from the black activist David Walker, whose goals and hopes and aspirations for his people were, among other things, an effort to make sure that Boston abolitionism would not bear an all-white stamp. For blacks and whites working separately and together not only would begin but also would continue to have an impact upon the brand of abolitionism that would endure over the years in Boston. The legacy of racial cooperation is there for all to see and celebrate, as historians try to go about the business of erasing the not-so-benign myths that for all too long inaccurately shaped many of the widely accepted interpretations of the American historical experience.

Heralds of Freedom. Boston abolitionists. Tinted lithograph by Leopold Grozelier (1857). William Lloyd Garrison (*center*), surrounded by (*clockwise from top*) Ralph Waldo Emerson, Wendell Phillips, Joshua R. Giddings, Theodore Parker, Gerrit Smith, Samuel J. May. The Boston Athenæum.

NOTES

1. W. E. Woodward, *Meet General Grant* (New York: H. Liveright, 1928), quoted in James M. McPherson, *The Negro's Civil War: How American Negroes Felt and Acted during the War for the Union* (New York: Vintage, 1965), p. viii.

2. Winthrop D. Jordan, *White over Black: American Attitudes toward the Negro, 1550–1812* (Chapel Hill: University of North Carolina Press, 1968), p. 67.

3. Ibid., p. 69.

4. Samuel Sewall, "The Selling of Joseph" and "Judge Saffin's Reply," in George Washington Williams, *History of the Negro Race from 1619 to 1880* (New York, 1883), vol. 1, pp. 210–17; Lawrence W. Towner, "The Sewall-Saffin Dialogue on Slavery," *William and Mary Quarterly* 21 (January 1964): 42.

5. Justin Winsor, *Memorial History of Boston,* vol. 3 (Boston, 1881), p. 371; Williams, *History of the Negro Race,* vol. 1, pp. 214–17; Towner, "The Sewall-Saffin Dialogue," pp. 46–47, 50–51.

6. John Daniels, *In Freedom's Birthplace: A Study of the Boston Negroes* (Boston: Houghton Mifflin, 1914), pp. 5, 8; Lorenzo Greene, *The Negro in Colonial New England, 1620–1776* (Port Washington, N.Y.: Kennikat Press, 1942), p. 84; Winsor, *Memorial History,* vol. 2, p. 185.

7. Williams, *History of the Negro Race,* vol. 1, pp. 233–35.

8. *Massachusetts Spy,* February 10, 1774, in *The Liberator,* April 29, 1859, p. 67.

9. Greene, *The Negro in Colonial New England,* p. 313.

10. Herbert Aptheker, *Essays in the History of the American Negro* (New York: International Publishers, 1964), pp. 77–78.

11. "Quock Walker Case," Massachusetts Historical Society, *Proceedings,* Second Series 13 (April 1874), p. 294.

12. Charles Stimpson, *Stimpson's Boston Directory* (Boston, 1825), p. 298.

13. Daniels, *In Freedom's Birthplace,* p. 36.

14. Henry Highland Garnet, *Walker's Appeal, with a Brief Sketch of His Life . . .* (New York, 1848), pp. v, vii.

15. James Brewer Stewart, *William Lloyd Garrison and the Challenge of Emancipation* (Arlington Heights, Ill.: Harlan Davidson, 1992), pp. 1–11.

16. *Freedom's Journal,* March 12, 1827, vol. 1, pp. 3, 4; March 28, 1829, vol. 2, p. 412.

17. *The Liberator,* January 1, 1831, p. 3.

18. Ibid.

19. *The Liberator,* February 12, 1831, p. 25.

20. David Walker, *Walker's Appeal in Four Articles, Together with a Preamble to the Coloured Citizens of the World, but in Particular and Very Expressly to Those of the United States of America,* 1st ed. (Boston: Printed for the Author, September 28, 1829), pp. 31–32; *The Liberator,* May 19, 1832, p. 77.

21. *Walker's Appeal,* 1st ed., pp. 33–36.

22. Ibid., p. 11.

23. *The Liberator,* January 8, 1831, p. 7.

24. Ibid., February 12, 1831, p. 26.

25. John Hilton et al. to William Lloyd Garrison, in *The Liberator,* February 12, 1831, p. 26.

26. James G. Barbadoes to William Lloyd Garrison, in *The Liberator,* February 12, 1831, p. 26.

27. Herbert Aptheker, *"One Continual Cry": David Walker's Appeal to the Colored Citizens of the World (1829–1830), Its Setting and Its Meaning* (New York: Humanities Press, 1965), p. 89.

28. *Genius of Universal Emancipation,* quoted in George W. Forbes, *Unpublished Papers,* "David Walker" (Boston Public Library), p. 6.

29. *The Liberator,* January 8, 1831, p. 6.

30. *The Liberator,* January 8, 1831, quoted in Truman Nelson, ed., *Documents of Upheaval* (New York: Hill and Wang, 1966), pp. 5–6.

31. Donald M. Jacobs, "William Lloyd Garrison's *Liberator* and Boston's Blacks, 1830–1865," *The New England Quarterly* 44, no. 2 (June 1971): 260–61.

32. Ibid., pp. 267–69.

33. Ibid., pp. 273–74.

34. *The Liberator,* April 30, 1831, p. 69; May 7, 1831, p. 77; May 28, 1831, p. 85.

CHAPTER TWO

William E. Gienapp

Abolitionism and the Nature of Antebellum Reform

*I*n this perceptive overview of abolition's impact amidst demands for all kinds of change, Professor Gienapp discusses the different cultural and ideological currents that helped shape the great variety of antebellum efforts to reorder society that historians have labeled the Age of Reform. It was a time when advocates for change, mainly from the North, were championing a whole array of causes, including temperance, women's rights, peace, and many others. But at the center of the struggle, and more controversial and divisive than the rest, largely because of the sectional schism it caused, was antislavery.

With Boston as the focal point, Gienapp carefully examines the role played by Garrisonian abolitionism, with its emphasis on immediatism, nonviolent moral suasion, anarchistic come-outerism, a radical brand of Christian perfectionism, and the notion that the Constitution was a proslavery document. He concludes that Garrison, by advocating these views and then choosing to act as spokesman for many different reform causes rather than concentrating on slavery alone, probably did more to divide the forces of antislavery than unite them.

Although very vocal and at times outrageously outspoken, Garrison's constituency of supporters, Gienapp argues, was quite limited. His strongest champions were northern free blacks, particularly those from Boston, whose subscriptions to The Liberator kept Garrison's abolitionist newspaper alive, especially during its early years of struggle. In turn Garrison gave strong backing to the many successful integration efforts of Boston's black community during the 1840s and 1850s. Ironically, at that time when the abolition movement was at its weakest, and as political events much more than moral concerns began to move the nation inexorably toward civil war, Boston's blacks were becoming more activist and were winning some of their most important victories. Implicit in Gienapp's thoughtful essay is the view that Garrison's

*stubborn dogmatism, while it proved to have a negative impact on abolition nation-
ally, did not damage him locally, particularly among Boston's black community, who
saw in him and in* The Liberator *valuable advocates in their ongoing struggle for
equality.*

New Year's Day 1863 was a special moment in Boston's history. Over three
thousand people, including a number of the city's leading literary figures, came
to Boston's Music Hall to hear Ralph Waldo Emerson read a poem that he had
written for the occasion and to listen to selections performed by the Symphony
Orchestra. An equally large gathering assembled at Tremont Temple, where the
prominent black leader William Cooper Nell opened the session. The ceremo-
nies, which had been organized by the predominantly black Union Progressive
Association, extended throughout the day and into the evening. "We were not
all colored," the renowned black abolitionist Frederick Douglass said of those
in attendance, "but we all seemed to be about of one color that day."[1]

These meetings had been called to commemorate the expected signing of the
Emancipation Proclamation by Abraham Lincoln. Several months earlier, the
president had announced that unless the rebellious southern states returned to
the Union by this date, he would issue the final Emancipation Proclamation
freeing the slaves in the Confederacy. Despite fears voiced by some abolitionists
that Lincoln might delay his promised action, both meetings were jammed to
overflowing, as the city's residents turned out in eager anticipation of this momentous act.

While the crowd at Tremont Temple waited impatiently for word that Lincoln had in fact issued the final proclamation, a parade of speakers, headed by
Douglass and Anna Dickinson, the famous abolitionist orator, discussed the
meaning of emancipation and its significance for the war that was still raging.
The crowd became increasingly restless as the hours ticked by, but finally a
messenger entered the hall and announced that word had arrived over the tele-
graph wires that Lincoln had signed the Emancipation Proclamation. Pande-
monium broke out as those present rose and cheered wildly. Later that evening,
after the text of the Proclamation was read, Douglass led the crowd in singing
the chorus of "Blow Ye the Trumpet Blow." When the building closed at midnight, the celebrants, unwilling to go home, moved to the Twelfth Baptist
Church, the leading black church in the city. It was several more hours before
the joyous crowd dispersed.[2]

William Lloyd Garrison, the most famous abolitionist in the country, had
been unable to participate in the evening's celebration. The following day, however, he hailed the Proclamation as "a great historic event, sublime in its magni-
tude, momentous and beneficent in its far-reaching consequences."[3] Shortly
thereafter, at a meeting of the Massachusetts Anti-Slavery Society, he summed

The Emancipation Proclamation, signed by Abraham Lincoln (1863). The Boston Athenæum.

up his feelings about this development. In doing so, he understandably glanced backward at the long road the abolitionists had traveled to this auspicious moment. "Thirty years ago, it was midnight with the anti-slavery cause," he observed. "Now it is the bright noon of day, with the sun shining in his meridian splendor."[4] While the end of slavery still lay in the future, the abolitionist movement, as Garrison's words suggested, had come a great distance since its beginnings in the 1830s. And no community had played a larger role in that movement than the city of Boston.

American slavery was considerably older than the republic. Racial slavery had evolved in the British colonies of North America during the second half of the seventeenth century and consequently antedated the republic by a century or more. Nevertheless, by upholding the doctrine of equality and natural rights, the American Revolution greatly stimulated antislavery sentiment in the new nation. Condemned by the Founding Fathers as incompatible with the ideals of the republic, slavery ceased to be a national institution during these years, as the northern states adopted various programs of emancipation. In the southern states, however, bondage continued to be a vital social and economic institution that resisted any easy solution; as a result, it not only survived the Revolution but pushed into new lands west of the Appalachians. By the early nineteenth century, after its initial success in the northern states, the antislavery impulse of the Revolutionary era had pretty much run its course.[5]

It was against this background that a new and much more militant form of antislavery, which took as its goal the immediate eradication of slavery, developed in the United States in the 1830s.[6] Abolitionism, as this movement came to be known, was confined to the northern states, and it was particularly strong in Massachusetts and the city of Boston. Part of the larger reform impulse of the antebellum period, abolitionism took root in a unique social and intellectual context.

The coming of the abolitionist movement was not the result of changes in the institution of slavery in the southern states. Throughout the antebellum period (1820–1860), slavery was essentially a static institution. The laws governing it, the way it functioned, and its material and psychological dimensions did not significantly alter during these decades. Instead, to understand the emergence and nature of abolitionism, we must look elsewhere in American society, particularly to the course of southern history and thought in these years, and to the intellectual and social changes that swept across the North beginning in the 1820s, which would lead to a new response to the South's "peculiar institution."

Prior to 1820, many southern leaders condemned slavery as a moral evil incompatible with the ideals of the republic. In the 1820s, however, southerners stopped apologizing for slavery, and some began to argue instead that it was a positive good. Such an argument shocked many Americans. This feeling was accompanied by a growing realization that slavery was not declining, but on the contrary was both flourishing economically and expanding geographically. It had crossed the Mississippi River into land not even owned by the United States at the end of the Revolution, and the slave population had doubled in the two decades from 1810 to 1830. More and more northerners were becoming convinced that southerners, even those who remained apologetic about the institution, intended to do nothing to end slavery. Southerners, in short, seemed to consider slavery not only a positive good but a permanent institution. And finally, southern legislatures refused to heed any of the criticisms of slavery and reform the institution. All of these developments stimulated a growing concern in the North about slavery and its future place in the republic.[7]

Even more important for the emergence of abolitionism were the religious, social, and intellectual changes that occurred in the North. Together, these changes produced a number of reform movements, of which abolitionism was only one. The period from 1830 to 1860 was truly the age of reform. Countless social problems were identified and organizations formed to deal with a host of problems that plagued the nation. Movements developed to end drinking, abolish war, establish tax-supported common schools, reform prostitutes, rehabilitate criminals, work with the deaf, blind, and insane, and promote women's rights, among other causes, as well as end slavery.[8]

This reform impulse grew out of two distinct sources. One was the intellectual and religious change that characterized the period. The first half of the nineteenth century was the heyday of romanticism, an intellectual movement that began in Europe but which had a particularly powerful impact on the United States. By emphasizing emotion and feeling as the source of truth and by glorifying the importance of the individual, romanticism strengthened greatly the reform impulse. With its belief in the dignity and self-worth of every person, it sought to free individuals from social restraints so that they could reach their full potential. Most important, it possessed a strong humanitarian component which stressed empathy for the oppressed and with suffering.[9]

Also critical was the development of so-called rational religion, of which Unitarianism was the major example. Appealing primarily to the elite and socially respectable elements in Massachusetts and New England, Unitarianism emphasized doing good works as the expression of true religion. Too socially respectable to be truly radical, Unitarians and similar sects nevertheless participated actively in efforts to eradicate social evils and help the unfortunate. Two prominent Massachusetts Unitarian ministers who were especially active in reform, including abolitionism, were Theodore Parker of Boston and Thomas Wentworth Higginson of Worcester.[10]

Most important, however, were the religious revivals that shook the North in the 1820s and 1830s, transforming American Protestantism and in the process spawning numerous reform movements.[11] Sharing much in common with the romantic movement, these revivals made emotion central to religion. The leading figure in this development was Charles Grandison Finney, who was from upstate New York. Lyman Beecher of Boston, whose children reflected the diversity of the reform impulse, was another important revivalist. Discarding traditional Calvinism, Finney and his fellow revivalists minimized original sin and preached instead the doctrine of free will. Sin was voluntary, and thus every individual could do good and become godly. Every person could be saved who

A religious revival at Eastham, Massachusetts (lithograph from 1851). Religious revivals were popular in the North during the 1820s and 1830s, and gave rise to many reform movements. The Boston Athenæum.

wanted to be, merely by accepting God's free offer of salvation. Employing a variety of techniques designed to stir the emotions of their congregations, they stressed the need for atonement and rebirth through a conversion experience.[12]

The northern revivalists also preached the ideas of millennialism and perfectionism. Perfectionism was the belief that individuals could become sanctified on earth, that a person could live without sin. As a result, a true Christian should aim to live by God's moral law and become perfect. Millennialism was the belief that the thousand years of peace and harmony prophesied in the Bible were at hand, and hence the end of the world, and with it eternal life for the faithful, was imminent.

Through their optimistic view of human potential, the revivalists made religion a major force for social reform. The greatest impact on American society of the Second Great Awakening stemmed from the way in which it linked religion and reform. The revivalists changed the whole emphasis of the religious experience by insisting that salvation was only the beginning. Having gained salvation, true Christians would undertake to perfect society by attacking sin wherever they found it. Their goal, Finney explained, was nothing less than "the universal reformation of the world."[13] Good works thus became a sign of salvation. The result was the launching of a host of reform movements led by clergymen and born-again Christians. The rise of evangelical Protestantism, with its focus on emotions and revivalism, provided a powerful impetus to the reform impulse, and support for reform was especially strong among members of the major evangelical churches (the Methodists, the Baptists, the Presbyterians, and the Congregationalists).[14]

The changes rapidly transforming the American economy and society in these years were the other major stimulus of the antebellum reform impulse. These included the beginnings of industrialization, increased urbanization, the rise of political democracy, and the expansion of the market economy with its overweening materialism. Accompanying these changes were a number of social problems. Cities, for example, were especially troubled by economic dislocation and social tensions, which the density of population made more noticeable. New technologies in communication facilitated propaganda efforts, and the new democratic political system perfected techniques of mass appeal that reformers adapted to their own purposes. Democracy, with its ideal of (white) manhood suffrage, made reforms such as temperance and public education seem imperative; with the franchise more widely distributed than before, a sober and educated citizenry was essential, it was thought, if American liberty was to be preserved. In addition, industrialization demanded a new type of worker who was self-disciplined, sufficiently educated, and reliable. Finally, the prosperity of the age created a class of men and women with the time to devote to reform. A person could choose reform as a career, and the reform movements were controlled and staffed by the middle class, the group that benefited most from these economic changes.

Reform also was a means to deal with the tensions and anxieties produced by rapid socioeconomic change. Those worried about the consequences of these changes could try to mitigate them through reform. Others, fearful of the impact of change on their own lives, could release this anxiety by throwing themselves into the cause of reform and helping others.

Women were particularly active in the reform movement. Northern society offered few outlets for educated or talented women, most of whom were largely confined to the home. But because women were expected to be active in religious work, they easily moved into the social reform movement as well. Reform offered them one way of upholding their position as moral leaders of society while at the same time actively influencing social change. Although men retained most of the positions of authority in reform organizations, middle-class women did much of the volunteer work these organizations required.

Men and women deeply alienated from this emerging competitive, market-oriented society, clergy and devout church members galvanized by the doctrines of millennialism and perfectionism, and community leaders anxious to preserve order and social control over the working class all turned to humanitarian reform. Organizations were formed to eradicate virtually every social evil. "In the history of the world," Ralph Waldo Emerson observed, "the doctrine of Reform never had such scope as at the present hour. . . . We are to revise the whole of our social structure, the State, the school, religion, marriage, trade, science, and explore their foundations in our own nature."[15] With its Puritan heritage, sense of mission, and educated citizenry, Massachusetts became a center of reform activity. And at the center of this larger reform impulse was abolitionism.

The most famous leader of the abolitionist movement was William Lloyd Garrison of Boston. Garrison personified the transition from the earlier, moderate antislavery movement to the more militant movement of the 1830s. He grew up in Massachusetts, a sober and religious youngster. In these qualities, he took after his pious Baptist mother rather than his drunkard sailor father. Apprenticed as a printer, he eventually got caught up in the reform movements of the 1820s, and while editor of a general reform paper he was much influenced by a talk by Benjamin Lundy, a prominent antislavery leader.

Although initially a supporter of the American Colonization Society, which aimed to send America's black population back to Africa, Garrison nonetheless embraced the antislavery cause and went to Baltimore to help Lundy edit his paper, *The Genius of Universal Emancipation*. Garrison brought a new aggressiveness to the paper, but he often leaped before he looked. In 1830 he was convicted of libel and imprisoned. Released after his fine was paid by Arthur Tappan, a wealthy New York City philanthropist, Garrison headed back to Boston, determined to publish a new kind of antislavery journal.[16]

Garrison's paper, *The Liberator,* debuted on the streets of Boston on January 1, 1831, with a press run of four hundred copies. From the first issue it brought a new tone and commitment to the antislavery crusade. Garrison was militant and uncompromising in his call for the abolition of slavery, and he was abrasive and vituperative toward all he considered opponents. In his first editorial in *The Liberator* he promised: "I will be as harsh as truth, and as uncompromising as justice. On this subject, I do not wish to think, or speak, or write, with moderation. No! No! . . . urge me not to use moderation in a cause like the present. I am in earnest—I will not equivocate—I will not excuse—I will not retreat a single inch—AND I WILL BE HEARD."[17]

Realizing that he needed to attract subscribers if his newspaper was to survive, Garrison made a strong appeal to northern free blacks, whom he began to view as a major constituency.[18] With an eye to securing black support, Garrison in his writings defined a new program and a new approach for ending slavery in this country. The principles he set forth served to define abolitionism and distinguish it from antislavery. The most important shift was toward immediatism: unlike earlier antislavery leaders such as Lundy, Garrison repudiated gradual emancipation and demanded that immediate steps be taken to end the institution.[19] "I know not by what rule of the gospel," he wrote, "men are authorized to leave off their sins by a slow process."[20] Garrison understood that abolition would not be instantaneous, but he insisted that it begin at once.

Garrison's brand of immediatism was partly a reaction to a growing black militancy, best symbolized by Boston abolitionist David Walker's *Appeal* (1829), which urged slaves to use violence to end their oppression, and the

A banner carried in antislavery demonstrations. The Massachusetts Historical Society.

slave revolt led by Nat Turner in Virginia in 1831. As an advocate of nonresistance, Garrison opposed such calls for violence, but he feared that this would be the inevitable result if blacks did not receive justice and something was not done about slavery.

Immediatism had religious overtones as well; it possessed close parallels to the doctrines of immediate conversion and personal holiness. Reflecting the idea that slavery was a sin, immediatism represented a personal commitment to make no compromise with sin, to tolerate no social evil. As such, it was an expression of the religious ideals of free will and moral responsibility, and it freed the individual from association with the national sin of slavery. In the eyes of the abolitionists, upholding slavery was as much a sin as owning slaves. To moral suasionists such as Garrison, it was possible to convince slaveowners to reject slavery and thus repent and renounce their sins. Amos A. Phelps, another Massachusetts abolitionist, argued that immediatism was synonymous with immediate repentance. "All that follows is the carrying out of the new principle of action, and is to emancipation just what sanctification is to conversion."[21]

Repudiating his earlier support for colonization, Garrison now denounced efforts to remove free blacks to Africa as an antiblack, proslavery movement. He leveled a withering attack on colonization both in his paper and in his pamphlet *Thoughts on African Colonization* (1832). Influenced by Garrison, who converted Arthur and Lewis Tappan on this question, most abolitionists no longer supported colonization, and opposition to it became a defining principle of the abolition movement.

In addition, Garrison rejected any compensation for slaveowners as part of a program of emancipation. His reasoning on this question was simple: slavery was a sin, and individuals should not be paid to give up sin. Christians gave up sin because it was wrong, not because it paid, although Garrison sometimes found himself forced to compromise this principle, as, for example, when he supported later efforts to purchase the freedom of Frederick Douglass.

In relying upon moral suasion as the proper means to end slavery, Garrison called upon abolitionists to persuade slaveholders to renounce slavery as a sin and free their slaves. He rejected the use of violence by either slaves or opponents to destroy the institution, nor did he favor political action against it. For emancipation to be correct, it had to be voluntary. The Declaration of Sentiments of the American Anti-Slavery Society announced that its members would work "for the destruction of error by the potency of truth—the overthrow of prejudice by the power of love—and the abolition of slavery by the spirit of repentance."[22]

Because of his leading role in defining the principles and approach of abolitionism, Garrison became a symbol of the movement. He was the most hated man in the South, and several southern legislatures offered a reward to anyone who would kidnap him and bring him south to stand trial for inciting slave insurrection. Yet for all the attention critics of the movement heaped on Garrison, *The Liberator*'s circulation remained low, and so did its influence. The paper had only a small number of white patrons, and it stayed in business initially only because of the faithful support of its free black subscribers, who mustered their limited financial resources to sustain this strong voice against slavery.

Outside the free black communities in the North, Garrison's circle of influence was limited largely to Boston and the surrounding area. His closest associate was Wendell Phillips, who came from a socially prominent family but braved the scorn of privilege in carrying on his fight against slavery. Garrison and Phillips complemented one another, for Garrison's skill was as a writer, while Phillips was a powerful public speaker. Other important white abolitionists in the Boston area included Stephen and Abby Foster, Parker Pillsbury, David and Lydia Maria Child, and Maria Weston Chapman. In addition, the area contained several prominent black abolitionists, including Frederick Douglass, who for many years remained a disciple of Garrison; Charles Remond of Salem; and perhaps Garrison's strongest black ally, William Cooper Nell, who led the fight to integrate Boston's schools.

Beyond Boston, others assumed leadership of the movement. One of the

Plaster bust by Edmonia Lewis of Boston abolitionist Maria Weston Chapman. Called by many "the workhorse of the abolition movement," Chapman was a staunch ally of Garrison. She was in the vanguard of the "new breed" of women who were taking an active part in the abolition movement. The Tufts Library, Weymouth, Massachusetts.

most important was Theodore Dwight Weld, who had been converted by Finney and eventually embraced abolition. Unlike Garrison, Weld was a superb organizer, and he eventually established the so-called Band of Seventy, a group of ministers who traveled throughout the West and Northeast lecturing on abolitionism. With the help of the Grimké sisters, he also anonymously wrote one of the most important pieces of antislavery propaganda ever published, *Ameri-*

can Slavery As It Is: Testimony of a Thousand Witnesses (1839), which documented the horrors of slavery from southern court records and newspapers.[23]

Another key figure in the abolitionist movement was Lewis Tappan, a wealthy New York City merchant who, along with his brother Arthur, devoted his fortune to funding various benevolent causes. Converted to abolitionism by Weld, Tappan was a proponent of evangelicalism (he was a Presbyterian) and advocated working through the churches to end slavery.[24]

James G. Birney was another major non-Garrisonian abolitionist. An Alabama slaveowner, Birney had been converted to abolitionism by Weld in 1832. Having freed his slaves, Birney moved to Kentucky in 1833 to publish an antislavery paper, only to be driven out by a proslavery mob. He then moved to Cincinnati, just across the Ohio River from Kentucky, and published the *Philanthropist,* which was devoted to abolitionism and other reform causes.[25]

Abolitionism was never a popular movement in the North, and consequently abolitionists were never very numerous. It has been estimated that they numbered no more than 200,000 in a northern population of more than 20 million in 1860. Moreover, becoming an abolitionist was very much a personal decision. Thousands of Americans with similar backgrounds, often from the same family, did not join the abolitionist movement. It took extraordinary courage and depth of conviction to embrace such an unpopular cause, whose supporters were ridiculed as extremists and subjected to social ostracism. Maria Weston Warren, a leader of the Boston Female Anti-Slavery Society, outlined the high price one paid to be an abolitionist: "It has occasioned our brothers to be dismissed from the pastoral charge—our sons to be expelled from colleges and theological seminaries—our friends from professorships—ourselves from literary and social privileges."[26]

Still, several generalizations can be made about the movement's supporters. Despite the efforts of Weld and others in the West, abolitionists were concentrated in the East, especially in New England. Elsewhere, they tended to be from areas settled by New Englanders, such as western New York and Ohio's Western Reserve. By and large they were young, having been born between 1790 and 1810, and thus were just coming of age, or had only recently done so, in the 1830s. They grew up in religious families and tended to remain quite religious as adults. Many had been influenced by the revivals of the Second Great Awakening and were members of the evangelical churches, especially the Congregationalists and Presbyterians. Abolitionism was primarily a middle-class movement, with its leadership drawn from the professions, particularly the clergy. Finally, abolitionists tended to be from rural areas and small towns rather than large cities. Their upbringing had exposed them to a stern emphasis on moral righteousness and social responsibility.[27]

While they were often successful in their careers and were not a displaced social elite, they were nevertheless deeply alienated from American society. They deplored the lack of religion in American life, the rampant materialism, and the crassness and pragmatism of American politics. They were shocked by the failure of the campaign in the 1820s to stop the movement of the U.S. mails on the Sabbath.[28] By the early 1830s their vague discontent began to come into sharp focus, as they concluded that slavery was the fundamental cause of the nation's degradation. Abolitionism became the means to save the country. The abolitionist cause "not only overshadows all others, but absorbs them into itself," Weld declared. "Revivals, moral Reform etc. will remain stationary until the temple is cleansed."[29]

Close links existed, in both leadership and membership, between abolitionism and other reform movements. Much to the chagrin of many black abolitionists who thought it would weaken the antislavery cause, white abolitionists were often active in a wide array of reform movements, and something approaching an interlocking directory existed among these various organizations. The Sabbatarian movement had attracted many future abolitionists in the 1820s. There were also strong ties between abolitionism and the temperance movement, both at the leadership level and in terms of mass support. Horace Mann, who was elected to Congress as a Free Soiler, was the most famous educational reformer in the country. He had attracted considerable attention for his efforts as secretary to the Massachusetts Board of Education. Samuel Gridley Howe, another prominent political abolitionist in Massachusetts, pioneered working with the blind; although he came under sharp condemnation from the Garrisonians because his school for the blind did not accept black students, he managed to weather the storm.

Abolitionism probably overlapped more strongly with women's rights than with any other reform movement except temperance. The first major tract in this era advocating women's rights was penned by a famous female abolitionist, Sarah Grimké. The women's rights movement was launched in 1848 at Seneca Falls, New York, by two prominent female abolitionists, Elizabeth Cady Stanton and Lucretia Mott. From the beginning, the movement focused on the question of equality and emphasized parallels between the oppression of the slaves and that of women in America.[30] Significantly, the only male allowed to deliver an address at the Seneca Falls convention was the black abolitionist Frederick Douglass.

With such strong religious overtones and such deep roots in the religious revivals of the period, abolitionism became a kind of surrogate religion. In the eyes of its members, support for abolitionism was a sign of Christian virtue. Participation in the movement became a supplement, even an alternative, to traditional religion. For those discontented with traditional religion, abolitionism satisfied religious yearnings and humanitarian impulses that established institutions, including the churches, failed to fulfill. Appealing to men and women troubled by flux and disorder, and disturbed by the apparent irrelevance of time-honored values in a changing society, the doctrine of immediatism fulfilled certain needs in its supporters and offered an outlet for their frustrations and uncertainty. It injected a sense of purpose and direction into their lives and gave concrete meaning to the abstract notions of sin, free will, and repentance.

And for African-Americans in the North, immediatism held out the hope that slavery would begin to be stripped of its power, and that its end might even be near.

The close links between various reform movements and abolitionism soon served to broaden and redefine the abolitionist program. Increasingly, the more radical abolitionists called for a program of thoroughgoing reform of American values and institutions. The movement's tendency toward ultraism was especially apparent in New England.

The Massachusetts Anti-Slavery Society, the first state abolitionist society in the country, was founded in 1832 by both blacks and whites. The following year Garrison, who controlled the state society, joined Lewis Tappan in founding the American Anti-Slavery Society. With the movement gaining converts and growing in strength, abolitionist leaders were quite optimistic. They predicted that they would rapidly convert the nation to their program of abolition and racial equality.

Instead the nation reacted harshly and often violently to the movement. There were a large number of anti-abolitionist mob actions in northern communities in the 1830s; in the most famous of these incidents, a mob in 1835 dragged Garrison through the streets of Boston with a rope around his body before he was rescued by the police. In Philadelphia, another mob set fire to the headquarters of the state abolitionist society and destroyed the building.[31] By this time, the South had clearly rejected moral suasion, and the proslavery argument had become more shrill. When abolitionists attempted to use the U.S. mails to reach southern whites, mainly because they could not travel with safety in the slave states, southern mobs destroyed the antislavery propaganda, and the Jackson administration acquiesced in this interference with the postal service.[32] With the mails closed to them, abolitionists launched a campaign to flood Congress with antislavery petitions. As a result, in 1836 Congress, under southern pressure, adopted the so-called gag rule, automatically tabling these petitions without consideration (this rule was finally repealed in 1844, thanks mainly to the efforts of John Quincy Adams, assisted by Theodore Dwight Weld).[33]

Abolitionists reacted in fundamentally different ways to these developments, which helps explain the eventual disruption of the national organization. Non-Garrisonian abolitionists, who were concentrated outside of New England, were more conservative, more oriented toward traditional institutions, and more supportive of using political means to attain their ends. They believed that the mob violence directed against them furthered the cause by giving the movement publicity and winning over additional sympathizers who were angered by this interference with civil liberties. Furthermore, they insisted that anti-abolitionist mobs, usually a coalition of the top and bottom of northern society, did not represent a majority of northerners. Consequently, they concluded that American society was basically healthy and that abolitionism could succeed by turning to political action, broadening its appeal, and then concentrating on converting the North.

GREAT MASSACHUSETTS PETITION.

To the Senate and House of Representatives of the State of Massachusetts:

The undersigned citizens of the State of Massachusetts, earnestly desiring to free this commonwealth and themselves from all connection with domestic slavery and to secure the citizens of this state from the danger of enslavement, respectfully pray your honorable body,

1. To forbid all persons holding office under any law of this state from in any way officially or under color of office, aiding or abetting the arrest or detention of any person claimed as a fugitive from slavery.

2. To forbid the use of our jails or public property of any description whatever within the Commonwealth, in the detention of any alleged fugitive from slavery.

3. To propose such amendments to the Constitution of the United States as shall forever separate the people of Massachusetts from all connection with slavery.

NAMES.

THE GREAT MASSACHUSETTS PETITIONS have been sent to Postmasters and known friends of human liberty in every town in the State. Many thousands have been printed. Let every freeman into whose hands they may fall, constitute himself an agent to obtain signatures. See that your own town and all the neighboring towns are supplied. Return them by forefather's day, Dec. 22d, or at any rate by Jan. 1, 1843. Hold your town meetings on the 22nd of December, and your county meetings on the first of January, throughout the state. Direct to the Latimer Committee, at their Head Quarters No. 3, Amory Hall, Boston. Let the parcels come, if possible, post paid, or free of expense. Sign under the word names, in a SINGLE Column.

GREAT PETITION TO CONGRESS.

To the Senate and House of Representatives of the United States of America:

The undersigned citizens of the State of Massachusetts, earnestly desiring to free their commonwealth and themselves from all connection with domestic slavery and to secure the citizens of their state from the danger of enslavement, respectfully pray your honorable body,

To pass such laws and to propose such amendments to the Constitution of the United States as shall forever separate the people of Massachusetts from all connection with slavery.

NAMES.

Petition forms urging Massachusetts senators and representatives to abolish slavery (1842). The Boston Athenæum.

Garrison and his followers advanced a quite different analysis. They denied that violent opposition helped the antislavery cause. Instead, the reaction of northerners and southerners to abolitionism indicated that both sections were morally corrupt and that national institutions were unregenerate. Like the more conservative abolitionists, the radical Garrisonian wing now concluded that moral suasion was not sufficient, but they decided that nothing less than a complete restructuring of American institutions and values was needed. Slavery was only part of a larger national disease that had to be rooted out. Led by Garrison, they formulated a program for the total reform of American society.[34]

Strongly influenced by John Humphrey Noyes's radical brand of Christian perfectionism, Garrison's growing extremism eventually split the national antislavery movement. Garrison endorsed a number of radical ideas, which constituted his "broad program" of reform. This program became known as root and branch abolitionism, because its advocates argued that all American institutions had to be destroyed root and branch. Alienated by what he saw as their failure fully to embrace abolitionism, Garrison became a bitter critic of the clergy and organized churches in the North. Even churches sympathetic to the antislavery crusade fell prey to his withering scorn for not coming up to his perfectionist standards. He called on abolitionists to leave the impure churches, and critics charged that he had convinced many blacks in Boston to follow his lead. Garrison further alienated traditional Protestants by rejecting the Sabbath as "an outworn and foolish superstition" (to Garrison, all days were holy).[35]

In addition, Garrison became a disunionist, calling on the North to secede from the South in order to free itself from complicity with slavery, and he put at the masthead of *The Liberator* the slogan "No Union with slaveholders." Proclaiming that the Constitution was proslavery, he denounced it as "a covenant with death and an agreement with hell."[36] It was probably this argument more than anything else that led Frederick Douglass to break with Garrison; reversing his earlier stand, the black leader now endorsed political means to achieve abolitionist ends. Garrison, in contrast, argued that the political system corrupted all who participated in it, and thus he opposed any political action as sinful. In particular, he rejected the idea of forming an antislavery third party. Furthermore, Garrison renounced all government as coercive and a constraint on individual conscience; even some of his earlier supporters considered him an anarchist. But the last straw for Garrison's opponents was when he took up the cause of women's rights.

Garrison's foes in the abolitionist movement did not necessarily oppose these ideas as separate reforms, but they would not accept his argument that these causes had to be part of a broad-based abolitionist program, and that no one could be a true abolitionist who did not support these reforms as well. The anti-Garrisonians also believed that linking abolitionism with other causes would inevitably weaken the abolitionist movement by alienating potential supporters.

The showdown between Garrison and his critics occurred at the national meeting of the American Anti-Slavery Society in 1840. The specific issue over which this larger struggle was fought was whether to allow women to hold office in the organization. By packing the meeting with a boatload of sympathizers from Boston, Garrison carried the day on this question, at which point his opponents seceded and formed a rival organization, the American and Foreign Anti-Slavery Society. The main leaders of this competing movement were Lewis Tappan, Theodore Dwight Weld, and James G. Birney. In addition, many anti-Garrisonians now turned to political action as the most effective way to combat slavery. They had already organized a new party, the Liberty party, and nominated Birney for president. Birney polled a scant seven thousand votes in the 1840 election, but the rift would not be healed.[37]

The schism within abolitionism marked the end of the initial phase of the movement. Crippled by this division, neither organization was very effective or exercised much influence after 1840. Instead, the antislavery struggle was increasingly fought within the political arena, where Garrison and his clique of six hundred followers were largely irrelevant, or over local issues, where the editor of *The Liberator* could always turn to Boston's black community for support. In opposing political action, Garrison had warned that any antislavery party would have to make all sorts of compromises in order to exert influence upon the political system. He preferred to remain pure and hold the abolitionists' banner aloft. Time would amply demonstrate the accuracy of his prophecy.

In the meantime, the political drive against slavery continued to gain strength. The Liberty party began running state and local candidates in certain areas of the North in order to drain off votes from the two major parties and put pressure on them to offer concessions to committed antislavery voters. In 1844, Birney again ran as the party's candidate for president. Aided by the issue of the annexation of Texas, he polled over sixty thousand votes, a dramatic increase over his showing four years earlier and a sufficient tally to determine the outcome of the national election.

Nevertheless, the Liberty party's strategy of holding the balance of power to exact concessions from the Whigs and Democrats failed. Thus in 1848, the political abolitionists joined with disgruntled Whigs and Democrats to organize yet another third party, the Free Soil party, which took as its major principle not hostility to slavery in the southern states but opposition to its expansion into the western territories. In a bid for additional support, the party also added various economic planks to its platform that had little to do with the slavery question. The party nominated former Democratic president Martin Van Buren, who had never previously displayed any sympathy with the antislavery movement, to head the national ticket. Van Buren received over 290,000 votes, almost a fivefold increase over Birney's showing in 1844. While political abolitionists were greatly encouraged, the Free Soil party was unable to sustain its power. In several states with significant antislavery constituencies, such as Massachusetts, New York, and Ohio, it continued to run state and congressional candidates, and even managed to win some offices, yet nationally its power eroded. The return of the Van Burenites to the Democratic party in 1852 cut the Free Soil vote in half and seemingly foreshadowed the party's ultimate demise.[38]

The Compromise of 1850, which was a series of laws aimed at settling all outstanding differences between the two sections over slavery, failed to revitalize the antislavery movement. The most controversial part of the Compromise in the North was the new Fugitive Slave Act. Designed to allow slaveholders to recover their runaway slaves from northern states, this statute was much more rigorous than the 1790 law it replaced. It had several controversial features, including denying the accused a jury trial, paying the U.S. commissioner additional fees if he ruled against the accused, authorizing U.S. marshals to call upon citizens for assistance in apprehending accused runaways, and providing for harsh punish-

A music sheet depicting a scene from Harriet Beecher Stowe's *Uncle Tom's Cabin*, whose portrayal of the slave condition moved thousands to join the abolition cause (1852). The Boston Athenæum.

ment of those who aided fugitives or interfered with their capture. Harriet Beecher Stowe, the daughter of Boston minister Lyman Beecher, wrote her famous novel *Uncle Tom's Cabin* (1852) in response to this law. An instant bestseller, the book was the greatest piece of abolitionist propaganda ever penned, but while it swayed popular emotions as few books ever have, it did not lead to a moral revolution against slavery.

Despite its controversial features, the Fugitive Slave Act was generally enforced in the North.[39] For the sake of the Union, most northerners, as Abraham Lincoln remarked, bit their lips and remained quiet following its passage. Well-publicized instances of forcible resistance to the law occurred in northern communities, however, in which Boston took the lead. Shortly after its passage, a meeting of Boston's black residents at the Belknap Street Church vowed to resist the law, and at a subsequent meeting at Faneuil Hall, Frederick Douglass urged that "we must be prepared . . . to see the streets of Boston running with blood."[40] The Boston Vigilance Committee, staffed by white and black antislavery reformers, intensified its activities to protect the city's black residents, and violent resistance soon broke out.

In February 1851 a band of blacks and whites stormed the Court House and freed Frederick "Shadrach" Wilkins, but in April of that year, efforts to rescue Thomas Sims, another fugitive, failed, and he was sent back to Georgia and slavery. Three years later, in May 1854, Anthony Burns, a runaway slave from Virginia who was living in the black community of Boston, was suddenly seized by U.S. authorities. In the wake of the just-completed passage of the Kansas-Nebraska Act, feelings ran high, and federal officials were anxious to reassure southerners that their property rights in human beings would be protected, even in Boston. The black community rallied against the law and in defense of Burns, and an antislavery mob, led by Thomas Wentworth Higginson, tried unsuccessfully to rescue him from the Court House, where he was being held. Despite legal efforts on his behalf, Burns was eventually returned to Virginia.

As Burns was marched through the city to the wharf, surrounded by U.S. troops, the church bells tolled their sorrowful dirge, buildings and homes were draped in black, and crowds lined the streets weeping or angrily denouncing the government and slavery. It had cost the federal government approximately fifty thousand dollars to return one fugitive to slavery. In addition, a federal officer had been killed during the failed rescue attempt. Despite the presence of a number of fugitives in Boston (perhaps as many as 400), there were no further attempts to enforce the law in the city, and the charges against Higginson, Theodore Parker, and other prominent Massachusetts abolitionists for their part in the effort to rescue Burns were eventually dropped, since it was obvious that no jury in the state would convict them. The Burns case made the city a national symbol of opposition to the law. Eventually Bostonians raised a fund and purchased Burns's freedom.[41]

The resistance of free blacks to the Fugitive Slave Act reflected growing black militancy in the North, especially in the city of Boston. Abolitionists promoted

Fugitive slave Thomas Sims. In 1851 Boston abolitionists unsuccessfully resisted efforts to return Sims to the South. The Boston Athenæum.

The Boston Court House encircled by a heavy iron chain during the trial of fugitive slave Thomas Sims in 1851. "Our temple of justice is a slave pen," commented Sims's lawyer, Richard Henry Dana. The Boston Athenæum.

BOSTON COURT HOUSE.

programs to aid free African-Americans in the North, attacked racial prejudice as well as slavery, and demanded that America live up to its promise of equality. Abolitionists' agitation for racial equality in the free states was the major reason for their unpopularity in the North. Backed by white abolitionists, blacks in Boston lobbied, petitioned, and sued in the courts in order to bring about the integration of public facilities. They conducted a legal battle against the city's segregated schools, sued to end segregation on railroads and other forms of public transportation, and carried on a steady campaign to integrate public accommodations and churches. Denying the prevailing belief that blacks were innately inferior, white abolitionists insisted that environment, and not inherent racial differences, accounted for African-Americans' condition.[42]

Although by the standards of the age abolitionists were remarkably advanced and enlightened on matters of race, they were never able to free themselves entirely from racial prejudice. The issue of social mixing always produced deep divisions in abolitionist meetings. Even the most liberal abolitionists, such as Garrison, were guilty of paternalism. They assumed that they knew what was best for blacks and should guide them to superior values. Antislavery societies, the black abolitionist Martin R. Delaney protested, always "presumed to *think* for, dictate to, and *know* better what suited colored people, than they know for themselves."[43]

This attitude, coupled with rising black militancy, precipitated a growing division between white and black abolitionists. Free blacks had always been an important source of support for the abolitionist movement. Garrison acknowledged on several occasions that without black subscribers *The Liberator* never would have survived. In return, white abolitionists encouraged and supported early black leaders in the movement. But by the 1840s, some black leaders began to complain that they were powerless in the abolitionist movement, that they had no influence on policy, and that they were excluded from responsible offices. The most famous black abolitionist in the country, Frederick Douglass, had begun his career under the tutelage of Garrison. But he chafed under Garrison's paternalism and became increasingly alienated over the latter's program to end slavery, which condemned the Constitution and disavowed political action against the institution. Finally, in 1847, Douglass began to move toward a break with Garrison, leaving Lynn for Rochester to found his own newspaper, *The North Star.*[44]

Douglass's break with Garrison was symptomatic of the growing divisions within the movement. By the 1850s, black abolitionists manifested fundamentally different attitudes from those of their white allies. Frustrated by the lack of progress, African-Americans were far more sympathetic toward the use of violence to end slavery, and they believed that antislavery should remain paramount under the canopy of reform, that other reforms were receiving too much attention, and that a more militant attack on racism in the North was needed. They favored an abolitionist program that was more practical and less abstract, and, manifesting their independence, more and more pursued their own course.[45]

This rising black militancy took shape against the growing moderation of the political antislavery movement. The passage of the Kansas-Nebraska Act in May 1854, which opened these territories previously closed to slavery, had revitalized the antislavery movement. That summer the first steps were taken to form a new party, the Republican party, dedicated to stopping the expansion of slavery. By 1856 the Republicans, aided by rising sectional tensions in Washington and the violence in Kansas, were the strongest party in the North. Political abolitionists and veterans of the Liberty party generally supported the Republican cause, while the Garrisonians continued to denounce political action.[46] As Garrison had predicted, increasing electoral support was accompanied by compromise and a steady lowering of the antislavery platform. Absent from the Republican platform was any reference to abolishing slavery in the District of Columbia, repealing the Fugitive Slave Act, extending civil rights to free African-Americans, or ending slavery in the states where it existed. Instead, Republicans called for a congressional prohibition on slavery in the territories and were careful to deny any intention of interfering with slavery in the southern states. Nor did the party's 1860 national platform, which denounced John Brown's abortive raid on Harpers Ferry, Virginia, in 1859 as "the gravest of crimes," outline any program to deal with slavery in the future.

In 1860, Abraham Lincoln became the first Republican to be elected president. Lincoln's election precipitated the secession of the states of the lower South and eventually led to the outbreak of the Civil War. Believing that the war would destroy slavery, most abolitionists rallied behind the Union cause, though not without considerable anguish. Even the pacifist Garrison supported the war effort, indicating that he was willing to sacrifice temporarily his peace views in order to promote the cause of black freedom. Abolitionists anticipated the rapid triumph of their cause, but as the conflict dragged on and Lincoln, who placed priority on maintaining the Union, refused to move against slavery, abolitionists went to work to rally northern public opinion to the cause of emancipation. Keeping up steady pressure on Lincoln and Congress, abolitionists assumed a vital role in the drive to make emancipation a Union war aim. In September 1862 Lincoln issued the preliminary Emancipation Proclamation, and on New Year's Day he announced the final version freeing the slaves in those areas of the country still in rebellion against the Union.

When the war began, northern black leaders urged the black community to support the war effort despite the discrimination to which they were subjected. Northern blacks lobbied for the right to serve in the U.S. military, and in 1862 the Lincoln administration agreed to accept black recruits, although in separate, all-black regiments commanded by white officers. Nonetheless, Douglass and other black leaders urged blacks to volunteer in order to end slavery in the South and secure civil rights in the North after the war. A number of northern free blacks volunteered. The most famous black regiment was the 54th Massachusetts, raised in Boston and commanded by Robert Gould Shaw, a member of a prominent Massachusetts abolitionist family. Reflecting the hopes and ide-

Abolitionist group at the home of Lucy Stone and Henry Blackwell, July 1886. *Seated, in front*: Harriet Sewall, Samuel Sewall. *First row*: Samuel May, William Lloyd Garrison, Jr., Wendell P. Garrison, Henry Blackwell, Theodore Weld. *On porch*: Elizabeth B. Chace, Francis J. Garrison, Sarah Southwick, Alla W. Foster, Abbey Kelley, Lucy Stone, George T. Garrison, Zilpha Spooner. The Sophia Smith Collection, Smith College.

als of antislavery opinion in the city, the regiment was given a rousing public send-off as it marched off to war. These black troops, most of whom were from Massachusetts, Pennsylvania, and New York, won enduring fame with their heroic charge against Fort Wagner in the unsuccessful campaign against Fort Sumter in 1863. Shaw died in the assault and the Confederates, seeking to dishonor him, buried the white commander with his fallen black troops. As a result of the Civil War, blacks became a permanent, albeit segregated, part of the U.S. military.[47]

The war undercut the alienation of many abolitionists from American society and institutions. Garrison, for example, who previously had held himself aloof from politics, now hailed Lincoln as the "chain-breaker for millions" and supported the president's reelection in 1864.[48] The culmination of the abolitionist movement was the adoption of the Thirteenth Amendment, abolishing slavery throughout the Union. Again, the abolitionists joined in the agitation for the amendment. The proposed amendment passed Congress in January 1865 and was ratified by the states the following December. Its ratification marked the successful culmination of more than three decades of agitation by white and black abolitionists in Massachusetts.

In the end, no city played a larger role in the antislavery movement than Boston. With its strong religious heritage, reform tradition, and active African-American community, the city served as the headquarters of the crusade against slavery during the antebellum period. During these years, as during the Revolution, Boston was in a very real sense the Cradle of Liberty.

NOTES

1. Quoted in Benjamin Quarles, *Lincoln and the Negro* (New York: Oxford University Press, 1962), p. 144.

2. For accounts of the celebration, see *The Liberator,* January 9, 16, 1863; Frederick Douglass, *Life and Times of Frederick Douglass* (New York: Collier Books, 1962; orig. pub. 1881, rev. 1892), pp. 351–54.

3. *Liberator,* January 2, 1863.

4. Wendell P. Garrison and Francis J. Garrison, *William Lloyd Garrison, 1805–1879: The Story of His Life Told by His Children* (New York: The Century Co., 1885–89), vol. 4, p. 71.

5. Arthur Zilversmit, *The First Emancipation: The Abolition of Slavery in the North* (Chicago: University of Chicago Press, 1967); David Brion Davis, *The Problem of Slavery in the Age of Revolution* (Ithaca: Cornell University Press, 1975).

6. The best history of abolitionism is James Brewer Stewart, *Holy Warriors: The Abolitionists and American Slavery* (New York: Hill and Wang, 1976). Other useful accounts include Louis Filler, *The Crusade against Slavery, 1830–1860* (New York: Harper and Row, 1960), and Merton Dillon, *The Abolitionists: The Growth of a Dissenting Minority* (DeKalb: Northern Illinois University Press, 1974).

7. For a fine history of the South in this period, see William W. Freehling, *The Road to Disunion: The Secessionists at Bay, 1776–1854* (New York: Oxford University Press, 1990). The literature on proslavery thought is voluminous. For a good introduction to the topic with a full bibliography, see Drew Gilpin Faust, ed., *The Ideology of Slavery: Proslavery Thought in the Antebellum South, 1830–1860* (Baton Rouge: Louisiana State University Press, 1981).

8. For reform movements in this period, see Ronald Walters, *American Reformers, 1815–1860* (New York: Hill and Wang, 1978), and Alice Felt Tyler, *Freedom's Ferment: Phases of American Social History from the Colonial Period to the Outbreak of the Civil War* (Minneapolis: University of Minnesota Press, 1944), which is fuller and more informative but less analytical.

9. John L. Thomas, "Romantic Reform in America, 1815–1865," *American Quarterly* 17 (Winter 1965): 656–81.

10. Henry S. Commager, *Theodore Parker: Yankee Crusader* (Boston: Beacon Press, 1947); Anne Rose, *Transcendentalism as a Social Movement, 1830–1850* (New Haven: Yale University Press, 1981).

11. Whitney Cross, *The Burned-Over District: The Social and Intellectual History of Religious Enthusiasm in Western New York* (Ithaca: Cornell University Press, 1950).

12. Finney's ideas are discussed in William G. McLoughlin, *Modern Revivalism: Charles G. Finney to Billy Graham* (New York: Ronald Co., 1959), pp. 3–165. For his career, see Keith J. Hardman, *Charles Grandison Finney, 1792–1875: Revivalist and Reformer* (Syracuse: Syracuse University Press, 1987).

13. Quoted in Walters, *American Reformers,* p. 26.

14. John R. McKivigan, *The War against Proslavery Religion: Abolitionism and the Northern Churches, 1830–1865* (Ithaca: Cornell University Press, 1984).

15. Ralph Waldo Emerson, "Man the Reformer," in *Selected Essays,* ed. Larzer Ziff (New York: Penguin Press, 1982), pp. 130, 142.

16. For Garrison's career, see John L. Thomas, *The Liberator: William Lloyd Garrison* (Boston: Little, Brown and Co., 1963), and Walter M. Merrill, *Against Wind and Tide: A Biography of William Lloyd Garrison* (Cambridge: Harvard University Press, 1963). Garrison has been the subject of a sharp debate among historians concerning his significance and contribution to the abolitionist movement. Aileen Kraditor, *Means and Ends in American Abolitionism: Garrison and His Critics on Strategy and Tactics, 1834–1860* (New York: Pantheon, 1969), is excessively laudatory. Extremely critical are Gilbert Hobbs Barnes, *The Anti-Slavery Impulse, 1830–1844* (Washington: American Historical Association, 1934), and Dwight L. Dumond, *Antislavery: The Crusade for Freedom in America* (Ann Arbor: University of Michigan Press, 1961).

17. *Liberator,* January 1, 1831.

18. Donald M. Jacobs, "William Lloyd Garrison's *Liberator* and Boston's Blacks, 1830–1865," *New England Quarterly* 44 (June 1971): 259–77.

19. For the doctrine of immediatism, see Anne C. Loveland, "Evangelicalism and 'Immediate Emancipation' in American Antislavery Thought," *Journal of Southern History* 32 (May 1966): 172–88, and David Brion Davis, "The Emergence of Immediatism in British and American Antislavery Thought," *Mississippi Valley Historical Review* 49 (September 1962): 209–30.

20. Quoted in Loveland, "Evangelicalism and 'Immediate Emancipation,'" p. 188.

21. Quoted in ibid., p. 185.

22. Quoted in Stewart, *Holy Warriors,* pp. 54–55.

23. Robert Abzug, *Passionate Liberator: Theodore Dwight Weld and the Dilemma of Reform* (New York: Oxford University Press, 1981).

24. Bertram Wyatt-Brown, *Lewis Tappan and the Evangelical War against Slavery* (Cleveland: Press of Case Western Reserve, 1969).

25. Betty L. Fladeland, *James Gillespie Birney: Slaveholder to Abolitionist* (Ithaca: Cornell University Press, 1955).

26. Quoted in Benjamin Quarles, *Black Abolitionists* (New York: Oxford University Press, 1969), p. 37.

27. Larry Gara, "Who Was an Abolitionist?" in Martin B. Duberman, ed., *The Antislavery Vanguard: New Essays on the Abolitionists* (Princeton: Princeton University Press, 1965), pp. 32–51; Betty L. Fladeland, "Who Were the Abolitionists?" *Journal of Negro History* 49 (April 1964): 99–115; Edward Magdol, *The Antislavery Rank and File: A Social Profile of the Abolitionists' Constituency* (Westport, Conn.: Greenwood, 1986). For a different emphasis, see David Donald, "Toward a Reconsideration of the Abolitionists," in *Lincoln Reconsidered: Essays on the Civil War Era* (New York: Alfred A. Knopf, 1956), pp. 19–36.

28. Bertram Wyatt-Brown, "Prelude to Abolitionism: Sabbatarian Politics and the Rise of the Second Party System," *Journal of American History* 58 (September 1971): 316–41.

29. Quoted in Quarles, *Black Abolitionists,* p. 43.

30. Ellen Carol DuBois, *Feminism and Suffrage: The Emergence of an Independent Women's Movement in America, 1848–1869* (Ithaca: Cornell University Press, 1978); Blanche G. Hersh, *The Slavery of Sex: Feminist Abolitionists in America* (Urbana: University of Illinois Press, 1978); Jean Fagan Yellin, *Women and Sisters: Antislavery Feminists in American Culture* (New Haven: Yale University Press, 1990).

31. Leonard Richards, *"Gentlemen of Property and Standing": Anti-Abolition Mobs in Jacksonian America* (New York: Oxford University Press, 1970).

32. Bertram Wyatt-Brown, "The Abolitionists' Postal Campaign of 1835," *Journal of Negro History* 50 (October 1965): 227–38.

33. The fullest discussion of this important but strangely neglected controversy is in Freehling, *Road to Disunion,* pp. 308–52.

34. Stewart, *Holy Warriors,* pp. 50–96.

35. Quoted in Russel B. Nye, *William Lloyd Garrison and the Humanitarian Reformers* (Boston: Little, Brown and Co., 1955), p. 109.

36. Quoted in Filler, *Crusade against Slavery,* p. 216.

37. For the Liberty party's history, see Richard H. Sewell, *Ballots for Freedom: Antislavery Politics in the United States, 1837–1860* (New York: Oxford University Press, 1976), pp. 43–165.

38. Ibid., pp. 152–253; Frederick J. Blue, *The Free Soilers: Third Party Politics, 1848–54* (Urbana: University of Illinois Press, 1973).

39. Stanley W. Campbell, *The Slave Catchers: Enforcement of the Fugitive Slave Law, 1850–1860* (Chapel Hill: University of North Carolina Press, 1970).

40. Quoted in Quarles, *Black Abolitionists,* p. 203.

41. Leonard W. Levy, "Sims' Case: The Fugitive Slave Law in Boston in 1851," *Journal of Negro History* 35 (January 1950): 39–74; Samuel Shapiro, "The Rendition of Anthony Burns," *Journal of Negro History* 44 (January 1959): 34–51; Harold Schwartz, "Fugitive Slave Days in Boston," *New England Quarterly* 27 (June 1954): 191–212; "Trial of Anthony Burns, 1854," *Proceedings of the Massachusetts Historical Society* 44 (December 1953): 353–90.

42. James McPherson, "A Brief for Equality: The Abolitionists Reply to the Racist Myth, 1860–1865," in Duberman, *Antislavery Vanguard,* pp. 156–77.

43. Leon Litwack, *North of Slavery: The Negro in the Free States, 1790–1860* (Chicago: University of Chicago Press, 1961), pp. 227–28. Also see William H. and Jane H. Pease, "Antislavery Ambivalence: Immediatism, Expediency, Race," *American Quarterly* 17 (Winter 1965): 682–95; Leon F. Litwack, "The Abolitionist Dilemma: The Antislavery Movement and the Northern Negro," *New England Quarterly* 34 (March 1961): 50–73.

44. William S. McFeely, *Frederick Douglass* (New York: W. W. Norton, 1991), pp. 146–53.

45. William H. and Jane H. Pease, *They Who Would Be Free: Blacks' Search for Freedom, 1830–1861* (New York: Atheneum, 1974), and "Ends, Means, and Attitudes: Black-White Conflict in the Antislavery Movement," *Civil War History* 18 (June 1972): 117–28.

46. For abolitionists' attitude toward the Republican party, see James McPherson, *The Struggle for Equality: Abolitionists and the Negro in the Civil War and Reconstruction* (Princeton: Princeton University Press, 1964).

47. Luis F. Emilio, *Brave Black Regiment: History of the Fifty-Fourth Regiment of Massachusetts Volunteer Infantry* (Boston: Boston Book Co., 1894); Peter Burchard, *One Gallant Rush: Robert Gould Shaw and His Brave Black Regiment* (New York: St. Martin's Press, 1965); Joseph Glatthaar, *Forged in Battle: The Civil War Alliance of Black Soldiers and White Officers* (New York: Free Press, 1990), pp. 135–41.

48. Quoted in Reinhard H. Luthin, *The Real Abraham Lincoln* (Englewood Cliffs, N.J.: Prentice-Hall, 1960), p. 574.

CHAPTER THREE

Bernard F. Reilly, Jr.

The Art of the Antislavery Movement

I f William Lloyd Garrison was not subtle in the way he chose to articulate the cause of antislavery, certainly neither were the various propagandists of abolition who relied upon both art and artifact to deliver their powerful message. Repelled by the institution of slavery, Bernard Reilly explains, these artists relied upon different media and crafted a variety of images in an effort to reach the consciences of the American people.

From small, often ornately decorated boxes made of wood to "shoes with 'Trample not the Oppressed' printed on the soles," from abolition newspaper mastheads to great majestic portraits to the many popular lithographs and prints, every visual effort possible was made to capture and shape the popular imagination. One major goal was to humanize the slave; another was to dehumanize the slaveholder. Thus, on the one hand we have the popular Wedgwood image imported from England of a slave seemingly praying to God for deliverance, captioned "Am I Not a Man and a Brother?" while on the other we have Frank B. Mayer's Leisure and Labor, portraying very negatively the landed gentry of the South.

Then, to make sure history would not soon forget, what were viewed as great events of the day were also effectively depicted, although at times in a rather exaggerated fashion. These included two portraits of Joseph Cinquez, the slave who commandeered the Spanish ship Amistad in 1839 in an effort to bring the slaves on board back to Africa and freedom, one drawn by James Sheffield and the other by Nathaniel Jocelyn; Theodor Kaufmann's Effects of the Fugitive Slave Law of 1850; and then Winslow Homer's Arguments of the Chivalry, which imaginatively portrays the violent 1856 attack upon Senator Charles Sumner of Massachusetts by Congressman Preston Brooks of South Carolina to avenge the verbal abuse publicly heaped by Sumner upon Brooks's uncle, Senator Andrew Butler, in a speech before the Congress.

While proslavery northerners of influence were at times able to prevent a public *display of some of this antislavery art, most of it successfully appeared and had significant visual and emotional impact. Reilly's narrative deals with a frequently overlooked weapon in the abolition arsenal, while at the same time offering up a rich array of powerful illustrations.*

In January 1838, a small wooden box containing one dollar and twenty cents was delivered to the office of the Anti-Slavery Society in Philadelphia. The money had been collected for the antislavery cause by a young boy—no doubt with some prompting from his elders—from relatives and friends. Painted or drawn on the lid of the box was a picture of the United States Capitol building in Washington, with a procession of manacled slaves passing before it. The contribution box does not survive today, but the scene portrayed on it was an episode recounted and illustrated many times during the history of the American antislavery movement. Nearly twenty years earlier, standing in the street near the U.S. Capitol, several members of Congress had watched a drove of African slaves passing by in chains. Just opposite the Capitol, one of the slaves stopped, raised his manacled hands as high as he could, and with no little irony began to sing the national hymn, "Hail Columbia! Happy Land."[1]

By this time slavery was long established in American society. The expansion of European settlements and the scarcity of inexpensive labor in the New World had by the 1660s largely put an end to the notion of free Africans, or even black indentured servants in the South, leading instead to the introduction of the idea of "perpetual servitude," or slavery. In 1790 the first national census counted 600,000 slaves in the five southern states, and the invention of the cotton gin three years later would soon begin to further accelerate the rate at which Africans were imported.

This explosive growth of slavery in the United States collided head-on with the many Christian reform movements that began to spring up during the early years of the nineteenth century. The reformers, black and white, were religious people, who saw in slavery a moral evil, a disease in American society on a par with alcoholism, dueling, and gambling. Their campaign against slavery set forces in motion which in three decades' time constitutionally brought about the emancipation of all American slaves and the permanent abolition of the institution in the United States.

But the abolition of slavery was accomplished with great difficulty. At first the overwhelming majority of Americans considered the abolitionists cranks and fanatics. Nonetheless, in their struggle to win people over to their cause, the antislavery forces would employ every available means of persuasion, not the least of which was visual art.

In the history of American art, the art of the antislavery movement is something of an anomaly. In many ways the young boy's contribution box epitomized its unusual character. The box was a common object, illustrated with a simple visual sermon. The identity of the artist is unknown, and in fact incidental. Most artists enlisted in the production of antislavery materials generally had little say in the design and development of the imagery. Much of the art used in the antislavery campaign was in fact either commissioned with specific guidelines or appropriated from earlier sources, usually British. While antislavery orators rose in prominence as the movement grew, the artists employed tended to occupy a much humbler and more tangential position in the movement, their work usually subordinate to the rhetorical center of abolition.

Perhaps most striking about the painted box is its inventiveness as a medium for antislavery propaganda. It typifies the often unconventional means employed by the antislavery people to spread their message. By the 1830s there were in the United States well-established channels of communication, including major newspapers, bookstores, print shops, and picture galleries. This network relied very heavily, however, on the patronage of the affluent merchants and businessmen of the Northeast, who were usually quite content to overlook the conspicuous moral failures of their southern trading partners, and considered the abolitionists wild-eyed radicals. This meant that the arts were largely subsidized by the merchants and industrialists of the North and the large agrarian landholders of the South, who shared a common indifference, if not hostility, toward those who were concerned about the plight of the African slave.

As a result, the abolitionists were forced to circumvent the usual channels in order to disseminate their views, and in this they became extraordinarily resourceful. Abolitionist prints were sold by mail order, through antislavery newspapers such as *The Liberator* in Boston, *The Emancipator* in New York, or the *Charter Oak* of Hartford, Connecticut, and also from the reading rooms and offices set up by the movement in the major northeastern cities. In addition, the movement produced or imported from England and then distributed a wide variety of ceramic pitchers, thimbles, purses, and pincushions adorned with all sorts of antislavery emblems and messages.

Women played a particularly significant role in the dissemination of this art. An account of the Boston Ladies Anti-Slavery Fair of 1836, published in *The Liberator,* described articles sold on the occasion such as shoes with "Trample not the Oppressed" printed on the soles, together with pens, bookmarks, quilts, and watchcases featuring antislavery insignia and mottoes. The intent in presenting such a range of items, *The Liberator* went on to explain, was "to keep the subject [of slavery] before the public eye, and by every innocent expedient to promote perpetual discussion."[2] A few of these kinds of items, in fact, have come down to us, such as a silk drawstring bag bearing the popular antislavery image of a supplicant female slave. This item was owned by Philadelphia Quaker abolitionist Elizabeth Margaret Chandler and is housed in the Museum of the Daughters of the American Revolution in Washington.

Like the contribution box, however, much of the art of the antislavery movement is now lost. Nor was it designed to endure beyond its immediate practical

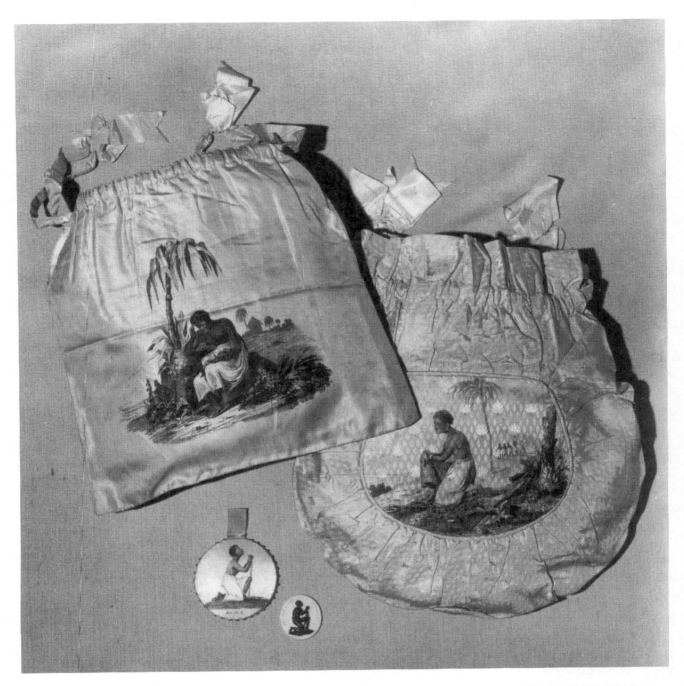

Two silk drawstring bags, a pinholder, and a cameo medallion, depicting abolition scenes (1820–1830). The DAR Museum, Washington, D.C. Gift of Mrs. Erwin L. Broecker and a Friends of the Museum Purchase.

and political use. Yet one can partly reconstruct the movement's efforts through objects such as this—the few surviving prints, the paintings, the broadsides, banners, purses, and household items—and through the abolitionists' own descriptions and portrayals of such items used in the struggle. What the art clearly shows is the influence of a three-part abolitionist rhetorical strategy. Therefore the aim of nearly all of these works was to create an ennobling image of the African, arouse the compassion of white Americans for the plight of the slave, or generate outrage among northerners toward the South. Apart from their specific message to the world of the 1830s, the representations on the contribution box reflected the abolitionists' abiding faith in the power of imagery and the belief that it could effectively convey the antislavery message.

SHAPING THE MESSAGE

The great African-American statesman and abolitionist Frederick Douglass reflected later in his life that "perhaps the greatest hindrance to the adoption of abolition principles by the people of the United States was the low estimate . . . placed upon the Negro as a man, that because of his assumed natural inferiority, people reconciled themselves to his enslavement and oppression, as being inevitable if not desirable."[3] This "low estimate" was nurtured and perpetuated (if not formed) by white American culture: by literature, the theater, the press, and even the visual arts.

Sketch for *Patrick Lyon at His Forge*, by John Neagle (ca. 1826). Ink wash drawing on paper. The Boston Athenæum.

tions which free blacks had begun to develop separately, the black Masons having been founded in Boston during the 1790s by the Negro abolitionist Prince Hall. In the early 1800s such institutions were often the objects of white scorn.

A series of broadsides issued in the 1820s cruelly lampooned the celebrations by Boston freedmen of the 1808 abolition of the African slave trade, here referred to as the "bobalition of slabery." Celebrated on the fourteenth of July, these colorful occasions were marked by parades, toasts, speeches, and other events, which were solemnly reported in detail in the newspapers. The author of these broadsides attempted to parody the dialect of Afro-Americans of the time, and the result, perhaps purposely, is nearly unreadable. The narrative features characters such as Scipio, Cesar, and Pompey, thus mocking the classical names that West Indian plantation owners were often known to give facetiously to their slaves, many of whom were now free blacks in the United States.

In Edward W. Clay's widely copied series of prints *Life in Philadelphia,* the attempts of free African men and women to adopt the fashions of white society were also ridiculed. Caricatures of "dandies" were a popular genre of the day, parodying the overdressed youthful fops of the new white middle class and the blacks that seemed to be copying their ways. These satires were not altogether playful; underlying them was a clear insinuation of immorality, as they depicted show, style, extravagance, and idleness—traits in opposition to the cherished traditional national values of modesty, economy, and industry.

In response the abolitionists set out to dismantle this grotesque, libelous representation, to strip away the disguise, remove the layers of assimilation, and reveal the basic humanity of the Africans. In an attempt to counter white biases, they offered up the best-known and probably the central image of the antislavery campaign—that of the supplicant slave. The image is of a kneeling African man, all but naked, his hands and feet chained, his gaze directed heavenward, and is usually captioned, "Am I Not a Man and a Brother?" It was originally adopted in the 1780s as the seal of the Society for the Abolition of Slavery in England, and appeared on several medallions for the society made by Josiah Wedgwood as early as 1787. (We know that a packet of these medallions was sent by Wedgwood to Benjamin Franklin in Philadelphia, probably for circulation among the few Americans who then supported the antislavery cause.)[5] Beginning in the 1820s, American abolitionists blanketed the Northeast with this image. It was printed on countless pamphlets, on stationery (advertised and sold through antislavery newspapers), and on handbills. It was also emblazoned on pottery and other goods.

The most famous version of this image appeared on a broadside of John Greenleaf Whittier's poem "My Countryman in Chains," first published in 1837 and sold, beginning in March of that year, from the Anti-Slavery Offices in Boston and New York (for two cents each or one dollar per hundred). The identity of the artist who engraved the woodcut is unknown. But he or she endowed the figure with a physical power and grace considerably greater than that in Wedgwood's original. The portrayal conveyed a sense of the innocence

ANTI-SLAVERY EVENTS

DURING THE YEAR ENDING 5th MARCH

1 8 6 3.

AM I NOT A MAN AND A BROTHER

AM I NOT A WOMAN AND A SISTER

" Can we behold, unheeding,
Life's holiest feelings crush'd ;—
While *Woman's* heart is bleeding,
Shall *Woman's* voice be hush'd ?"

"Am I Not a Man and a Brother? Am I Not a Woman and a Sister?" The central image of the antislavery campaign (1820). The Boston Athenæum.

of the black in his natural state, before the corrupting impact of slavery and Western society. To this is added a poignant sense of vulnerability. The slave's pose and the implied menace of his situation, as suggested by his plea "Am I Not a Man and a Brother?" cast him as a modern Daniel in the lion's den of slavery, his sole recourse being to God or to the divine spirit in man.[6]

The abolitionists also looked for real models to belie the stereotype, and to show the potential of Africans for advancement and ennoblement. Some found these models in history. Portraits of two such outstanding Africans from the past were presented in an engraving published in New York in 1836: Hannibal, the Carthaginian general and worthy military adversary of the great Roman leader Scipio Africanus; and Cyprian, Bishop of Carthage, an articulate and eminent figure in early Christianity. Their portraits appear here in aureoles of light. Accompanying them and reinforcing this meditation on African nobility are two scenes depicting the more recent fortunes of Africans: *Treatment of the Africans* (above) shows African natives beaten and abducted by slave traders, and *Hospitality of the Africans* (below) shows a party of whites shipwrecked on

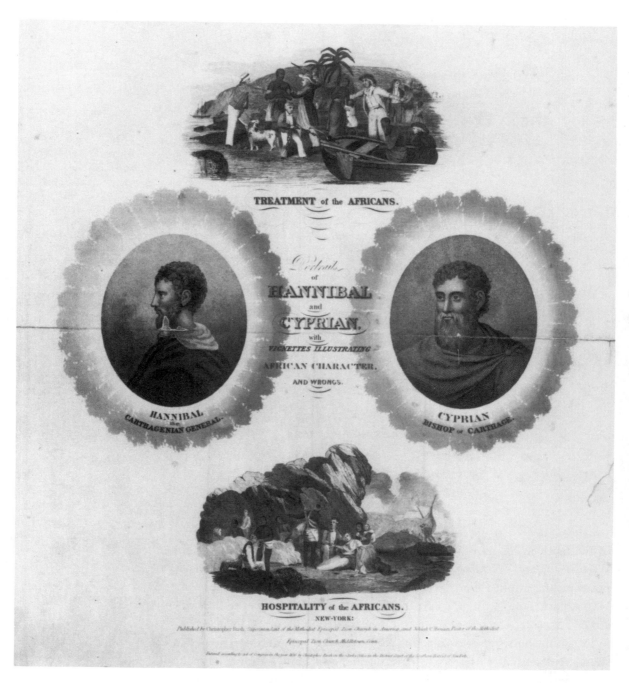

Portraits of Hannibal and Cyprian. Engraving (1836). The Library of Congress.

some African or Caribbean coast rescued and tended to by African natives. (In keeping with the heavy reliance of American abolitionist art on English models, the two vignettes were copied from late eighteenth-century engravings after the British artist George Morland.)[7] The print was published by two black clergymen, Christopher Rush, superintendent of New York's African Methodist Episcopal Zion Church, and Jehiel C. Beman, pastor of the Episcopal Zion Church of Middletown, Connecticut, and soon after of the Zion Methodist Episcopal Church of Boston.

In 1839, a new black hero appeared on the American scene. In June of that year the Spanish brig *Amistad* set sail from Havana, Cuba, after picking up a cargo of approximately fifty slaves who had been illegally kidnapped and transported to Cuba from Africa. While en route to Haiti, the black captives overpowered the white crew of the *Amistad.* Led by an African chieftain's son, Joseph Cinquez (Cinqué), the slaves killed the captain and three of the crew and took control of the vessel. Intending to sail the *Amistad* back to Africa, the mutineers were in fact misled by two of the surviving crew into landing off Long Island. Here their vessel was boarded by the U.S. Navy, and the Africans were promptly arrested and taken to New Haven, where they were charged with piracy and murder.

The event aroused enormous popular interest, resulting not only from public curiosity over what seemed the extreme violence of the act, but also from the fact that it was committed by Africans who yearned to be free.[8] In August 1839, Moses Beach, editor of the New York *Sun,* published a lithographed portrait of Joseph Cinquez, probably the first image of the man to be seen by the American public. It was titled *Joseph Cinquez, the brave Congolese Chief, who prefers death to Slavery, and who now lies in jail in Irons, in New Haven Conn. awaiting his trial for daring for Freedom.* The portrait was drawn by James Sheffield, a New London miniature painter, and was commissioned by Beach while Cinquez was imprisoned on board ship in New London Harbor.[9] Despite the highly charged atmosphere surrounding the *Amistad* mutiny, Sheffield's portrait is sympathetic, informal, and unromanticized. It shows a composed Cinquez, wearing a simple Western shirt, probably borrowed, gazing directly if guardedly at the viewer. An accompanying text quotes Cinquez's sober and moving speech to his comrades on board ship after the mutiny: "Brothers, we have done that which we purposed, our hands are now clean for we have Striven to regain the precious heritage we received from our fathers. . . . I am resolved it is better to die than to be a white man's slave. . . . "

Surely there was an opportunity here for the abolitionists, and they were not slow to seize it. The defense of the *Amistad* captives was undertaken by no less a personage than former president and now congressman John Quincy Adams. The abolitionists fanned the flames of sensationalism surrounding the case, focusing public attention on the issue of the nobility of the African race. In 1839, at the height of the controversy, Robert Purvis, a wealthy black abolitionist from Philadelphia, commissioned New Haven artist Nathaniel Jocelyn to paint a portrait of Cinquez.[10] Jocelyn's painting shows Cinquez not in the borrowed shirt of the prisoner depicted in Sheffield's portrait, but clad in a simple tunic. Here Cinquez is a commanding presence; he stands in an African landscape, holding a bamboo pole or lance, clearly a free man.

Jocelyn's portrait became widely known. A mezzotint copy of the work was engraved by Philadelphia artist John Sartain.[11] Sartain generously contributed

Joseph Cinquez, Brave Congolese Chief. Portrait by James or Isaac Sheffield (1839). The Library of Congress.

five hundred impressions of the engraving to the *Amistad* Committee to be sold to raise funds for the defense and support of the captives. It is probable that even more copies of the work were in circulation, since in March 1841, the *American and Foreign Anti-Slavery Reporter* announced that the engraved copper plate had in fact been purchased by the committee, and that prints from it were being sold at several antislavery offices.[12]

In the spring of 1841, after the captives' release as the result of a decision handed down by the U.S. Supreme Court, Jocelyn's painting was submitted by

Cinque. Joseph Cinquez. Mezzotint by John Sartain after Nathaniel Jocelyn (1840). The National Portrait Gallery.

Purvis to the annual exhibition of the Artists Fund Society in Philadelphia. The hanging committee, headed by society painter and prominent Whig John Neagle, barred the painting from the exhibition. Neagle explained the committee's decision, noting that it was "contrary to usage to display works of that character" and that "under the excitement of the times, it might prove injurious both to the proprietors and the institution." Enraged, the local abolitionist newspaper, the *Pennsylvania Freeman,* took up the issue:

> Why is the portrait denied a place in that gallery? . . . The negro-haters of the north, and the negro-stealers of the south will not tolerate a portrait of a negro in a picture gallery. And such a negro! His dauntless look, as it appears on canvas, would make the souls of slaveholders quake. His portrait would be a standing anti-slavery lecture to slaveholders and their apologists.[13]

In his defense of the work, the writer no doubt aggravated the worst fears of the slaveholders and their "apologists." Fear of slave rebellion was pervasive at the time. Several things had happened to justify that fear. The history of the slave system in North America in fact was a succession of abortive but damaging revolts. Most recently, in August 1831, Nat Turner's rebellion had killed nearly sixty white men, women, and children before being put down by federal and state troops, who responded by executing approximately one hundred blacks.

Neagle's concern reflected the fact that in many parts of the North, people were not ready for the spectacle of a strong, young African man, armed and at liberty. Under the circumstances the idea of the "noble savage" remained problematic, and after the Cinquez incident, the image of the empowered black man vanished from the propaganda of the abolitionists.

The moment was important for another reason. It marked the decisive banishment from the usual places of exhibit and display, at least for the time being, of art conveying an antislavery message. In these genteel halls the subject of slavery was, to say the least, embarrassing, and even dangerously volatile. It would be another decade before this situation would change.

USING IMAGERY TO CREATE EMPATHY

But the abolitionists had other means of conveying their message. One of the most horrifying and (probably) effective weapons in their arsenal was the successful effort to publicize and build a strong negative emotional response to the plan for packing the slaves being transported by the notorious slave trading ship the *Brookes*. First issued in England during the campaign for parliamentary regulation of the slave trade in 1788, it appeared in several manifestations in the United States. It initially appeared as an anonymous broadside in 1789, and repeatedly thereafter in editions of Thomas Clarkson's popular book *The History of the Rise, Progress and Accomplishment of the Abolition of the African Slave Trade* (Philadelphia, 1808), even after the British traffic in slaves directly from Africa had ended.

The plan was actually intended to make the voyage to slavery less claustrophobic, as it followed the rule that only three slaves would be transported for each tonnage displacement. Nonetheless, the plan surpassed all other abolitionist images in its grimness, providing in graphic terms a clear, albeit horrifying, picture of the conditions faced by slaves transported along the Middle Passage. At times over six hundred persons had been carried in these slave-trading vessels, which were actually designed to accommodate only half that many, and even then in deplorable, subhuman conditions. The plan vividly conveys the suffocating crowding of men, women, and children—"human cargo," as they were called in abolitionist sermons—into coffinlike ships. These *were,* in fact, floating coffins for many, as probably at least one out of every four slaves transported did not survive the voyage across the Atlantic.

The sense of dreadful confinement was developed further in pictures of the face masks, gags, manacles, and irons diagrammed with care in Samuel Wood's

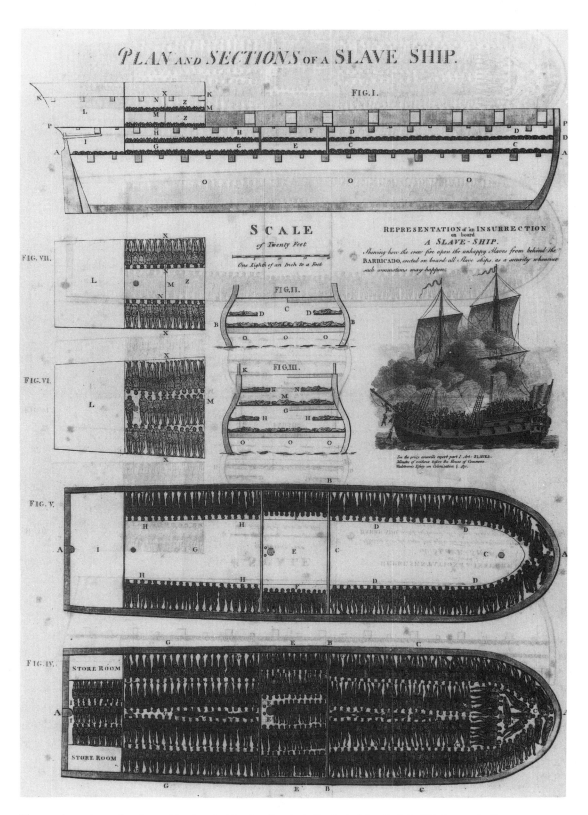

Plan and section of a slave ship (probably the *Brookes*). Included in Carl B. Wadstrom's *Essay on Colonization* (1790). The Boston Athenæum.

UNITED STATES SLAVE TRADE.

United States Slave Trade.
Engraving (1830). The
Historical Society of
Pennsylvania.

broadside *Injured Humanity,* published in New York in 1805. The theme of
suffocation was in fact widespread in American antislavery rhetoric. Profoundly
disturbing on a physical level, it served also as a powerful metaphor for the
spiritual death that was slavery.

In a further effort to generate sympathy for the slave, the abolitionists produced a flood of images of suffering; flogging scenes and scenes of the slave
markets were particularly prevalent. As real as the sufferings were, there seems
to have been an ulterior religious motive at work. The recurrent biblical cycles
of suffering, sacrifice, death, and resurrection can be seen as the underpinning
for both the rhetoric and the art of this campaign. The slave was often portrayed
in the Christlike role of the innocent sufferer who silently endures mortifica-
tion, flagellation, and a spiritual death in slavery. Accordingly, his sufferings as
portrayed in abolitionist art are reminiscent of scenes from sacred history.
Many slave market scenes, a staple of antislavery pamphlets and medallions,
played on marked thematic and compositional similarities to the portrayals of
Christ before Pilate common as the subject of Christian meditation (and visual-
ization in art) since the Middle Ages. Probably the most widely known image of
this sort at the time was the 1831 illustrated masthead of William Lloyd Garrison's radical abolitionist newspaper *The Liberator.* Common also were scenes of
floggings of slaves, which to Christian Americans of the time would have
brought to mind the flagellation of Christ.

Similarly, emancipation was often portrayed in terms strikingly similar to
those traditionally used with the risen Christ—not surprising given the rhetorical linking of the theme of freedom with that of resurrection and new life. One
engraving circulated widely in the United States by abolitionists was *The Eman-*

cipated Family, after a painting by the British artist Edward Villiers Rippingville, in which the freed slave, central to the composition, strikes the pose of the risen Savior. Such pictures reflect the fundamentally religious character of the abolitionist movement.

In 1849 a Virginia slave named Henry Brown succeeded in escaping by having himself packed in a crate and shipped via Adams Express from Richmond to Philadelphia. In a popular lithograph of the time, we see him "resurrected" in the office of the Pennsylvania Anti-Slavery Committee. An account of his escape and ordeal published at the time is filled with images of death and burial.[14] It describes his travel in the dark, tomblike box, and his joyous resurrection into a new life of freedom in the North. Another print, bearing the same title but issued by one less sympathetic to the antislavery cause, parodies the theme, showing the attending figures in the biblical role of the Marys at the Tomb. Although several prints were inspired by the escape of this modern-day Lazarus, the most poignant commentary on the subject was a broadside published in Philadelphia simply showing the box itself. Consistent with the resurrection theme, the third masthead for *The Liberator,* designed by Boston illustrator Hammatt Billings in 1850, again stresses the parallel between emancipation and resurrection by placing Christ himself in the central position formerly reserved for the slave.[15]

This imagery of suffering worked on many levels, aside from that of purely eliciting human sympathy. Integral to the religious imagery of suffering and resurrection is the idea, traditional in Christian art and writings, of the implied complicity of the viewer in the perpetration of this suffering. In her recent study of women and the antislavery movement, Jean Yellin has pointed out the implicit accusation in the supplicant slave's appeal "Am I Not a Man and a Brother?"[16] The question cannot be answered in the affirmative without necessitating Christian action. The views of the slave markets and the flagellations, like those devotional images and sermons of Christian tradition, place the viewer in a world polarized by the forces of good and evil. Listeners to religious sermons were held accountable for the sufferings of Christ through their sins. And as the religious images demanded personal penitence and reform, the abolitionist images demanded both political and moral action.

THE SOUTH SEEN THROUGH A GLASS DARKLY

Overall, perhaps the most effective strategy of the antislavery press was the unremitting campaign of attacking the southern character and way of life. In their newspapers and journals, the abolitionists carefully developed and cultivated an image of the South as a world in decline, a place of deteriorating physical and moral conditions, exhausted soil, and a dispirited working class. As the *Maine Cultivator and Weekly Gazette* put it,

It is common opinion here in the North, that if you go South where the seasons are warm and climate more favorable to the growth of certain products, you will find

Final masthead of *The Liberator*, by Alonzo Hartwell after Hammatt Billings. First used May 31, 1850. The Boston Athenæum.

fields almost like paradise, and the people rioting in plenty which is burdensome. Go and see the mistake. . . . We have travailled some in the sunny South, and we say deliberately, that in the southern states, agriculture does not begin to compare with the agriculture amongst us. The fences are bad, the fields are skimmed over and appear sterile, the buildings are miserable compared with ours, the poor slaves lift and let fall their hoes as if they cared not a fig how little and poorly the work was done, whilst the lordly whites, too proud to work, are wasting their time in idleness, and those vices which idleness seldom fails to induce.[17]

An implicit link was made between a declining agricultural economy and degenerate behavior, lawlessness, and decay. The South was presented as a kind of moral quagmire. The prevalence of dueling and gambling, for example, was viewed by abolitionists as proof of the general decadence of the southern character. This was the view of the region fostered by one of the most ubiquitous antislavery publications, Samuel Bourne's *Picture of Slavery,* illustrated with woodcuts of southern cruelties.

Arrayed in opposition to this were images of a preposterously idyllic South presented and maintained by the many northern apologists for slavery, such as artist Edward Williams Clay in his 1851 lithograph *America,* published in New York, and the Boston publisher of the 1850 print *Slavery As It Exists in America/Slavery As It Exists in England.*[18]

For the abolitionists the South clearly represented a political as well as a moral menace because of its designs on Texas, Mexico, and even Central America in order to expand slavery. For obvious reasons, the spread of the power and influence of the planters was widely feared.

During the 1830s, much had occurred to reinforce these fears. The decade saw the passage in every state in the South of measures that seriously infringed upon the constitutional liberties of Americans. These laws included prohibiting the formation of antislavery societies and preventing the dissemination of abolitionist literature through the establishment of vigilance committees for meting out extralegal punishment to those accused of fomenting "emancipationism."

SOUTHERN IDEAS OF LIBERTY.

Sentence *passed upon one for supporting that clause of our Declaration viz. All men are born free & equal.*
" *Strip him to the skin! give him a coat of Tar & Feathers!! Hang him by the neck, between the Heavens and the Earth!!! as a beacon to warn the* Northern Fanatics *of their danger!!!!* "

There were also many instances in which antislavery activists were tarred and feathered, and even hanged in Georgia, Louisiana, and Mississippi.

Two lithographs originally published in Boston in 1835, anonymous but no doubt from the abolitionist mill, portray these very real examples of southern violence. The first, *Southern Ideas of Liberty,* was advertised as

> a lithographic print, representing Judge Lynch, as seated on a cotton bag, bolstered up with boxes of sugar and tobacco, trampling the Constitution under his feet, presiding over a court, (a mob) of slaveholders, pasing [*sic*] sentence upon "Northern Fanatics. . . ."[19]

On the print itself, the text reads

> Sentence passed upon one for supporting that clause of our Declaration viz. All men are born free and equal. "Strip him to the skin! Give him a coat of Tar & Feathers!! Hang him by the neck, between the Heavens and the Earth!!! as a beacon to warn the Northern Fanatics of their danger!_!!"

The second print, *New Method of Assorting the Mails,* portrays the nocturnal raid on the Charleston Post Office in July 1835 and the burning by a mob of citizens of abolitionist mail found there. In the print, mail sacks are handed through the forced window of the ransacked post office, torn open, and burned. Bundles of newspapers such as Garrison's *The Liberator,* the *Boston Atlas,* and the *Commercial Gazette* are removed and strewn about. All this in a public square within sight of a church. A sign reading "$20,000 Reward for Tappan" hangs on the wall of the post office, referring to the bounty placed by the city of New Orleans on the head of Arthur Tappan, founder and president of the American Anti-Slavery Society.

Abolitionists sought to make a convincing case that such examples of repression were a dangerous threat to civil liberties in the North. They were sure that such actions led to mobs in the North violently disrupting antislavery meetings and lectures, destroying the homes and presses of advocates of abolition, and tarring and feathering, beating, threatening, and even killing northern supporters of the antislavery cause. During the summer of 1835, anti-abolition mobs roamed the streets of New York City. They ransacked the home of Lewis Tappan (Arthur Tappan's brother) and then invaded a black neighborhood, wrecking three churches, a school, and twenty houses. Abolition propagandists retaliated by offering up artistic images of these mob actions.

The threats posed by judicial compliance with the slaveholders struck an even more deeply responsive chord in the North. In 1855 a large print was issued depicting antislavery activist Passmore Williamson in his cell in Pennsylvania's Moyamensing Prison.[20] Williamson had been jailed by order of a Philadelphia judge for his part in freeing the three personal slaves of U.S. Minister to Nicaragua John Hill Wheeler.

Of all the tactics of the abolitionists, expounding on the theme of the degeneracy of southern society and its threat to the North proved the most successful, helping shape what eventually became the prevailing image of the South. The picture of the South as brutal, degenerate, and politically threatening was critical to the decisive turn taken in the tide of northern opinion against the South, effected by the great crises of the 1850s that eventually led to the Civil War.

THE 1850s: THE TRIUMPH OF POLITICS OVER MORALITY

The first of these crises was the passage by Congress of the Fugitive Slave Act as part of the Compromise of 1850. The act was seen as a transgression of their civil rights that the people of the North could not ignore. It obliged the northern states, the federal government, and even private citizens to assist in the capture and return to the South of fugitive slaves, an unprecedented intrusion on personal freedom, upheld by national legislation, northerners argued. As the number of fugitive slave cases multiplied in northern courts, resentment increased. And as these cases drew more and more attention, portraits of the unfortunate fugitives captured and returned were published and circulated widely.

NEW METHOD OF ASSORTING THE MAIL, AS PRACTISED BY SOUTHERN SLAVE-HOLDERS, OR

ATTACK ON THE POST OFFICE, CHARLESTON, S.C.

New Method of Assorting the Mail, portraying the nocturnal raid on the Charleston, S.C., Post Office and the burning of abolitionist mail in July 1835. The Library of Congress.

An elaborate and highly polemical portrait of one such fugitive, Anthony Burns, was published anonymously in Boston in 1855. Burns's arrest and trial in Boston under the Fugitive Slave Act had touched off riots and protests by abolitionists and other residents of the city in May 1854. The 1855 wood engraving, published under Burns's name, features a bust portrait copied by Boston painter James Barry from a daguerreotype. Surrounding the portrait are scenes from Burns's recent life, including the ever-present auction scene, his arrest, and his poignant departure from Boston in chains and under armed guard.

The lithograph *Effects of the Fugitive Slave Law,* drawn by painter Theodor Kaufmann, conjures up a vivid picture of slavecatchers rampant in the North. Here there is real sympathy for the free black men, ambushed in a northern

Passmore Williamson.
Lithograph (1855). The
Library of Congress.

PASSMORE WILLIAMSON,

IN MOYAMENSING PRISON FOR ALLEDGED CONTEMPT OF COURT

cornfield by a posse of southern bounty hunters and their agents. Kaufmann, a
Dusseldorf-trained painter, based the poses of the victims here on the tor-
mented figures in the well-known classical sculpture of Laocoon and his sons,
which to the nineteenth-century viewer epitomized the ideal of heroic and noble suffering. In this way he conveyed a heart-rending sense of tragedy, of a
nobility of spirit destroyed by the workings of an unjust law. Kaufmann's print
was, in a significant way, different from the earlier images discussed here. It was

the independent product of an artist, created evidently as an act of individual conscience. It was also sold, not through the mails but in an art gallery near Broadway in New York.

During the early 1850s, the popular success of Harriet Beecher Stowe's *Uncle Tom's Cabin* revealed the high pitch of emotion and sympathy for the slaves (be it genuine or based upon sentimentality) which had taken root in the North. First published in book form in 1852, the novel generated a groundswell of feeling for the slaves. By this time Victorian sensibilities were well prepared for a novel that would recount with vividness the sufferings endured by slaves at the brutal hands of the overseer. The book appeared in numerous illustrated editions, and inspired a raft of popular prints of scenes from the story, many of them cloyingly sentimental.

An actual event that captured several artists' imaginations was South Carolina Representative Preston Brooks's nearly fatal beating of Massachusetts Senator Charles Sumner on the floor of Congress in May 1856. Brooks's act was provoked by Sumner's earlier public remarks against his uncle, South Carolina Senator Andrew Pickens Butler, whose love of slavery Sumner likened to the love of a prostitute. In an early and uncharacteristic venture into political commentary, Winslow Homer produced a scathing pictorial condemnation of Brooks's act. In Homer's lithograph *Arguments of the Chivalry,* an enraged Brooks (*right*) looms over the seated, unsuspecting Sumner in the Senate chamber, about to land a heavy blow of his cane. On the left stands Brooks's fellow South Carolinian, Representative Lawrence M. Keitt, raising his own cane menacingly to prevent any intervention by the other legislators present. Clearly no help for Sumner is forthcoming. Behind Keitt's back, concealed in his left hand, is a small pistol, a weapon often viewed in the nineteenth century as an instrument of treachery. Above the scene is a quote from an inflammatory speech made by minister Henry Ward Beecher. Speaking before a rally in New York just days after the event, Beecher had proclaimed, "The symbol of the North is the pen; the symbol of the South is the bludgeon."[21] Sumner's beating outraged many in the North, in the process helping to galvanize majority opinion there against the South.

Beecher in his speech and Homer in his print both expressed a view of southern society that two decades earlier had been dismissed as the ranting of fanatics, but in 1856 was becoming conventional wisdom in the North. Another work from the 1850s, Maryland painter Frank B. Mayer's *Leisure and Labor,* also reflects a marked antipathy toward the landed gentry of the South that had become ingrained in northern thinking. Here a southern squire stands idly by as the northern blacksmith goes about his honest toil. The greyhound crouching at the southerner's feet is a symbol of idle pursuits, such as the racing and breeding of practically useless animals, often associated with the southern gentry. (The greyhound later became a symbol of the Confederacy in antisouthern political satires published during the Civil War.) The emblem on the wall behind the planter, "Tempus fugit," ensures that the judgmental point of the painting is not overlooked by the viewer.

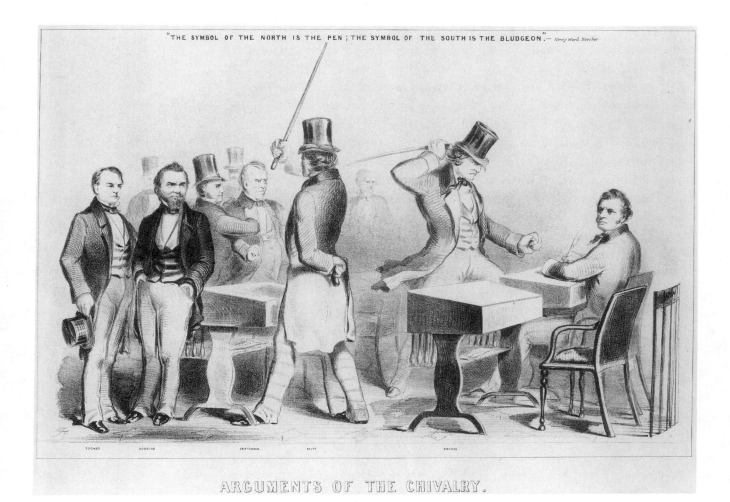

"THE SYMBOL OF THE NORTH IS THE PEN; THE SYMBOL OF THE SOUTH IS THE BLUDGEON." — *Henry Ward Beecher*

ARGUMENTS OF THE CHIVALRY.

Arguments of the Chivalry, Winslow Homer's depiction of the attack by Rep. Preston Brooks upon Massachusetts Senator Charles Sumner on the floor of the U.S. Senate, May 22, 1856. The Library of Congress.

Such works represent a victory of sorts for the abolitionists. They reflect a new northern outlook toward the South fueled by both events and rhetoric. The issue of slavery was now argued openly and widely, but on terms quite different from those articulated by the early abolitionists. Nor was it the purer humanitarianism advocated by the early antislavery advocates that caused the downfall of slavery, but instead a complex system that combined political fears, angry prejudices, and self-proclaimed high ideals.

By now Senator William Seward of New York and others were engaged in orchestrating the founding of a nascent Republican party, formed from groups of political abolitionists, northern Democrats, and assorted remnants of the Whig party that had virtually been destroyed by the Kansas-Nebraska Act of 1854. Then the Republicans forced the issue of slavery into the national forum during the presidential campaign of 1856. The Republican strategy in this election was to portray the Democrats as the agents of the slaveocracy, pawns of the evil, threatening power of "King Cotton," the landed gentry whose wealth was built upon the labor of slaves and which threatened to supplant the industrial

Frank Blackwell Mayer: *Leisure and Labor* (1858). In the collection of The Corcoran Gallery of Art, Gift of William Wilson Corcoran.

power of the North and dominate the frontier by allowing slavery in the western territories.

Abraham Lincoln's election in 1860 marked the triumph of the Republicans' determination, if not to rescue the oppressed black man, at least to crush the slave power of the South. Within weeks of Lincoln's election, South Carolina and six other southern states declared themselves independent of the Union. In April 1861, with the firing on Fort Sumter, the Civil War began, a war not to free the slaves, Lincoln insisted, but to preserve the Union. Under pressure, however, to take a stronger stand against slavery, in September 1862, after the long and costly Battle of Antietam, Lincoln issued his Proclamation of Emancipation. Not a meaningful measure against slavery, the Proclamation called for the freeing only of slaves in areas of the South controlled by the Confederacy. Nonetheless an important beginning had been made, for if the North won the Civil War, slavery would then be destroyed.

EPILOGUE

No stranger to the power of symbolism, Lincoln had ordered resumption of the enlargement of the U.S. Capitol in Washington, which had lapsed soon after the beginning of the war. Placed atop the newly enlarged dome of the Capitol in December 1864 was Thomas Crawford's statue *Freedom.* The statue faced east, toward Europe and the Old World, as a beacon and symbol of American liberty. But it became an important symbol for the people of the North as well. As the North entered the final excruciating phase of the war, the Capitol itself became a symbol of the Union, born again, transformed, replacing the image of the old Capitol, which had appeared on the small abolitionists' contribution box back in 1838, presiding tacitly over the commerce in human flesh transacted in the heart of the nation's government.

Now, with the full realization of the meaning of Lincoln's Emancipation Proclamation, the Civil War had become a holy war, a national redemption in which the soul of the body politic was being cleansed in a holocaust of fire and blood. The moral evil that the abolitionists of the 1830s had condemned, had pointed out as a cancer, was now finally being purged on the battlefield. As the war ground on, many of the abolitionists were gone or declining. But their cause seemed finally to be coming to fruition, a cause aided and fostered along the way by an array of symbols and artifacts that demonstrated so well how critically important could be the blending of history, politics, and art.

NOTES

1. For the account of the boy and his contribution box, see *National Enquirer and Constitutional Advocate of Universal Liberty* (Philadelphia), January 25, 1838. The account also credits the source of the story illustrated on the box as Charles T. Torrey.

2. *The Liberator,* January 17, 1831.

3. Frederick Douglass, *My Bondage and My Freedom: Life and Times of Frederick Douglass* (Boston: DeWolfe, Fiske and Co., 1892).

4. For the treatment of African-Americans in painting during the early nineteenth century, see Hugh Honour, *From the American Revolution to the Civil War,* vol. 4 of the series The Image of the Black in Western Art (4 vols., Cambridge, Mass.: Harvard University Press, 1989), and Guy McElroy, *Facing History: The Black Image in American Art, 1710–1940* (Washington, D.C.: Corcoran Gallery of Art, 1990).

5. *Wedgwood Portraits and the American Revolution* (Washington, D.C.: National Portrait Gallery, 1976), pp. 116–17.

6. Honour, *From the American Revolution to the Civil War,* pp. 63–64.

7. Morland's works are reproduced and discussed in ibid., pp. 66–74.

8. "The Whole of the Particulars concerning the Piracy, Mutiny, and Murders, on Board the Spanish Schooner *Amistad,* . . . " *New York Sun,* August 31, 1839.

9. The events surrounding the capture and trial of the *Amistad* captives is well documented and summarized in Eleanor Alexander's "A Portrait of Cinqué," *Connecticut Historical Society Bulletin* 49, no. 1 (Winter 1984): 31–51.

10. Ibid., pp. 38–43.

11. For a discussion of Sartain's work and his relationship to the antislavery campaign, see Katherine Martinez, "The Life and Career of John Sartain (1808–1897): A Nineteenth Century Philadelphia Printmaker," unpublished dissertation, George Washington University, May 1986, pp. 69–83.

12. "Portrait of Cinqué," *American and Foreign Anti-Slavery Reporter,* March 15,

1841, p. 16. This notice states that "a superb portrait of Cinqué . . . was painted last winter by Mr. N. Jocelyn, of New Haven. . . . It was painted for Mr. Robert Purvis, of Philadelphia. Mr. J. Sartain has made a mezzotinto engraving of it, which is very handsomely executed. . . . The plate has been purchased by the committee acting on behalf of the Africans, with a view to devote the profits to their benefit. . . . "

13. Quoted in Martinez, "The Life and Career of John Sartain," p. 77.

14. Henry "Box" Brown, *Narrative of Henry Box Brown, Who Escaped from Slavery Enclosed in a Box* (Boston: n.p., 1849).

15. On this commission, see James F. O'Gorman, *A Billings Bookshelf: An Annotated Bibliography of Works Illustrated by Hammatt Billings (1818–1874)* (Wellesley, Mass.: Wellesley College, Grace Slack McNeil Program in American Art, 1986), pp. 15–16.

16. Jean Fagan Yellin, *Women and Sisters: The Antislavery Feminists in American Culture* (New Haven: Yale University Press, 1989), p. 21. The rhetorical strategy of the words is discussed by Yellin with reference to the female version of the supplicant slave image.

17. *Maine Cultivator and Weekly Gazette,* quoted in *The Liberator,* February 20, 1840.

18. The two prints are reproduced and discussed in Bernard F. Reilly, Jr., *American Political Prints, 1766–1876: A Catalogue of the Collections in the Library of Congress* (Boston, 1991).

19. *Charter Oak* (Hartford, Conn.), May 1838.

20. Reilly, *American Political Prints,* no. 1855–8.

21. The best discussion of the caning of Sumner and the many prints it inspired appears in David Tatham's "Pictorial Responses to the Caning of Senator Sumner," in *American Printmaking before 1876: Fact, Fiction, and Fantasy* (Washington, D.C.: Library of Congress, 1975).

CHAPTER FOUR

Robert L. Hall

Massachusetts Abolitionists Document the Slave Experience

Often as powerful, both in its detail and in its antislavery message, as the art of the abolition movement was the literature, especially the slave narratives. Many of these works were published in Massachusetts and appeared initially in Boston, probably the most vibrant center of antislavery thought in the nation.

Here, as Robert L. Hall explains, there developed a very rich collaboration between blacks and whites, as runaway slaves fled to the North and began to relate the often harrowing stories of what it was like to live one's life in chains. White antislavery publishers were willing to do everything possible to get these exciting tales into print.

Also playing a key role in this biracial collaboration, Hall explains, were the abolitionists, many of whom were involved in the Underground Railroad as well. After a runaway had successfully escaped, it was usually the railroad conductor in the North, often a black, who helped that person become established in freedom. Once this had been accomplished, some ex-slaves chose to tell of their adventures from the antislavery lecturer's platform, while others chose a successful alternate route, the autobiographical slave narrative. Some would do both, such as Frederick Douglass, for example, who in the process was soon able to establish himself as the nation's preeminent black abolitionist.

Hall also emphasizes the important role played by women such as Lydia Maria Child in spreading the slave's message. In addition to editing a major abolitionist newspaper, Child oversaw the publication in Boston of more than twenty slave narratives, including that of Harriet Jacobs, one of the few slave women to make public her story. Ironically, the credibility of her narrative was very early called into question and, as Hall tells us, has only recently been substantiated as a result of careful scholarship.

Blacks and whites, men and women—together they spread the words of antislavery protest, words, as Hall explains, that the black ex-slaves willingly shared with abolition's forces in a joint effort to destroy slavery once and for all.

Like their counterparts elsewhere in the United States, Massachusetts-based abolitionists, black and white alike, contributed significantly toward the documentation of the American slave experience by collecting, preserving, authenticating, and publishing eyewitness testimony about the physical and social realities of the United States' "peculiar institution." The materials they gathered in various publications were intended for propagandistic purposes in the sense that they were attempting to persuade listening and reading audiences that slavery was evil and that they should engage in actions that would hasten its demise. But this does not necessarily mean that the materials were falsified, inaccurate, or unsuitable as sources of documentation in reconstructing the slave experience. Despite a recent resurgence of interest in folklore, oral tradition, and material culture as means of reconstructing the actual day-to-day experiences of enslaved antebellum blacks, the bedrock of evidence upon which our modern understanding of the slave experience rests is the massive, detailed, and varied body of documentation about slavery itself, most of which was reduced to writing in the process of agitating against the institution.

There is a direct line between David Walker's *Appeal,*[1] the fiery condemnation of slavery published in 1829 by a Boston free black dealer in clothes, and the rhetoric of such twentieth-century black agitators as El Hajj Malik el Shabbaz (alias Malcolm Little and Malcolm X). While serving a sentence at Norfolk Prison Colony in Massachusetts for burglary, Malcolm X chanced upon several boxes of books, papers, and pamphlets that had been willed to the prison library. These materials included slave narratives, scattered issues of Garrison's *The Liberator,* and other publications gathered by Massachusetts abolitionists about a century before Malcolm's incarceration. By that time, having copied a dictionary from cover to cover, he had also become a voracious reader. Malcolm X's headlong plunge into this material clearly contributed to his powerful oratory, particularly his verbal depictions of the slave experience which electrified audiences who listened to him during the early 1960s. In his autobiography Malcolm X related his encounter with the literature of antislavery:

> Parkhurst's collection also contained some bound pamphlets of the Abolitionist Anti-Slavery Society of New England. I read descriptions of atrocities, saw those illustrations of black slave women tied up and flogged with whips; of black mothers watching their babies being dragged off, never to be seen by their mothers again; of dogs after slaves, and of the fugitive slave catchers, evil white men with whips and clubs and chains and guns. I read about the slave preacher Nat Turner, who put the fear of God into the white slavemaster.[2]

Walker's *Appeal,* published in Boston in September 1829 at his own expense, was a galvanic document in its own time and punctuated a turning point in the struggle against slavery. Two years earlier, Walker, already a leading figure in the recently established Massachusetts General Colored Association, had met at his home with a group of other blacks, including the Baptist preacher Thomas Paul, Sr. They had come together to pledge their support for *Freedom's Journal,*

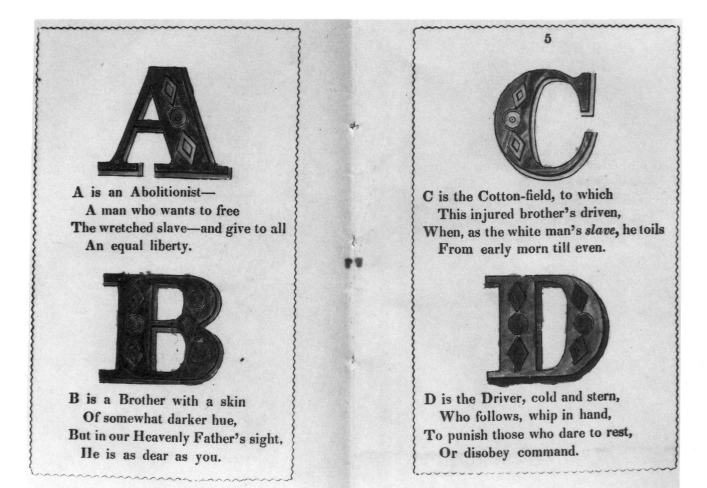

A is an Abolitionist—
A man who wants to free
The wretched slave—and give to all
An equal liberty.

B is a Brother with a skin
Of somewhat darker hue,
But in our Heavenly Father's sight,
He is as dear as you.

C is the Cotton-field, to which
This injured brother's driven,
When, as the white man's *slave*, he toils
From early morn till even.

D is the Driver, cold and stern,
Who follows, whip in hand,
To punish those who dare to rest,
Or disobey command.

Two pages from *The Anti-Slavery Alphabet*, a children's book (1847). The Boston Athenæum.

the nation's first black newspaper, which the Reverend Samuel E. Cornish and John B. Russwurm were about to launch.[3] Later in 1827, Walker and Paul signed on as the paper's Boston agents.[4] *Freedom's Journal* and Walker's *Appeal* demonstrated the growing black awareness of the need to make the fullest use of the written word in an effort to destroy slavery.

Partly because Boston was an educational and publishing center from very early in the colonial period, long before it came to be identified as a hotbed of Garrisonian abolitionism, it comes as no great surprise that many slave narratives were published there. Marion Wilson Starling, a careful student of the slave narrative, estimates that between 1703 and the publication of the scientist George Washington Carver's autobiographical record in 1944, over six thousand narratives of enslaved black Americans were published, including over one hundred narratives which appeared in book form between 1760 and the end of the Civil War.

The first of these known to be published, the narrative of Adam, "servant of John Saffin, Esquire," was printed in Boston in 1703. A collection of pam-

Harriet Beecher Stowe. Carte de visite taken by Black and Batchelder about 1860. The Boston Athenæum.

phlets, court documents, and diaries known collectively as "Adam Negro's Try-all" was published between 1701 and 1710, but contained no material purported to have been written by Adam. In 1701 Judge Samuel Sewall of Boston had published the humanitarian tract *The Selling of Joseph*, considered by many to be the first identifiable piece of abolitionist literature in this country.[5] In 1760 Briton Hammon's *A Narrative of the Uncommon Sufferings and*

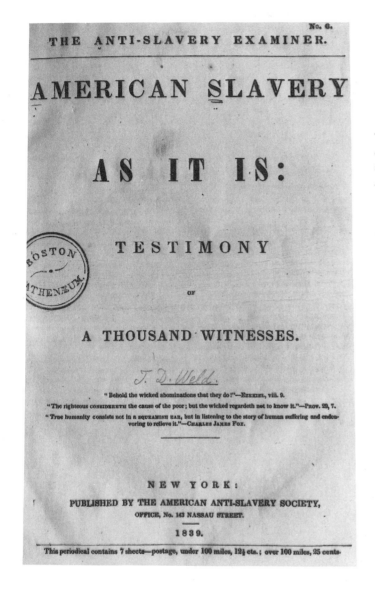

Title page of *American Slavery As It Is*, compiled by Theodore Weld and Angelina and Sarah Grimké (1839). The Boston Athenæum.

Surprising Deliverance of Briton Hammon, A Negro Man, etc., probably the first autobiographical account by someone who had been enslaved, was published in Boston by Green and Russell.

Between the 1830s and the outbreak of the Civil War, abolitionists did a good deal of research and writing about slavery. They actively sought out former slaves, eliciting and recording, sometimes stenographically, the ex-slaves' accounts of bondage, and they reprinted material in pamphlet form that had appeared previously in newspapers and magazines. During the 1830s, much of their research involved extracts from southern newspapers and the testimony of whites who had seen slavery firsthand. Perhaps the best-known and most influential example of this genre was *American Slavery As It Is: Testimony of a Thousand Witnesses, As Taken from Southern Papers*, published in 1839 by the American Anti-Slavery Society. It was the work of Theodore Dwight Weld, his wife, Angelina Grimké Weld, and her sister Sarah Grimké and was based on hours of research in over twenty thousand issues of newspapers.

Abolitionist organizations and individuals would soon intensify their efforts to gather and disseminate eyewitness testimony by blacks who had themselves been slaves and who often worked in the antislavery movement as speakers and agents. In the 1840s, as increasing numbers of former slaves rose to prominence on the antislavery lecture circuit, additional narratives were published in Massachusetts, usually either in Boston or in New Bedford, but also occasionally in Worcester. Among those printed as books in Boston were the narratives of Lunsford Lane (printed for the author by abolitionist J. G. Torrey in 1842 and by Hewes and Watson in 1848), Moses Grandy (Oliver Johnson, 1844), Lewis Clarke (D. H. Eli, 1845), William Wells Brown (published by the American Anti-Slavery Office in 1847),[6] Henry Watson (Henry Holt, 1848), Josiah Henson (narrated to Samuel Eliot and published by Arthur D. Phelps, 1849), Henry "Box" Brown (Brown and Stearns, 1849),[7] and Peter Randolph (published for the author, 1855).[8] Among the slave narratives published in New Bedford was that of Leonard Black (Press of Benjamin Lindsay, 1847). A few narratives, such as that of John Thompson (by the author, 1856), were published from Worcester.

By as early as 1830, almost one-fourth of the blacks in the state of Massachusetts lived in Boston, while another significant concentration resided in New Bedford. When Anna and Frederick Douglass arrived in New Bedford in 1838, 1,051 of its 12,354 inhabitants were black.[9] Later, when Henry "Box" Brown was smuggled out of Philadelphia after having himself shipped by the Adams Express Company from Richmond to Philadelphia in a crate, he went to the home of the New Bedford abolitionist Joseph Ricketson. Like cities in New York, Pennsylvania, and Ohio, Boston was a hub of black antislavery activism in New England.[10]

Another milestone in the story of abolitionism in Massachusetts was reached on January 1, 1831, when William Lloyd Garrison, who previously had worked on Benjamin Lundy's *Genius of Universal Emancipation* in Baltimore before rejecting colonization and moving to Boston, published the first issue of *The Liberator*. In 1832, at the urging of black abolitionists, Garrison, a native of Newburyport, Massachusetts, published his pamphlet *Thoughts on African Colonization,* which sold 2,750 copies in nine months.[11] On January 6 of that same year, Garrison and about a dozen of his white friends established the New England Anti-Slavery Society in Boston's African Baptist Church (also known as the African Meeting House, the Abolition Church, and the black Faneuil Hall).[12] According to the historians August Meier and Elliott Rudwick, "only after the plans had been formulated were Negroes invited to participate."[13] But participate they did! By the time the constitution of the new organization was approved, one-fourth of the seventy-two persons present to sign the document were black.

In the late 1820s and early 1830s, the antislavery struggle shifted from gradu-

RESURRECTION OF HENRY BOX BROWN.

alism (usually coupled with colonization of freed blacks in Africa) to immediat-ism. Once Garrison came out forcefully against colonization, the Garrisonian wing of abolitionism received widespread support among blacks, and it contin-ued to do so until 1839–40, when disagreements emerged over whether to move beyond Garrison's strict adherence to moral suasion and engage in politi-cal action to end slavery. Clear evidence of that early support is Garrison's esti-mate that 90 percent of *The Liberator's* subscribers in its first year of publication were black, and that in 1834 blacks constituted three-fourths of its 2,300 sub-scribers. Almost immediately blacks began publishing numerous essays, notices of meetings, and letters there. Among *The Liberator's* black agents in New Eng-land was New Bedford's Richard Johnson.

Another towering figure in the abolitionist struggle was the free black Bosto-nian William Cooper Nell, a frequent contributor of articles to *The Liberator* and a loyal Garrisonian. Born in Boston in 1816, Nell had graduated from an all-black school in 1829 but because of his color was denied the citywide recog-nition that he had earned as an honor student. Years later Nell recalled: "The

Resurrection of Henry Box Brown, the slave who shipped himself north to freedom in 1849. From William Still's *The Underground Railroad* (1872). The Boston Athenæum.

impression made on my mind, by this day's experience, deepened into a solemn vow that, God helping me, I would do my best to hasten the day when the color of the skin would be no barrier to equal school rights."[14] When, in 1831, he was inspired by Garrison's *Liberator* to plunge into abolitionist activities, he retained vivid memories of the discrimination he had experienced as a schoolboy and made the desegregation of Boston's schools a major goal.

In addition to writing articles for *The Liberator,* working in the paper's Negro Employment Office, and serving on the Committee of Vigilance, Nell never missed an opportunity to challenge the segregation of public schools. His central role in the protracted struggle against this practice was recognized by Massachusetts blacks and their white allies with a banquet in his honor in December 1855, following the abolition of segregated schools by the Massachusetts legislature the previous April.[15]

Also among the black Bostonians working actively to abolish the twin evils of slavery and race prejudice was James G. Barbadoes, one of three black signers of the Declaration of Sentiments when the American Anti-Slavery Society was created at Philadelphia in December 1833.[16] He addressed the 1834 convention of the New England Anti-Slavery Society, excoriating the practice of kidnapping free blacks and selling them as slaves. Barbadoes knew of this all too well, as one of the five cases he discussed in his address was that of his own brother, Robert, who had been kidnapped in New Orleans eighteen years earlier while working as a seaman.[17] James Barbadoes was often among the delegates representing Boston blacks at meetings of the National Negro Convention.

Although insufficient scholarly attention has been devoted to the participation of black women in antislavery and other antebellum reform movements, there is no doubt that black women in Massachusetts joined their counterparts in other states in the new organizational trends emerging in the abolitionist movement during the early 1830s. One of the earliest "colored female societies" was formed in Philadelphia in November 1831, and by 1834 such groups had been established in Nantucket and Salem, Massachusetts. While some impetus to the formation of these societies derived from the simple desire of black women to come together in the antislavery cause, they were also inspired by their awareness of the profound ambivalence felt by white abolitionists about black membership in antislavery societies.

When the Quaker sisters Elizabeth Buffum Chace and Lucy Buffum Lovell invited several black women to join the Female Anti-Slavery Society they had formed in Fall River, Massachusetts, they ignited a firestorm of controversy that almost broke up the organization. Although white women abolitionists in Fall River eventually decided to admit black members, some female societies in other states chose not to admit blacks.[18] Boston's Susan Paul—whose father, Thomas Paul, had in 1805 founded the city's first black Baptist church—was a counselor of the Boston Female Anti-Slavery Society and in 1835 became a life member of the Massachusetts Anti-Slavery Society.[19] Sarah Parker Remond, a Salem native and the sister of Charles Lenox Remond, joined the antislavery lecture circuit with her brother in July 1842. Before leaving the United States in 1858, she served in various capacities in the Salem Anti-Slavery Society, the New England Anti-Slavery Convention, the Essex Anti-Slavery Society, and the American Anti-Slavery Society.[20]

During the 1830s, blacks and whites worked together in the effort to abolish slavery and oppose colonization in Africa, but by the late 1830s and early 1840s, blacks within the abolitionist movement began to challenge racial prejudice among white abolitionists, to object to subordination within those struggles, and to push for independence. The Reverend Samuel Snowden of Boston, who was one of nine counselors of the New England Anti-Slavery Society, was the exception rather than the rule when it came to black representation in the highest echelons of antislavery organizations. When the free-born Charles Lenox Remond—the son of a Salem hairdresser, caterer, and merchant from Curaçao—was appointed a lecturer by the Massachusetts Anti-Slavery Society in 1838, he became the first black to hold such a position.[21] Some black activists in the antislavery struggle earned a living through their reform activities: lecturing, editing newspapers and journals, and writing and selling their own slave narratives. Many of them were what the historian Larry Gara has called "professional fugitives." As former slaves, they brought to the task a fresh firsthand experience with the hated "peculiar institution," and their speeches and writings carried a special authority.[22]

This direct evidence about the nature of the institution itself was absolutely crucial to the battle being waged for northern white public opinion. In reviewing a selection of narratives in the *Christian Examiner* in 1849, Ephraim Peabody found them "calculated to exert a very wide influence on public opinion."[23] In that sense the context in which these accounts were generated and disseminated was a propagandistic one. During the 1830s a chink in abolitionist armor was the proslavery assertion that abolitionists were largely either northern whites or free blacks who had no direct knowledge of slavery as it was. There developed in response a kind of rank order that determined which antislavery speakers were most convincing to northern white audiences; fugitives topped the list, followed by free blacks and then whites.

In 1842 John A. Collins, general agent for the Massachusetts Anti-Slavery Society, told Garrison: "The public have itching ears to hear a colored man speak, and particularly a *slave*. Multitudes will flock to hear one of this class speak."[24] Lecturers displayed dioramas and artifacts such as bullwhips. Standard equipment on the lecture circuit for Henry "Box" Brown, the fugitive who had arranged to be shipped from Richmond to Philadelphia, was an exact replica of the crate that he used to reenact his dramatic escape from slavery. It was common for fugitive slave lecturers who had published memoirs to display panoramas depicting slave life, to read from their memoirs, and then to sell copies of those memoirs to the assembled crowds. Traveling mainly in New England, William Wells Brown first publicly told his story in Boston. Hearing and seeing a black antislavery orator in a church or lecture hall, especially one who had

SLAVERY IN AMERICA.

Illustration from *Slavery in America*, a tract published about 1841. The Boston Athenæum.

personally experienced bondage, was an exciting firsthand experience. These renderings might, in retrospect, be called oral narratives. Printed versions of these narratives, while sometimes lacking the immediacy of the lecture hall, nonetheless could reach readers who might otherwise never have ventured to a public gathering. Gara believes that "written accounts were almost as valuable as the appearance of a living fugitive."[25]

Thus the published narrative came to be viewed by abolitionists as an "infallible means of abolitionizing the free states." Stories of escape and self-purchase were the stock-in-trade of the abolitionist press, and many narratives were also published in the annual reports of antislavery societies. As early as 1836, brief narratives of fugitives from slavery were appearing in at least a dozen newspapers. One clear example of how this dynamic operated was the publication, with the help of Boston's Lydia Maria Child, of James R. Bradley's short narrative. Bradley had purchased his own freedom in Arkansas and had entered Lane Seminary in Cincinnati. Two fellow students at Lane, abolitionists Henry B. Stanton and Theodore Dwight Weld, recruited Bradley to participate in debates over slavery.[26] Admitted to Lane in May 1833, he soon became manager of the student antislavery society at the seminary. Stanton was so impressed with Bradley that he wrote a short biographical sketch of him that was published in *The Liberator* the following March.[27] When Child and other Boston abolitionists heard about Bradley's stunning speeches, Child asked him to write an account of his slave experience, which he did in a letter to her.[28] An edited version of Bradley's account was published in an abolitionist gift book, *The Oasis,* later that year, and thereafter was reprinted often in antislavery publications.[29] In the process of editing, publishing, and disseminating these narratives, the abolitionist societies and individual ex-slaves created a detailed, verifiable permanent record of the slave experience.

Clearly, though hundreds of life stories of fugitives and other former slaves were published, uncounted others that would have been valuable ammunition in the abolitionist war for minds were suppressed for the sake of the safety of fugitives wishing to conceal both their real identities and their whereabouts. In an 1840 letter to her sister, Maria Weston Chapman of the Boston Female Anti-Slavery Society, the New Bedford abolitionist Deborah Weston mentioned the arrival of a fugitive but lamented that the need for secrecy would make it unsafe to publish his story, which, she said, "is a great pity, for there never was a prettier one."[30]

Prominent among the Boston blacks who were active in the movement but who had not personally experienced slavery was Robert Morris, generally acknowledged to have been the first black man to practice law in the city (he was admitted to the bar in February 1847). Although not a former slave himself, Morris was aware that his African-born grandfather, Cumono, had been transported to Ipswich, Massachusetts, as a young child. Morris was active in the Boston Vigilance Committee as a member of its finance committee and also served as assistant legal counsel to Charles Sumner in the *Roberts v. Boston* school desegregation case (1850).

Other black activists in the antislavery movement, notably the black Boston-based printer Benjamin F. Roberts, made a living from the movement in a slightly different way. Roberts printed speeches, reports, pamphlets, and other items for antislavery and black organizations. When he launched a black newspaper, the *Anti-Slavery Herald,* in 1838, however, he met with opposition from white abolitionists and received little support from blacks in Boston. As a result, the paper failed within six months. A decade and a half later Roberts made another effort, but his attempts to sustain the *Self-Elevator* suffered a similar fate. Roberts traveled through New England with Henry "Box" Brown and narrated scenes in a diorama depicting Brown's escape from slavery. In the 1840s Roberts joined William Cooper Nell and other Bostonians in protesting the all-black Smith School, eventually offering his daughter as plaintiff in the unsuccessful *Roberts* school desegregation case.[31]

Frederick Augustus Washington Bailey, later known to the world and to his-

The Life of Gustavus Vassa, a slave narrative (frontispiece, 1837). The Boston Athenæum.

tory as Frederick Douglass, first learned that there were people called "abolitionists" when, at about the age of thirteen, he overheard snatches of conversation between his master and other slaveholders in which this group was vilified and blamed for every escape attempt, crime, or other act of violence committed by a slave. Still, prior to escaping to freedom, Douglass had only the vaguest notion of who these people were. By about February 1839, he had bought the first copy he had ever seen of Garrison's *The Liberator,* which, Douglass would later write, "took a place in my heart second only to the Bible."[32] In his narrative published in Boston in 1845, Douglass described his first encounter with *The Liberator:*

> In about four months after I went to New Bedford, there came a young man to me, and inquired if I did not wish to take the "Liberator." I told him I did; but, just having made my escape from slavery, I remarked that I was unable to pay for it then.

I, however, finally became a subscriber to it. The paper came, and I read it from week to week with such feelings as it would be quite idle for me to attempt to describe. The paper became my meat and my drink. My soul was set all on fire. Its sympathy for my brethren in bonds—its scathing denunciations of slaveholders—its faithful exposures of slavery—and its powerful attacks upon the upholders of the institution—sent a thrill of joy through my soul, such as I had never felt before![33]

Douglass soon began attending regular informal meetings hosted by John Bailey, a black fellow abolitionist in New Bedford, as well as more-public gatherings in which antislavery matters were discussed. In March 1839 he actively participated in a black meeting at the Christian Church of New Bedford, and later in the year he chaired a similar meeting. Two years later, in August 1841, Douglass first heard Garrison speak at an annual meeting of the Bristol Anti-Slavery Society, and a few days after that at an abolitionist meeting in Nantucket. By this time Douglass was being urged to make public his own views by William C. Coffin, "a gentleman who had heard me speak in the colored people's meeting at New Bedford." After Douglass spoke at Nantucket, William Lloyd Garrison commented on how his speech had excited "extraordinary emotion." Immediately after that meeting, John A. Collins, general agent of the Massachusetts Anti-Slavery Society, asked Douglass to become a lecturer for the society. Traveling with George Foster to obtain subscriptions to the *Anti-Slavery Standard* and *The Liberator,* Douglass lectured throughout eastern Massachusetts:

Much interest was awakened—large meetings assembled. Many came, no doubt, from curiosity to hear what a Negro could say in his own cause. I was generally introduced as a *"chattel"*—a *"thing"*—a piece of southern *"property"*—the chairman assuring the audience that *it* could speak. Fugitive slaves, at that time, were not so plentiful as now; and as a fugitive slave lecturer, I had the advantage of being a *"brand new fact"*—the first one out. Up to that time, a colored man was deemed a fool who confessed himself a runaway slave, not only because of the danger to which he exposed himself of being retaken, but because it was a confession of a very *low* origin![34]

The launching of Douglass's career as an antislavery lecturer and agent in 1841 resulted in the creation of "a new type: the slave lecturer whose closeness to the peculiar institution quite captured public imagination."[35] Most previous black lecturers against slavery, including the Salem barber Charles Lenox Remond, had themselves been raised as free persons, and others—such as Henry Highland Garnet, Samuel Ringgold Ward, and James W. C. Pennington—though they had once been enslaved, tended to conceal or minimize their backgrounds for security reasons. Henry Bibb, formerly enslaved in Kentucky, hit the abolitionist lecture circuit in 1843 and later made a swing through New England. By the time his narrative was published in 1849, he had told his story "publicly all through New England and the Western states to multiple thousands."[36]

Lectures delivered before various antislavery societies, such as William Wells Brown's talk before the Female Anti-Slavery Society of Salem, were also published (1847). Consisting of "females of color," that organization had been in existence since 1832.[37] In May 1847, after separating from his wife, Elizabeth Schooner, Brown had moved from Farmington, New York, to Boston, where he had been hired as a lecturer by the Massachusetts Anti-Slavery Society. Later that year he composed his autobiographical memoir with assistance from Garrisonian Edmund Quincy.[38] Brown's narrative sold eight thousand copies in less than eighteen months. He went overseas in 1849 and, because of the passage of the Fugitive Slave Act in 1850, did not return until abolitionist friends in England had purchased his freedom. He then lived the remainder of his life in the Boston area.

Another fugitive slave who lectured in Massachusetts was James L. Smith.[39] One of eleven children born to Charles and Rachel Smith in Northern Neck, Northumberland County, Virginia, Smith escaped in May 1838 with two friends. Upon reaching Philadelphia, he became separated from the others, but was soon befriended by black and white abolitionists and given a letter of introduction to David Ruggles, the black abolitionist of New York who had actively assisted many fugitives out of bondage, including Frederick Douglass. After spending a few days with Ruggles, Smith boarded a boat for Hartford, Connecticut. Later, in Springfield, Massachusetts, an antislavery lecturer named Dr. Hudson engaged Smith to travel with him for one year through parts of Massachusetts and all of Connecticut. Accompanying Hudson throughout the winter of 1842, Smith lectured to large audiences in Wilbraham and South Wilbraham, Massachusetts. At the Methodist Episcopal Church in South Wilbraham, said Smith, "many that heard of the sufferings of the poor slave, wept like children; many turned from slavery to anti-slavery." During that tour he also spoke in Worcester and addressed a large gathering at the Spring Street Church in Boston.[40]

Upon occasion, abolitionists were known to have withdrawn slave narratives from publication because their inaccuracies had been lampooned in southern newspapers. In 1838 the executive committee of the American Anti-Slavery Society withdrew from sale the narrative of James Williams as told to John Greenleaf Whittier.[41] The controversies that arose over this and several other books originally thought to be authentic slave narratives, while causing abolitionists much embarrassment, did make them more vigilant. Following these controversies, abolitionists redoubled their efforts to confirm the authenticity of any future narratives that they sought to publish. Abolition society committees frequently interrogated the fugitives and surprisingly sometimes even wrote letters to former masters and their neighbors requesting information.

The abolitionist periodical press, particularly the weekly newspapers, regularly carried excerpts from the published book-length narratives. These papers

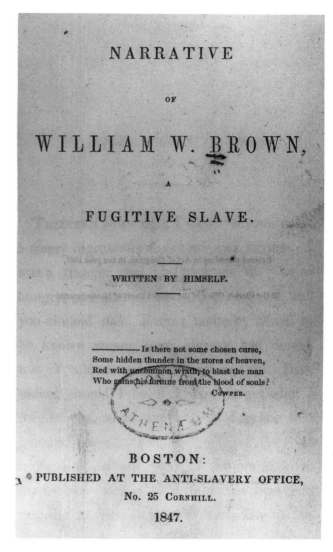

Slave narrative of William Wells Brown, with portrait frontispiece (1847). The Boston Athenæum.

were also fond of publishing escaped slaves' letters to their former masters. One example is Frederick Douglass's letter to Thomas Auld in which he described his service to the antislavery movement as a lecturer:

> After remaining in New Bedford for three years, I met Wm. Lloyd Garrison, a person of whom you have *possibly* heard, as he is pretty generally known among slaveholders. He put it into my head that I might make myself serviceable to the cause of the slave by devoting a portion of my time to telling my own sorrows, and those of other slaves which had come under my observation. This was the commencement of a higher state of existence than any to which I had ever aspired.[42]

Douglass's first autobiographical narrative, *The Narrative of the Life of Frederick Douglass, an American Slave, Written by Himself,* considered by some to be among the premier slave narratives, was published in Boston at the Anti-Slavery Office at 25 Cornhill in 1845 and sold thirty thousand copies in its first five years. In a preface to the volume, William Lloyd Garrison assured the readers that it was the work of Douglass's own hand:

> Mr. Douglass has very properly chosen to write his own Narrative, in his own style, and according to the best of his ability, rather than to employ some one else. It is, therefore, entirely his own production; and, considering how long and dark was the career he had to run as a slave,—how few have been his opportunities to improve his mind since he broke his iron fetters,—it is, in my judgement, highly creditable to his head and heart.[43]

The publication of *The Narrative of the Life of Moses Grandy, Late a Slave in the United States of America* by Oliver Johnson of Boston in 1844 stemmed from Grandy's participation in the antislavery movement. In setting down his life story, Grandy—a native of Camden County, North Carolina, who had purchased his freedom—was responding partly to the encouragement of his fellow abolitionists and partly to the desire to raise money to free his wife, children, and other family members.

In 1849 a Boston publisher brought out *The Life of Josiah Henson, Formerly a Slave, Now an Inhabitant of Canada, as Narrated by Himself to Samuel Eliot.* Eliot was a graduate of the College and the Divinity School at Harvard, a member of the state legislature, a three-term mayor of Boston, the treasurer of Harvard (1842–53), and later a member of Congress (1850–51). As a member of the Boston Board of Aldermen during the 1830s, he had been the primary force behind the effort to build the Smith School for black children on Beacon Hill, which was completed in 1835.

During the extradition hearings of the fugitive slave Anthony Burns in May 1854, the Boston lawyer and journalist Charles Emery Stevens took down the details of Burns's life; he published them in 1856. Burns had been born in bondage to Colonel Charles Suttle in Stafford County, Virginia, in 1834. While enslaved, and despite laws prohibiting the teaching of reading to slaves, he had learned how to read from white children. Converted to the Baptist denomination at age ten, Burns was preaching to other enslaved black folk as a teenager. While being hired out to a mill owner in Richmond, he stowed away on a ship, landed in Boston, and found work in a clothing store. He managed to keep his fugitive status secret between February and May of 1854, when his former master intercepted a letter intended for Burns's brother, permitting Suttle to locate Burns. As the former slave walked home from work, he was arrested on a bogus charge of breaking into a jewelry store. His seizure by a U.S. deputy marshal threw Boston into turmoil for nine days.

Protest meetings were held at Faneuil Hall, and a group of blacks and whites

Slave narrative of Frederick Douglass, with portrait frontispiece (1845). The Boston Athenæum.

attacked the courthouse, but they failed to rescue Burns. During these demonstrations a federal officer was killed, but significantly, no one, either black or white, was ever brought to trial. The Reverend Leonard A. Grimes, who pastored the church Burns attended (the Twelfth Baptist Church) and who had persuaded him to contest the case in the first place, raised $1,200, which was Suttle's asking price.[44] By that time, however, the case had become embroiled in a national political debate over the enforcement of the Fugitive Slave Act of 1850, and the U.S. district attorney blocked the sale. Burns was returned to bondage in Virginia. Suttle had taken a symbolic stand and secured Burns's return with the aid of federal authorities, but he was not particularly eager to retain such a troublesome property, and he soon sold him to a slave trader for $905. In 1855 the Reverend Grimes and his parishioners were finally able to purchase Burns's freedom for $1,300.

Twelfth Baptist, which had begun as an offshoot of the First Independent Church during the 1840s, took a special interest in fugitives from slavery. Born free in Virginia, Leonard A. Grimes had moved to New Bedford, Massachusetts, in 1840, and in 1848 he was one of twenty-four founding members of the new church, sometimes called "the fugitive slaves' church." Earlier he had spent two years in a Washington, D.C., jail for assisting escaped slaves.[45] The preponderance of fugitive slaves among its early members made it a precarious undertaking, especially after the passage of the Fugitive Slave Act of 1850, when about forty of its members, fearing for their safety, fled to Canada.

Burns, angered by an allegation printed in a Richmond newspaper that after legally obtaining his freedom he had been sentenced to a term in the Massachusetts Penitentiary, wrote a letter that was published in *The Liberator* saying he had been studying for two years at the Oberlin Institute and the Fairmount Theological Seminary in Ohio. Now he was in Maine, he said,

> making preparations to travel with a panorama, styled the Grand Moving Mirror— scenes of real life, startling and thrilling incidents, degradation and horrors of American slavery—for the purpose of selling my book, a narrative giving a full account of my life in slavery from childhood, with many other facts connected with the system of slavery. The proceeds are to enable me to complete my studies, at which time friends will have the opportunity of seeing, hearing, reading and knowing for themselves.[46]

Only twenty-four years old when he wrote that letter, Burns did succeed in completing his theological studies, was ordained, and took charge of a congregation of fugitives from slavery at Zion Baptist Church in St. Catherine's, Ontario, but there is no evidence he ever published the promised autobiography before his death in 1862 at age twenty-eight.

In 1855 the Boston publisher John P. Jewett issued Benjamin Drew's *The Northside View of Slavery: The Canadian Refugees' Own Narratives.* Based on interviews with fugitives residing in Canada, it contained 191 narrative sketches of people who had been enslaved in the United States. That same year Peter Randolph's *Sketches of Slave Life; or, Illustrations of the Peculiar Institution* appeared. Born in slavery in Virginia about 1825, Randolph was freed in 1847 and moved to Boston, where he became a Baptist minister. He remained active in Baptist ministerial work, studied law, and eventually served as a justice of the peace in Boston. In 1893 he published a vastly expanded autobiographical narrative of two hundred pages (his 1855 narrative was eighty-two pages long) entitled *From Slave Cabin to the Pulpit: The Autobiography of Rev. Peter Randolph—The Southern Question Illustrated and Sketches of Slave Life.*

Of course, not every escapee from the "Southern prison house" of bondage who lived in Boston left an autobiographical account or published narrative, but many of them, such as Lewis Hayden, made significant contributions to the antislavery effort and to the building of Boston's black community. Born in slavery about 1815 in Lexington, Kentucky, Hayden had escaped to Canada via the Underground Railroad with his wife, Harriet, and their ten-year-old son. The Haydens lived in Canada and Detroit before moving to Boston about 1850. The Boston city directory for 1849–50 listed Lewis Hayden's occupation as "lecturer." He soon became a leader among Boston's blacks, serving as one of five blacks on the Boston Vigilance Committee, which contained a total of 207 members. During the 1850s the Hayden home was a "station" on the Underground Railroad. An estimated seventy-five fugitives from slavery, about one-fourth of all the fugitives believed to have passed through Boston, stopped at the Haydens' house at 66 Phillips Street.[47] Prominent among those he assisted were William and Ellen Craft, who had escaped from Macon, Georgia, in 1848, with Ellen dressed as a man and passing as William's master.[48] Hayden was also among the group of black Bostonians who rescued the fugitive Shadrach in February 1851.[49]

During the first six months of 1849, over a decade before the narrative of their escape was published in London, William and Ellen Craft were on a New England speaking tour arranged by William Wells Brown. In a letter to Garrison, Brown described the couple and asked him to announce in *The Liberator* their upcoming speaking engagements in Worcester, Nantucket, and New Bedford in January 1849.[50] In Boston they addressed the convention of the Massachusetts Anti-Slavery Society that month and the annual meeting of the New England Anti-Slavery Society the following May.[51] The Crafts settled briefly in Boston, where William worked as a carpenter and Ellen as a seamstress. After learning that in compliance with the Fugitive Slave Act of 1850, federal writs had been issued for them, William bought a gun and sent Ellen into hiding. Finally, upon hearing that federal militia were on their trail bearing presidential orders to arrest them, they went into exile from their native land. In 1852, after he and his wife had moved to England, William Craft informed a Mr. May (probably Samuel J.) that on October 22 his wife had given birth "to our first free born babe," a boy whom they named Charles Estlin Phillips, "after our kind friend Mr. Estlin of Bristol, and after Mr. Wendell Phillips, the eloquent champion of liberty."[52]

Lydia Maria Child, besides encouraging James R. Bradley to prepare and publish his short narrative in 1834, was one of the most tireless writers against slavery and, according to Jean Fagan Yellin, "perhaps the most important of the free white female abolitionist writers."[53] During the previous year her *Appeal in Favor of That Class of Americans Called Africans* was published in Boston, causing such a stir that the trustees of the Boston Athenæum revoked her membership. That book was merely the first in a long line of Child's publications attacking slavery. From 1841 to 1843 she was the managing editor of the weekly *National Anti-Slavery Standard*.

Child's tract *The Duty of Disobedience to the Fugitive Slave Act: An Appeal to the Legislators of Massachusetts* was published in Boston in 1860 by the American Anti-Slavery Society and contained five narrative sketches of former slaves. Her *The Patriarchal Institution, As Described by Members of Its Own Family,* also

William and Ellen Craft, fugitive slaves. From William Still's *The Underground Railroad* (1872). The Boston Athenæum.

WILLIAM CRAFT.

ELLEN CRAFT.

published in Boston in 1860 by the American Anti-Slavery Society, contains seven such sketches, and her *The Freedmen's Book,* published by Boston's Ticknor and Fields in 1865, contains nine more. In addition, Child was the editor for Harriet Jacobs's *Incidents in the Life of a Slave Girl,* published for the author in Boston in 1861 under the pseudonym "Linda Brent." Previously categorized as a fictionalized slave narrative and once considered "not credible" even by some recent historians of the black experience, Jacobs's narrative has been authenticated as a genuine self-written piece through Jean Fagan Yellin's painstaking research.[54]

Clearly the body of literature that included book-length personal narratives, supplemented by biographical and autobiographical sketches of thousands of

Lydia Maria Child, eloquent advocate of emancipation. From a carte de visite taken by John G. Whipple in 1865. The Boston Athenæum.

former slaves, was a potent propaganda tool in the struggle against slavery. But after the end of slavery, and partly because of its origin as propaganda, this documentary record would be ignored by most historians for almost a century. Fortunately, it has reemerged as a valuable tool in reconstructing slave life from the point of view of the slaves.

As recently as 1971, Kenneth M. Stampp, author of the landmark study *The Peculiar Institution* (1956), stated that "direct evidence from the slaves themselves is hopelessly inadequate."[55] Yet, as John W. Blassingame and others have demonstrated, black eyewitness testimony on the slave condition can be found in a wide range of sources, including letters written by slaves, speeches, interviews conducted by journalists and scholars, and autobiographies published in periodicals and rare books. In comparative perspective, Stampp's statement notwithstanding, efforts such as those described in this essay ironically resulted in blacks enslaved in the United States leaving "more extensive documentary records than any other group of slaves in history."[56] Such records, clearly the product of a significant biracial effort, not only helped shape the direction of the antislavery movement during the antebellum years, but continue to inform the present generation's understanding of what it was like to be enslaved in these United States.

NOTES

1. See Clement Eaton, "A Dangerous Pamphlet in the Old South," *Journal of Southern History* 2 (1936): 323–24. See also Sterling Stuckey, "David Walker (1785–1830)," in Rayford W. Logan and Michael R. Winston, eds., *Dictionary of American Negro Biography* (New York: W. W. Norton, 1982), pp. 622–23, and the biographical sketch of Walker by Jason H. Silverman in Randall M. Miller and John David Smith, eds., *Dictionary of Afro-American Slavery* (Westport, Conn.: Greenwood Press, 1988), pp. 791–92.

2. Malcolm X, *The Autobiography of Malcolm X (As Told to Alex Haley)* (New York: Ballantine Books, 1965), p. 176.

3. Many Black Bostonians knew Russwurm, as he had taught briefly at the African School that met on the first floor of the African Meeting House. An independent school for black children had moved its location to the church soon after the edifice was completed in 1806. *Freedom's Journal* was the first of twenty-four black newspapers to be published in the United States before the Civil War.

4. So potent was the "diabolical Boston Pamphlet," as Walker's *Appeal* was called in the South, that the states of Georgia and North Carolina passed laws outlawing its distribution, and the mayor of Savannah and the governor of Georgia wrote letters of protest to Boston's mayor, Harrison Gray Otis. Although William Lloyd Garrison's response to the pamphlet's initial circulation had been lukewarm because of its call for slave violence, he reprinted most of Walker's work in *The Liberator* several months after its founding in January of 1831. In the meantime, Walker had died at his Bridge Street residence on June 28, 1830, a victim, certain of his contemporaries felt, of poisoning.

5. Lorenzo Dow Turner, *Anti-Slavery Sentiment in American Literature Prior to 1865* (Port Washington, N.Y.: Kennikat Press, 1966), pp. 1–3.

6. Within two years of its initial publication, Brown's autobiography had gone through four American editions and sold ten thousand copies. See biographical sketches of Brown by Carter G. Woodson in the *Dictionary of American Biography,* vol. 2, pt. 1, p. 161, and William Edward Farrison in Logan and Winston, *Dictionary of American Negro Biography,* pp. 71–73. See also Farrison's *William Wells Brown: Author and Reformer* (Chicago: University of Chicago Press, 1969).

7. The full title of Henry Brown's narrative is *Narrative of Henry Box Brown, Written from a Statement of Facts Made by Himself* (Boston: Brown and Stearns, 1849).

8. The title of Peter Randolph's narrative was *Sketches of Slave Life* (Boston, 1855).

9. William S. McFeely, *Frederick Douglass* (New York: W. W. Norton and Co., 1991), p. 77.

10. The statement about population is derived from William H. Pease and Jane H. Pease, *They Who Would Be Free: Blacks' Search for Freedom, 1830–1861* (1974; reprint, Urbana: University of Illinois Press, 1990), p. 27.

11. The full title of the publication was *Thoughts on African Colonization; or, An Impartial Exhibition of the Doctrines, Principles & Purposes of the American Colonization*

Society. Together with the Resolutions, Addresses & Remonstrances of the Free People of Color (Boston, 1832).

12. See *The African Meeting House: A Sourcebook* and Beth Anne Bower and Byron Rushing, "The African Meeting House: The Center for the 19th Century Afro-American Community," in Robert L. Schuyler, ed., *Archaeological Perspectives on Ethnicity in America: Afro-American and Asian American Culture History* (Farmingdale, N.Y.: Baywood Publishing Co., 1980), pp. 69–75. According to Bower and Rushing, "The African Meeting House was built in 1806 by black craftsmen under the direction of Ward Jackson, master builder" (p. 69). A more general treatment of the material culture aspects of the African-American experience in Boston, including the African Meeting House, is Beth Anne Bower, "Material Culture in Boston: The Black Experience," in Randall H. McGuire and Robert Paynter, eds., *The Archaeology of Inequality* (Cambridge, Mass.: Basil Blackwell, 1991), pp. 55–63.

13. August Meier and Elliott Rudwick, "The Role of Blacks in the Abolitionist Movement," in *From Plantation to Ghetto*, rev. ed. (New York: Hill and Wang, 1970), excerpted in John H. Bracey, August Meier, and Elliott M. Rudwick, eds., *Blacks in the Abolitionist Movement* (Belmont, Calif.: Wadsworth Publishing Co., 1971), p. 112.

14. *The Liberator*, December 28, 1855. Nell made this statement at a banquet held in his honor on December 17, 1855, celebrating the end of school segregation in Boston. See Louis Ruchames, "Race and Education in Massachusetts," *Negro History Bulletin* (December 1949).

15. Robert P. Smith, "William Cooper Nell: Crusading Black Abolitionist," *Journal of Negro History* 55 (July 1970): 182–99. See also Carleton Mabee, "A Negro Boycott to Integrate Boston Schools," *New England Quarterly* 41 (September 1968). In addition to being an ardent abolitionist, Nell was also a pioneer black historian who published *Colored Patriots of the American Revolution* (Boston: Robert F. Wallcut, 1855; with an introduction by Harriet Beecher Stowe).

16. There were sixty-two signers of the society's Declaration of Sentiments. The other two black signatories, in addition to James G. Barbadoes, were Robert Purvis and the dentist James McCrummell, both of Philadelphia.

17. Barbadoes's speech to the 1834 convention of the New England Anti-Slavery Society was reprinted in *The Liberator* June 7, 1834.

18. For a fuller treatment of the hesitancy of some abolitionists to extend equality of social intercourse to northern blacks in the antislavery movement, see Leon F. Litwack, "The Abolitionist Dilemma: The Antislavery Movement and the Northern Negro," originally published in *New England Quarterly* 34 (March 1961): 50–73, reprinted in Dwight W. Hoover, ed., *Understanding Negro History* (Chicago: Quadrangle Books, 1968), pp. 138–58.

19. Charles H. Wesley, "The Negro in the Organization of Abolition," *Phylon* 2 (Third Quarter 1941), as reprinted in Bracey, Meier, and Rudwick, *Blacks in the Abolitionist Movement*, p. 58. On the Paul family see J. Carleton Hayden's sketch of Thomas Paul, Sr., in Logan and Winston, *Dictionary of American Negro Biography*, pp. 482–83, and J. Marcus Mitchell's "The Paul Family," *Old Time New England* (Winter 1973). The edifice of the African Meeting House, generally regarded as the oldest standing black church building in the United States, was completed by black artisans in 1806.

20. Dorothy B. Porter, "Sarah Parker Remond, Abolitionist and Physician," *Journal of Negro History* 20 (July 1935), and Porter's biographical sketch of Remond in Logan and Winston, *Dictionary of American Negro Biography*, pp. 522–23.

21. See Dorothy B. Porter, "Charles Lenox Remond," in Logan and Winston, *Dictionary of American Negro Biography*, pp. 520–22, and William L. Usury, "Charles Lenox Remond, Garrison's Ebony Echo," *Essex Institute Historical Collections* 106 (April 1970).

22. Larry Gara, "The Professional Fugitive in the Abolition Movement," *Wisconsin Magazine of History* 26 (Spring 1965): 196–204.

23. Ephraim Peabody in the *Christian Examiner* 47, no. 67 (July 1849), as quoted in Larry Gara, *The Liberty Line* (Lexington: University of Kentucky Press, 1961), p. 124.

24. John A. Collins to William Lloyd Garrison, January 18, 1842, quoted in Philip S. Foner, ed., *The Life and Writings of Frederick Douglass,* 4 vols. (New York, 1950–55), vol. 1, p. 46.

25. Gara, *The Liberty Line,* p. 122.

26. Theodore Dwight Weld would later help produce the influential *American Slavery As It Is,* published in 1839.

27. *The Liberator,* March 29, 1834.

28. James R. Bradley's letter to Lydia Maria Child of June 3, 1834 is reprinted in C. Peter Ripley et al., eds., *The Black Abolitionist Papers,* vol. 3 (Chapel Hill: University of North Carolina Press, 1991), pp. 136–40.

29. Another edited version of Bradley's narrative was published in the *Herald of Freedom,* March 7, 1835. That version appears in John W. Blassingame, ed., *Slave Testimony* (Baton Rouge: Louisiana State University Press, 1977), pp. 686–90.

30. Deborah Weston to Maria Weston Chapman, March 4, 1840, Weston Papers.

31. In terms of desegregated schooling, Boston lagged behind most other cities and towns in Massachusetts; by 1845 black parents could send their children to integrated public schools in Salem, New Bedford, Nantucket, Worcester, and Lowell, but not in Boston. See Leon F. Litwack, *North of Slavery: The Negro in the Free States, 1790–1860* (Chicago: University of Chicago Press, 1961), pp. 143–44, and Donald M. Jacobs, "The Nineteenth-Century Struggle over Segregated Education in the Boston Schools," *Journal of Negro Education* 39 (Winter 1970): 76–85. On the case *Sarah Roberts v. Boston,* see Leonard W. Levy and Harlan B. Phillips, "The *Roberts* Case: Source of the 'Separate but Equal' Doctrine," *American Historical Review* 56 (April 1951): 510–18.

32. Frederick Douglass, quoted in Waldo E. Martin, Jr., *The Mind of Frederick Douglass* (Chapel Hill: University of North Carolina Press, 1984), p. 20.

33. Frederick Douglass, *The Narrative of the Life and Times of a Slave Written by Himself* (Boston, 1845), pp. 118.

34. Frederick Douglass, *My Bondage and My Freedom* (New York, 1855), reprinted by the Johnson Publishing Company in its Ebony Classics series (Chicago, 1970), p. 281.

35. Pease and Pease, *They Who Would Be Free,* p. 5.

36. *The Narrative of the Life and Adventures of Henry Bibb, an American Slave* (1849).

37. *The Liberator,* November 17, 1832.

38. Quincy's introductory letter to the book states that his role was limited to correcting "clerical" errors. William Wells Brown, *Narrative of William W. Brown, a Fugitive Slave, Written by Himself* (Boston, 1847), p. vi.

39. Smith did not publish his autobiography until 1881, when he was "broken down by the infirmities of age." *Autobiography of James L. Smith* (Norwich, 1881), reprinted in Arna Bontemps, ed., *Five Black Lives* (Middletown, Conn.: Wesleyan University Press, 1971), p. 144. By purchasing the narrative, he said, readers would be helping to support him in his "declining years."

40. Ibid., p. 187.

41. The controversy over the Williams narrative is discussed in such contemporary sources as *Emancipator,* August 30, 1838 and October 25, 1838, and in Charles H. Nichols, *Many Thousands Gone: The Ex-Slaves' Accounts of Their Freedom and Bondage* (Leiden, 1963).

42. Frederick Douglass to Thomas Auld, *The Liberator,* September 22, 1848, reprinted in *Journal of Negro History* 10 (July 1925): 390.

43. Douglass's 1845 narrative has been analyzed vigorously in great detail and from many angles. See, for example, Donald B. Gibson, "Reconciling Public and Private in Frederick Douglass' Narrative," *American Literature: A Journal of Literary History, Criticism, and Biography* 57, no. 4 (December 1985): 549–69; Ann Kibbey, "Language in Slavery: Frederick Douglass' Narrative," *Prospects: An Annual Journal of American Cultural Studies* 8 (1983): 163–82; and John Sekora, "Comprehending Slavery: Language and Personal History in Douglass' Narrative of 1845," *College Language Association Journal* 29, no. 2 (1985): 157–70.

44. On the history of the church pastored by the Reverend Leonard A. Grimes, see

William H. Hester, *One Hundred and Five Years by Faith: A History of the Twelfth Baptist Church* (Boston: Published by the Twelfth Baptist Church, 1946). I thank Ava Baker for bringing this publication to my attention.

45. Samuel Shapiro, "The Rendition of Anthony Burns," *Journal of Negro History* 44 (January 1959): 39, n. 20.

46. *The Liberator,* August 13, 1858, reprinted in *Journal of Negro History* 10 (1925): 453.

47. Stanley J. Robboy and Anita W. Robboy, "Lewis Hayden: From Fugitive Slave to Statesman," *New England Quarterly* 46 (December 1973): 591.

48. The Crafts' narrative was eventually published in London in 1860 as William and Ellen Craft, *Running a Thousand Miles for Freedom; or, The Escape of William and Ellen Craft from Slavery.*

49. Many of the details summarized in this paragraph appear in Kenneth Wiggins Porter, "Lewis Hayden," in Logan and Winston, *Dictionary of American Negro Biography,* pp. 295–97.

50. *The Liberator,* January 12, 1849.

51. Benjamin Quarles, *Black Abolitionists* (New York: Oxford University Press, 1969), p. 63.

52. William Craft to Mr. May, November 10, 1852, published in *The Liberator,* December 17, 1852, reprinted in *Journal of Negro History* 10 (July 1925): 447–48.

53. Jean Fagan Yellin, *Women and Sisters: The Antislavery Feminists in American Culture* (New Haven: Yale University Press, 1989), p. 53.

54. See, for example, Jean Fagan Yellin, "Written by Herself: Harriet Jacobs's Slave Narrative," *American Literature* 53, no. 3 (November 1981): 479–86, and a voluminously annotated edition of the narrative prepared by Yellin and issued by the Harvard University Press in 1987. An anonymous reviewer of the original publication claimed to know the author personally: "Linda: Incidents in the Life of a Slave Girl. Written by Herself," *The Anti-Slavery Advocate* 2, no. 53 (May 1, 1861): 1. See also Joanne M. Braxton, "Harriet Jacobs' Incidents in the Life of a Slave Girl: The Re-definition of the Slave Narrative Genre," *Massachusetts Review: A Quarterly of Literature, the Arts and Public Affairs* 27, no. 2 (Summer 1986): 379–87.

55. Kenneth M. Stampp, "Rebels and Sambos: The Search for the Negro's Personality in Slavery," *Journal of Southern History* 37 (August 1971): 367–92.

56. Peter Kolchin, *Unfree Labor: American Slavery and Russian Serfdom* (Cambridge: Harvard University Press, 1987), p. 379.

CHAPTER FIVE

James Brewer Stewart

Boston, Abolition, and the Atlantic World, 1820–1861

I n *James Brewer Stewart's original and thought-provoking essay, Boston's historical past, going back to the days of the Revolution, takes center stage as the clash of ideologies between England and her colonies is played out again over issues related to slavery. Clearly some feared that the "cradle of liberty" might soon become a "graveyard for freedom." But while abolitionists such as William Lloyd Garrison and David Walker began to lionize English values tied to emancipation and immediatism, they loudly called into question the new breed of American values all too evident even in Boston, values that strengthened the unfortunate alliance between the lords of both loom and lash.*

This resulted, Stewart believes, in a confusing array of historical contradictions as anti-abolition mobs and their supporters began to offer up examples of heroic Revolutionary rhetoric against British tyranny and the activities of groups such as the Sons of Liberty as justification for often violent attacks upon the forces of abolition. Here David Walker and William Lloyd Garrison come together ideologically, loudly calling into question the growing power of the proslavery forces in the United States, with Walker angrily citing the racist notions set forth in Thomas Jefferson's Notes on Virginia *and Garrison offering up in the masthead of* The Liberator *the radical words of Thomas Paine.*

In Boston it became a struggle between the entrenched brahmin leadership, fearful of losing their power, who were soon joined by a variety of elements opposed to all efforts aimed at black freedom, and the surprisingly strong biracial abolitionist coalition epitomized by the coming together of the followers of both Walker and Garrison. As Stewart points out, while in some respects the abolitionists might have "helped make Boston an even more deeply divided city, they also created some profound elements of unity" whereby "black Bostonians and white" could find "in abolitionism a common sense of the past" that they could in turn use in an effort to create a better future.

In the three decades before the Civil War, Bostonians found themselves constantly reminded of their forebears' struggles against British "tyranny." Scattered throughout their city were many more historical symbols than remain today of the city's rich associations with the "Spirit of '76." Boston's streetcorner atmosphere in those days *"breathed resistance,"* recalled Henry Adams, grandson of John Quincy Adams and great-grandson of John Adams, who himself spent much of the 1840s and 50s in the city, pondering his family's revolutionary past.[1]

What provoked the young Adams to these historical contemplations was Boston's intense three-decade debate over the morality of slavery and the relationship of "inalienable rights" to people of the black race. Past always fused tightly with present in this self-consciously historic city whenever these disagreements flared. All parties, rich and poor, black and white, claimed allegiance to the values of 1776. All insisted that they were fighting against terrible conspiracies threatening their personal liberties, conspiracies that were linked in some fashion to the influence of Great Britain. In the course of their disputes, Bostonians from all walks of life also revealed deeply divided opinions over the directions in which their city was developing, together with antagonistic visions of Boston's place in the Atlantic world of commerce and culture.

An exploration of these matters, however, first requires an evocation of the historical terrain so familiar to Henry Adams and his contemporaries. More than anything else, perhaps, it was this streetcorner environment, thick with visible history, that conditioned Bostonians to relive their parents' revolution when colliding over the subject of slavery.[2]

Near the city's center, Henry Adams could not have helped but notice the headstone of his great-uncle, that leading "Son of Liberty" Sam Adams, whenever he passed by the Common burial ground. It stood prominently in the front row, flanked by the monument of James Otis. Casting his vision across the Common and up the east side of Beacon Hill, young Adams could also make out John Hancock's old barn, standing as sturdily as when it had been built, and behind it, off to the left, the State House, once the proud seat of King George's authority, and now the site of republican government for the Commonwealth of Massachusetts.

As Adams walked through the city, still other monuments to the Revolution came into view. A fast stroll across Tremont Street and into the business district took him past the spot where the patriots' first martyr, the African American Crispus Attucks, had fallen in the massacre of 1770. A bit farther west stood Paul Revere's house and workshop. Slightly farther still, close by the wharves and within sight of the steeple of the Old South Church, was Peter Faneuil's precious gift to Boston, Faneuil Hall, Boston's enduring temple of free speech, patriotic resistance, and civic activism. "One lived in the atmosphere of the Stamp Act, the Tea Act, and the Boston Massacre," Adams recalled of the 1840s and 50s. "Within Boston a boy was first an eighteenth-century politician. . . . If violence were a part of complete education, Boston was not incomplete."[3]

The Boston Athenæum's Beacon Street building, completed in 1849. The Boston Athenæum.

What made young Adams and his contemporaries so acutely conscious of these reminders of their ancestors' rebelliousness was neither simple nostalgia nor innocent civic pride. Instead, their sense of history was sharpened by the unsettling new directions being taken as a result of both the city's day-to-day affairs and its long-term development. Boston, all agreed, had since the start of the 1820s gone far to transform itself into an extraordinarily sophisticated city, one which was exploring the promises of large-scale manufacturing, compounding capital investment, and global commerce. But as their city's wealth grew, Bostonians from all walks of life began to encounter evidence of the human cost of their growing affluence, cosmopolitanism, and transatlantic interdependence. These trends seemed to undermine the civic virtue and harmonious republican order that they so prized as their city's special legacies from the Revolution. Such concerns, in turn, would be deeply influential when the conflict over slavery forced Bostonians to link present with past.

Starting in the 1820s, signs of widening rifts between the opulent and the poor became increasingly difficult for Bostonians to ignore. Below the great mansions of Beacon Hill, expanding neighborhoods of transient laborers began to rupture the traditional boundaries of domestic privacy with increased noise, crowding, and crime. Tensions multiplied dangerously between unskilled black and white workers in Boston's ever more competitive labor market, a trend that would be complicated in the 1840s by new ethnic and religious conflicts as streams of Irish Catholic immigrants began arriving in the otherwise Protestant city. While civic leaders lauded their city's progress in "an age of improvements"—modern new libraries, hospitals, schools, and other fine public works—the wealthiest families were fleeing Boston by building summer estates in the countryside. Meanwhile, they expanded their social dominion by foreclosing admission to Harvard College to all but the most affluent, and by replacing Boston's traditional system of Faneuil Hall town meetings with a city council chosen through at-large elections. By 1830, old Boston "town" had been transformed into a much more complex urban society. Its traditional "leading families," joined by representatives of newer wealth, were emerging as the fabled "brahmin aristocracy" that would dominate the city until well after the Civil War. In the meantime, its many more ordinary citizens had begun increasingly to constitute a racially polarized, ethnically divided, and economically hard-pressed working class.[4]

Deeply unsettled by this sweeping change, Bostonians of every sort, rich as well as poor, Catholic as well as Protestant, black as well as white, sensed disturbing parallels between past and present, between their understanding of their parents' revolution against English tyranny and their own growing misgivings over the direction of current trends. As they did so, they began to fear that latter-day equivalents of tyrannous royalty, corrupted parliamentarians, and traitorous local collaborators were conspiring to subvert the personal liberties and public virtues that had always been the hallmarks of their republican city. It is little wonder, then, that Bostonians began to see disturbing new meanings in

Beacon Hill mansions at 63–61 Mt. Vernon Street. Photograph by J. J. Hawes (1857–1867). The Boston Athenæum.

the hallowed sites that embodied the memories of their parents' revolution. Were they, the sons and daughters of the founding generation, witnessing an effort to squander the moral endowment that their history had bequeathed them by creating in its place a city in which greed and despotism flourished, spreading vice, corruption, and enslavement in their wake?[5]

The moral crisis that most sharply focused these general fears was set off by the accumulating impact of black slavery in the South on the life and values of Boston. It was surely no coincidence that local controversies over the morality of slaveowning first began to explode here during the early 1830s, just as the disturbing consequences of the city's plunge into modernity were becoming so apparent. Indeed, a persuasive case could easily be made that much of Boston's new affluence and the consequent malaise of its citizenry arose from the growing ties between the city's evolving economy and the plantations of the slave states.

From the 1820s onward, Boston's political economy and that of the slaveholding South were clearly becoming more tightly intertwined. Various Lowells, Appletons, and Lawrences were only the most prominent of the

Massachusetts Senator Charles Sumner in a photograph taken by J. W. Black in 1874. The Boston Athenæum.

emerging "brahmins" to add new fortunes to old by linking their assets with those of "king cotton." By developing sophisticated textile factories outside Boston that processed vast amounts of raw cotton, these powerful entrepreneurs linked their city's banking, shipping, trading, and investment enterprises to the economy of the slave states. Soon many of the same families had also become principal investors in Massachusetts' burgeoning shoe industry, which came to depend increasingly on southern markets.

As the scions of these "leading families" pooled capital and coordinated investments through organizations such as the "Boston Association," they also increased their political influence in their city and the Commonwealth, emphasizing views of public policy to which many southern planters also subscribed, views stressing the importance of "gentlemanly" leadership, an orderly approach to society's problems, and a skeptical view of ideas that might inflame and divide society. By the 1840s it had become common to equate Boston's "lords of the loom" with the "lords of the lash" who held sway in the Deep South, and to read the politics of Beacon Hill in the speeches of Daniel Webster, Robert C. Winthrop, and Abbott Lawrence—"Cotton Whigs," as everyone now called them.[6]

But if upper-crust Bostonians were involving their city ever more deeply with the slave states, they also ensured that it remained part of the rich elite culture of "mother" England, and the vast imperial system over which the British presided. Since 1776 Boston's high-toned patriots had made it clear that their quarrel was with a tyrant-king and a corrupted Parliament, not with venerable and venerated British traditions, customs, or markets, a persuasion that remained unshakable on Beacon Hill until at least the Civil War. Boston's commercial enterprises, after all, relied increasingly after 1815 on networks of lineage, trade, commerce, and credit that criss-crossed from London, Liverpool, Glasgow, and Bristol to the West Indies and India.

In clothing, art, and literature as in architecture and manners, "brahmin" pacesetters looked constantly for direction to England's leading families. But at the same time they could not help but notice that Great Britain had become the world's most powerful force for abolishing slavery. As the lives of Bostonians became enmeshed with the politics and economics of the American South, many of the city's residents also had to acknowledge the expansive influence of abolition-minded England, a trading and commercial colossus whose navy suppressed the worldwide slave trade, and whose Parliament, in 1831, decreed black emancipation throughout its sprawling empire.[7]

Linked increasingly to these conflicting Atlantic worlds of production and culture, Bostonians likewise began to divide. While commerce and capitalism, propelled by southern cotton and British investment, continued to remake the traditional social fabric of their city, Bostonians began contesting among themselves over the moral meanings of slavery and freedom not only within the wider limits of their world, but within their own neighborhoods as well. As they did so, they began to invoke in a myriad of ways what they believed to have been the lessons of their forebears' revolution.

Generalizations such as these mean little without flesh-and-blood historical figures to give them substance. Black abolitionist David Walker was certainly one of these. The community to which Walker belonged was seemingly ill provisioned to defend any claims to liberty, for black Bostonians were always few (no more than 3 percent of the city's 1830 population), poor, and seemingly segregated. They lived together on the back side of Beacon Hill ("nigger hill,"

Two samples of seamen's protection papers, carried by free black sailors in southern ports where they risked being captured and sold into slavery. The New Bedford Free Public Library.

as whites scornfully referred to it), within sight of the "brahmin" mansions on its crest and close by the State House. Most of its residents were unskilled laborers, small shopkeepers, or domestic servants, except for the many seamen who shipped out to far-flung ports.

But if they were poor in material resources, black Bostonians possessed rich traditions of political militancy and communal self-help, rooted historically with Crispus Attucks and Prince Hall in the days of the Revolution and embodied in the 1820s by people such as David Walker. And as Walker understood it, Boston's expanding involvement in commerce and cotton only intensified the oppression against which he, his neighbors, and his predecessors had always been forced to struggle. As trade with the South expanded, for example, Boston's black sailors found themselves forced to lay over in unfriendly ports such as Charleston, Savannah, and Baltimore, where they could be, and often were, jailed for the duration of their visits, and where they risked being captured and sold into slavery.

Still more terrifying was the sudden increase of kidnapping at home that began in the 1820s, once slave traders and their agents discovered how profitable it could be to capture African American citizens on the streets of Boston and sell them in the South. Meanwhile, Boston's skilled black craftsmen found their prospects diminishing even as the city's commercial growth continued. Competition with white artisans intensified in a market increasingly requiring primarily unskilled laborers of both races, inflaming racial animosities among working-class Bostonians as never before. Viewed from the perspective of David Walker, Boston's developing ties with the cotton South were, quite literally, allowing slavery to poison the lifeblood of his community while jeopardizing his own personal freedom. He was, after all, a North Carolina expatriate with a poorly documented past.[8]

Walker's *Appeal to the Coloured Citizens of the World . . . ,* first published in Boston in 1829, has long been noted for its unvarnished anger, vibrant Christian vision, blunt commentary on the free African American community's shortcomings, and bold endorsement of violent responses to racist tyranny. Less noticed are the tensions evident in Walker's exposition between his fervent application of America's revolutionary values and his heartfelt endorsement of imperial England as black Americans' most resolute ally against what he felt was a tyrannous America, corrupted by grasping slaveowners and their unprincipled northern collaborators. When faced with the choice between Boston's two worldwide commercial cultures, Walker did not hesitate.

Walker's description of the cultural sources of good and evil soon took on truly subversive dimensions, not only as history but as an analysis of his present. For example, Walker concluded the *Appeal* by quoting verbatim Jefferson's preamble to the Declaration of Independence, and then challenged the republican sensibilities of his white readers by declaiming: "Compare your own language . . . with your cruelties and murders inflicted by your cruel and unmerciful fathers and yourselves on our fathers and on us. . . . I ask you candidly, was your suffering under Great Britain, one hundredth part as cruel and tyrannical as you have rendered ours under you?"[9]

Throughout the *Appeal,* moreover, Walker attacked the "Sage of Monticello" as a malicious bigot, quoting liberally from *Notes on Virginia* to document Jefferson's belief in the natural inferiority of blacks and the necessity of banishing them, through colonization, beyond the borders of the republic. Clearly, Walker believed deeply in the ideals espoused in the Declaration and wanted them applied to the oppressed for whom he spoke. Just as clear, however, was Walker's wholesale rejection of the idea that Americans of his day were living out the legacy of their patriot-forebears' devotion to human rights.

That the American Colonization Society continued vigorously throughout the 1820s to promote its programs only confirmed to Walker the enduring tragedy of the patriots' compromised vision. It listed among its sponsors Massachusetts' Daniel Webster, Harrison Gray Otis, and other leading New Englanders, as well as many slaveholding notables, while proclaiming "safe" solutions to the problems of slavery and race. But to Walker, its program of gradually emancipating and deporting the nation's black population was a threatening racist insult that African Americans must reject at every turn. Instead he demanded complete citizenship, a full extension of the "inalienable rights" of 1776 to all Americans of his race. Walker, the political moralist, therefore held fervently to the "self-evident truths" of the Declaration of Independence, while his sense of history left him profoundly at odds with the fashion in which white Americans had lived out their revolutionary creed.

Reflecting these conflicting feelings of patriotism and alienation, Walker looked to Great Britain, the "soulless oppressor" of Jefferson's Declaration, and saw instead a civilization that was helping African Americans achieve liberation and citizenship: "The English are the best friends the colored people have on this earth," Walker declared. "They have done one hundred times more for the melioration of our condition, than all the other nations of the world put together. . . . There is no intelligent **black man** who knows anything, but esteems a real Englishman, . . . for they are the greatest benefactors we have."[10] For critics such as David Walker, upholding the historic principle that "all men are created equal" now seemed to require turning to the British in a crusade to overturn tyranny in America. By so radically revising the moral equations between nations, Walker had propounded a truly revolutionary view of the two commercial cultures that connected Bostonians to the Atlantic community. England, he believed, worked for the liberation of America, while within the United States slavery was leading to ever-increasing despotism. It was a reversal of moral perspectives to which others in Boston responded, quickly and emphatically.

Some who may have done so were those possibly responsible for Walker's demise (he was found dead in 1830 under circumstances suggesting foul play). But another, the youthful white newspaper editor William Lloyd Garrison, converted Walker's singular visions into an enduring crusade for black freedom. In the process he also provoked Bostonians of all sorts to begin expressing their deepening social and economic differences, and to weigh the impact of modernity on the condition of their city.

The most revealing clue to the focus of Boston's abolitionist movement is found in the slogan that Garrison chose for the masthead of his newspaper, *The Liberator,* when it first appeared in 1831: "OUR COUNTRY IS THE WORLD—OUR COUNTRYMEN ALL MANKIND." Rich with internationalist implications and boldly transcending standard definitions of American citizenship, it was a phrase of which David Walker would have approved. For Garrison, like Walker, instinctively aligned his vision with the expansive British world of commerce, empire, and abolition, while scorning the morality of his own nation's history and his city's ties to the South. Like Walker, Garrison measured America's hypocrisy by the patriotic standards of Jefferson's Declaration. (He had borrowed *The Liberator*'s motto from Thomas Paine.) To Garrison, as to Walker, all American claims to traditions of human freedom had been hopelessly corrupted long ago by slavery, not just in the South but in the daily affairs of northerners, Bostonians included.

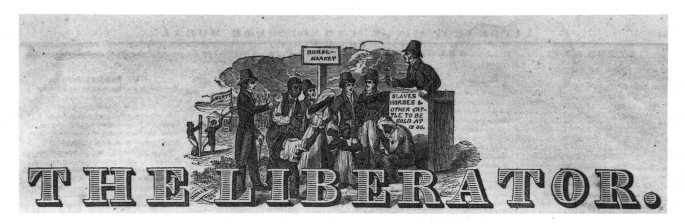

The Liberator's first masthead (first used April 23, 1831). By David Claypoole Johnston. The Boston Athenæum.

Garrison proposed to remedy this disaster with two simple words borrowed without apology from Great Britain's most influential reformers—IMMEDIATE EMANCIPATION—a demand, like Walker's, that embraced English values, condemned colonization, and registered contempt for American pretensions of liberty. From its inception by Garrison and Walker, Boston's abolitionist crusade was thus irrevocably anglophile, subversively patriotic, and based on an African American view of history's moral direction set in transatlantic terms. In 1833, for example, Garrison toured in England, making himself the subject of admiring commentary among the powerful peers and parliamentarians who had just legislated the slaves' emancipation throughout their empire. His way had been paid by donations from ordinary African Americans in Boston and other northern cities, friends, acquaintances, and readers of David Walker, who subscribed heavily to *The Liberator* and who clearly were relying on Garrison to represent them to their most important allies.[11]

To fulfill this mandate, Garrison promulgated extensive exposés of the American Colonization Society, demanded immediate emancipation, and lauded the British for their efforts in the cause of abolition: "You and your people," he assured a group of English peers, "are, in the sight of the Almighty, a people who have truly worked His will. . . . We, in America, look to you, as to Him, for our emancipation." As if to emphasize just how fully he equated his admiration of England with his alienation from American political culture, Garrison also declared that the United States was "insulting the majesty of Heaven" by "professing to be the land of the free and the asylum of the oppressed" while disenfranchising half a million free blacks, starving and plundering two million bondsmen, kidnapping and selling untold numbers of newborn slaves, "ruthlessly invading the holiest relations of life and cruelly separating the dearest ties of nature." Announcing that "my soul sickens when turning over this mass of corruption," Garrison went on to criticize the federal Constitution for protecting slavery and to castigate Americans in general for their hypocrisy when proclaiming all men as equals while upholding slavery.[12]

To hostile critics back in Boston, Garrison seemed to be calling for the overthrow not only of slavery but also of the government of the United States. Before long his detractors would hurl his words back at him, charging him and the abolitionists in general with being traitors who conspired with the British to destroy America's liberties by promoting slave insurrection, racial "amalgamation," and political disunion under the guise of "immediate emancipation." To certain other Bostonians, however, Garrison's elaborations on David Walker's internationalism represented a spiritually inspiring call to action that they felt compelled to embrace. As Bostonians began dividing over the meaning of international abolitionism, they also started to explore the deeper tensions created by their city's simultaneous embrace of southern slavery, British commercialism, and economic modernity.

Garrison unintentionally supplied a perfect occasion for Bostonians to begin expressing their conflicting views by inviting his new English friend, the radical abolitionist George Thompson, to tour New England and give antislavery speeches. Thompson, in many Americans' eyes, offered perfect confirmation that Garrisonian abolitionists had sold out to the English and had joined in their conspiracy to reenslave the United States by inflaming race relations and domestic politics. Thompson, who exuded English arrogance, was a sarcastic and vehement speaker who jeered at American claims of equality and carried Garrison's most fulsome endorsements. Soon after he arrived, on October 14, 1835, Boston found itself embroiled in riot. Mobs roamed the streets looking to bring the "British cut-throat" to justice by applying a full dose of tar and feathers, vowing to suppress the "niggers, firebrands and harpies" of the abolitionist movement suddenly so active in their city. The first person who "should lay violent hands" on "that foreign scoundrel" and bring him "to the tar kettle before dark" was to be rewarded with "a purse of $100," declared a handbill that appeared on the city's streets.[13] Boston's black citizenry, fearing the worst, hid in their homes while white abolitionists attempted, without success, to preserve their rights to free speech and assembly against the threat of mob rule. Garrison, chased by an angry crowd, was forced to take refuge in the Boston city jail. Thompson, sensing danger, simply refused to enter Boston.

Abolitionists always painted their riotous attackers as a wicked amalgam of aristocracy and rabble, the "head and tail" of society, as they often put it. As modern research has shown, their analysis was reasonably accurate. As in New York, Philadelphia, Utica, Cincinnati, and other sites of anti-abolitionist rioting in the mid-1830s, Boston's mobs were clearly encouraged by the city's "gentlemen of property and standing," its "brahmin elite," while poorer elements of the white working class eagerly enlisted as members. It is important, then, to examine the specific motives and grievances of each of these groups in the 1835 Boston riot, for thereby the larger relationships between the slavery controversy and Boston's interactions with the Atlantic world of commerce and cotton become clearer. So do its citizens' deepening disagreements over the continuing meaning of the city's revolutionary past.[14]

The Abolition Garrison in Danger and the Narrow Escape of the Scotch Ambassador, Boston, October 21, 1835. Cartoon depicting the riot that occurred to protest Garrison's announced intention to bring Scottish abolitionist George Thompson to speak in Boston. Garrison eventually had to be locked in the Leverett Street jail for his own safety. The New York Historical Society.

Boston's "gentlemen of property and standing" accurately perceived abolitionism as igniting a wholesale rebellion within their own so proudly constructed "aristocracy." While Boston's first abolitionist leaders were obscure individuals (the printer Garrison and the rag peddler Walker), the movement quickly began to enroll some of the city's most prestigious members. Within the rising generation of "great families," possessing such names as Quincy, Phillips, Loring, Chapman, May, Greene, Sewall, and Weston, young men and women with impressive educations, great inherited wealth, pronounced anglophile tastes, and extraordinary personal qualities began mingling with the free blacks and little-known white religious visionaries who gathered in *The Liberator*'s dingy office in Merchants' Hall. While David Walker and William Lloyd Garrison had already challenged the brahmins' southern allegiances from below, this direct confrontation from the "aristocracy's" own sons and daughters was a far more serious matter.

What impelled each of these young "aristocrats" to embrace immediate emancipation is far too complex a question to answer here, though modern biographers have done much to enlighten us.[15] It is clear, however, that among their motives, these rebels all saw themselves as carrying forward the fundamental principles of human liberation that had been formulated in the American Revolution (if not earlier) and bequeathed to them by their forebears. For some, these were easy claims to make. Boston attorney Samuel Sewall, for example, needed only to refer to the Puritan ancestor for whom he was named, whose *Selling of Joseph* (1701) constituted one of the earliest published protests against slavery in America. Edmund Quincy, son of one of Boston's most influential public officials, Josiah Quincy, could read in his father's writings dating from the 1790s deep misgivings about slavery's effect on American political behavior. For the Weston sisters, Deborah, Caroline, Ann, and Maria Weston Chapman, abolitionism greatly extended the parameters of female activism first established by upper-class women such as Abigail Adams, Mercy Warren, and their own female relatives during the American Revolution. Wendell Phillips, on the other hand, drew his inspiration not only from the august Puritan traditions of public service, but also from his intense identification with the great revolutionaries he associated with the Anglo-American past—Oliver Cromwell, Sir Henry Vane, Sam Adams, Edmund Burke, John Hancock, and Thomas Paine.[16]

Other examples could be cited, but the main point should be as clear to us as it was to the shocked elite of Boston. By rallying for "immediate emancipation" in the South and an end to white supremacy within Boston proper, these young renegades were openly denying all orthodox "brahmin" claims to moral leadership, historical authority, and economic legitimacy. The sons and daughters of these "leading families" now sneered at their elders as "lords of the loom," enslaved by their dependence on cotton to the "lords of the lash" on southern plantations. Worse still, they cheered and laughed when Wendell Phillips (the most polished, eloquent, and aristocratic rebel of them all) publicly insulted the "brahmins" as "narrow men, ambitious of office, fancying that an inheritance of millions entitles them to public advancement . . . some without the wit to keep the money they stole. . . . Old families run to respectable dullness. Snobbish sons of fathers lately rich, anxious to show themselves rotten before they are ripe."[17]

Worst of all, these upper-class rebels defied established conventions at every turn, consorting familiarly with activist blacks from "nigger hill" such as William Cooper Nell, *The Liberator*'s office manager, with plebeian zealots such as Garrison, and soon enough with militant women such as Maria Weston Chapman who blended with their abolitionism uncompromising demands for gender equality. By 1834 they had launched campaigns to repeal Massachusetts' statutes prohibiting racial intermarriage, to found integrated private schools, and to further discredit the American Colonization Society, to which so many of Boston's elite still subscribed. Such behavior, as every Bostonian knew, registered a wholesale rejection of the increasing southern orientation of Boston's

Antislavery rally on the Boston Common. Wendell Phillips addresses a crowd during the trial of fugitive slave Thomas Sims in 1851. The Boston Athenæum.

commercial and political life, and a deepening suspicion that the city had strayed far from its heritage as the "Cradle of American Liberty."

While these were sufficient reasons for Boston's civic leaders to applaud mob action against the abolitionists, the list of their "offenses" hardly ended here. Most disturbing of all to Boston's "gentlemen of property and standing" was their fear that the presence of a strong local abolitionist movement meant that their city had fallen under attack by a vast conspiracy. Judged from a neutral perspective, Boston's abolitionists gave the city fathers ample reasons for this belief. The most important of these was the fact that they did, indeed, collaborate feverishly with like-minded reformers, not only throughout the North but (more ominously) in Great Britain as well. The letters that passed back and forth between abolitionists in Boston and their allies in the British Isles fill scores of thick folios in the Boston Public Library, weighty evidence of the networks of personal contact that constantly renewed Boston Garrisonianism as the truly Anglo-American movement that David Walker had envisioned. So did the constant news from Great Britain that filled the abolitionist press, the incessant reprinting in Boston periodicals of antislavery speeches delivered on the floor of Parliament, and the constant travel of American abolitionists across the Atlantic. The "brahmin rebels" Phillips, Quincy, the Westons, and the rest, like Garrison and Walker, looked from the first to the British while struggling to realize their vision of Americans' "inalienable rights."

To Boston's established leadership, however, agitators such as these, in league with visiting subversives such as George Thompson, were hardly patriots. Instead, they were simply a confirmation of well-planned British plots to destroy civic harmony in Boston and scatter seeds of insurrection in the South. The rapine, pillage, and carnage that were to follow would foretell the collapse of all social order and the "reenslavement" of America. These fears also reflected the recognition that upstart local radicals now chose to ignore the historic prerogatives of leadership claimed by the Boston elite and appeal directly to the people at large. As the Boston *Courier* complained in 1835, the abolitionists had embarked upon "a systematic and, as far as practicable simultaneous effort" to stir up the most dangerous passions of the masses "through organized societies, public meetings, authorized agents, foreign emissaries, regular publications, and the incessant circulation of cheap tracts, pamphlets, handbills, etc."[18]

To these dire warnings, Harrison Gray Otis, Boston's great old Federalist leader, added his own. Addressing an overflow crowd in Faneuil Hall, which convened six weeks before the October anti-abolition riot, Otis spoke out against a "dangerous association" organized "from afar . . . , a *revolutionary society*—combined and affiliated with auxiliary societies in every state and community, large or small." Not only did this far-flung organization invite "all men" to subscribe to the immediatist crusade, said Otis, but it also enticed women to "turn their sewing parties into abolition clubs" and to seduce small children into the movement with gifts of "sugar plums." Soon, he predicted, the conspiracy would move into politics, eventually plunging the nation into civil war and servile insurrection. "I pray," he concluded, "that my grave will close over me before the union descends into hers."[19]

Otis had stated an important truth. The long-presumed right of patriarchal "brahmins" to rule uncontested over their social "inferiors," including women and children, and to set the direction of their city's affairs, was now being challenged in wholesale fashion. They were suddenly faced with a volatile alliance between militant residents of "nigger hill," elite British reformers, obscure white Garrisonians, and some of the most promising young "bluebloods" raised in their own neighborhoods. As his Faneuil Hall audience registered strong approval, Otis appealed to their "patriotic sentiments" as "descendents of the Sons of Liberty" and as "citizens of our beloved city." Oppose and ignore the abolitionist conspirators, he urged, and thereby protect American freedoms from terrible threats both at home and abroad.[20]

Although his mansion was furnished in sumptuous English decor and he measured his position by the standards of the peerage, Otis had now responded to the challenge of abolitionism by rejecting British internationalism. Instead, he had embraced a nationalist alliance with the South. In his version of patriotic history, honest citizens must recognize that duty called upon them to resist once again British corruption and efforts at internal subversion, disguised this time as "humanitarian" abolitionism, which was seeking as in 1776 to obliterate America's freedoms. His was a formulation of citizenship, of the revolutionary past's relationship to the duties of the present, that completely inverted the values of David Walker, William Lloyd Garrison, Maria Weston Chapman, and the rest who sought to expand American equality by collaborating openly with the British. Several weeks after Otis concluded, the mob began gathering and calling for Garrison and Thompson. When taking the law into their own hands, Boston's anti-abolitionists would always insist that they were living out the traditions of Sam Adams and the Sons of Liberty.

Needless to say, the dignified "Harry" Otis did not stride forth from Faneuil Hall, coattails flapping, the mob forming behind him. The vast majority of Otis's approving listeners lived well below his exalted social station and traced their lineages to the years before 1776 in a far different fashion than did he. While the memory of James Otis loomed large in the mind of his direct descendant, some in "Harry's" audience saw England through a very different lens. These were the sons and daughters of immigrants who had poured into Boston after 1815, fleeing the economic and political oppression of post-Napoleonic Great Britain. Others were recent refugees from New England's declining farm economy who entered Boston poorly skilled and deeply suspicious of any who proposed to assist their black competitors in Boston's tightening labor market. Still others were hard-pressed craftsmen, especially in the building trades, who found their independence being undermined by "brahmin" investment cartels that hired gang labor to construct their ambitious projects. In the 1820s, members of all these groups had already founded a Workingman's party to protest the worsening prospects of the "producing classes" in Boston's modernizing economy. All looked with hostility upon those who trafficked with English peers and who endangered the prospects of the humble still further by freeing and equalizing African Americans.

England, after all, had an international reputation for being no friend to the working poor, or to those politically active on labor's behalf. The "dark satanic mills" of Birmingham, London, and Leeds bore witness to the devastating impact of the industrial revolution on ordinary people. Moreover, the repressive policies of post-1815 governments toward dissenting groups in England remained a vivid memory for many immigrants and their children. To some critical observers, English industrialists had unleashed their own terrible form of slavery, "wages slavery," and were now exporting it to the factories of nearby Lynn, Lowell, and Waltham, and to vast capitalist enterprises within Boston itself. While Garrison, Walker, and the other abolitionists lauded British philanthropists for their liberation of black labor, working-class Bostonians saw the matter quite differently. Never would they have considered appealing to imperial England to advance their rights as working Americans. In the Atlantic world of commerce, their allegiances would always lie elsewhere, specifically with powerful men such as Otis who condemned the abolitionists and their British sympathizers, even denying their rights to free speech.[21]

Abolitionists, it must be emphasized, gave Boston's working people reasons aplenty for distrusting them, apart from their blatant anglophilia. The Westons, Chapmans, Quincys, and Phillipses in particular reeked of snobbishness and harbored deep aversions to the grittiness and spontaneity of working-class culture—its drinking, gambling, loudness, and general lack of polish. (One English visitor, after encountering Wendell Phillips and Edmund Quincy strolling together down Park Street, reported that they were the only two Americans he had ever seen that actually "looked like gentlemen.")[22] Worse still, from the perspective of the laboring poor, Boston's abolitionist leaders adamantly rejected the Workingman's party claim that industrial impoverishment was, in itself, "enslavement." In letters to the editor in the earliest issues of *The Liberator,* labor spokesmen pressed Garrison hard, asking, "Is not poverty itself slavery?" Garrison's answer, a confident "No," expressed the orthodox abolitionist conviction that the master/slave relationship was unique in its violations of God's will and elemental human justice. "They may go in rags, it is true," Garrison remarked of the working poor, "but their bodies and souls belong to them, not others." Indeed, he continued, poverty could actually be a blessing in disguise, challenging people to transform themselves into "self-made" individuals, by exercising "piety, self-denial, perseverance and education."[23]

Such patronizing advice was small comfort to Boston's laboring poor, since it also revealed how deeply committed most of the abolitionists were to the values of economic individualism and self-discipline, values that were propelling New England into an economy of industrial capitalism. For all their suspicions of the motives of the "lords of the loom," Boston's abolitionists harbored few reservations about the consequences of textile factories for those who worked long hours in them. With their pro-English biases, attitude of cultural superiority, and hostility toward workingmen's demands, abolitionists seemed fit subjects for mobbing by ordinary folk who feared for their own basic rights. It is little wonder that they roused to action when "gentlemen" such as Otis cried "Conspiracy!"

The "tail" of Boston's white social order, its laboring poorer whites, had now united with its "head," the Otises and their Beacon Hill associates, solid in the belief that an Anglo-abolitionist conspiracy threatened and that patriotic duty called them to arms. As the rioters stormed the meetingplace of the Boston Female Anti-Slavery society on October 21, 1835, searching for Thompson and Garrison, Bostonians commenced three decades of bitter internal struggle over which version of American history, patriotism, and citizenship would prevail. Would it be the one that linked the city to the expansive commercial world of British reformers, or the one that aligned Boston with realms where "cotton was king"?

NEW ENGLAND FACTORY LIFE.—"BELL-TIME."—DRAWN BY WINSLOW HOMER.

New England factory life. *Bell Time*, by Winslow Homer. Wood engraving from about 1868. The Boston Athenæum.

The struggle itself has been richly chronicled by some of America's most gifted historians and needs no repeating here.[24] However, some statements about its salient features and illustrations of its most important long-range dynamics are worth developing. Boston's history of struggle over the problems of slavery and white supremacy was truly unique in its scope and intensity, and could have been driven only by the aforementioned fundamental clashes of world view and historical understanding.

In the absence of these powerful influences it seems impossible, for example, to explain the tenacity and endurance of Boston's biracial coalition, let alone to account for all that it accomplished before the start of the Civil War. Whenever blacks and whites attempt to collaborate against racial injustice, tension, misunderstandings, and deep psychological wounds always result, and Boston's community of activists fell prey to all of these. Meanwhile, the anti-abolition forces within the city were strengthened manyfold after 1840 as thousands of Irish Catholic immigrants joined those already implacably hostile to anglophile "nigger lovers." Nevertheless, through years of demonstrating, boycotting, litigating, testifying, and editorializing, black and white Bostonians did succeed in ending segregation in public conveyances and in the public schools, and banded together to protect the city's African American citizens by identifying and resisting slavecatchers. In these endeavors, local black leaders such as William Cooper Nell, John Hilton, Robert Morris, Samuel Snowden, and Charles Lenox Remond worked closely with their various white associates. In the end, by 1860, Boston's interracial activists could justly claim that they had expanded beyond all expectations Bostonians' fundamental understanding of Jefferson's Declaration.[25]

Through it all, their sharp sense of their city's revolutionary history and their place among the international community of transatlantic reformers continued to infuse Boston's abolitionists with convictions that were vividly seen, tangibly felt, and immediately acted upon. For example, they spent decades contesting with their anti-abolitionist foes for dominion within that most revered of all monuments to the Revolution, Faneuil Hall. While these meetings were often disrupted by the bellowing of outraged laborers, Irishmen, and "Cotton Whigs," they succeeded by the 1850s in transforming the building into a temple of patriotic Bostonian resistance to slavecatchers and "northern men with southern principles." Occasionally city officials would try to deny them access. The hue and cry that inevitably resulted soon convinced everyone that it was wiser to let the abolitionists in.

In 1837, Wendell Phillips commenced this contest over the symbol that was Faneuil Hall when facing down Massachusetts attorney-general James T. Austin at an overflow meeting called to discuss the murder of abolitionist Elijah Lovejoy by proslavery rioters in Alton, Illinois. Austin spoke first, comparing Lovejoy's killers to John Hancock, Sam Adams, and the Sons of Liberty, for they, like their patriot forerunners, he claimed, had also been forced to take the law into their own hands (as "an orderly mob") to purge their city of "the disgusting instruments of their degradation."

Phillips followed. Possessing perhaps the most eloquent voice in America during its golden age of oratory, he charged Austin with giving terrible "insult to the memory of those patriot fathers." He then looked up and, gesturing toward the large oil portraits of Hancock, Adams, and Otis that hung at the back of the hall, vividly described not only his first reaction upon hearing Austin's words, but also the sudden collapse of the present into the past that always took place when Bostonians truly confronted slavery. "I thought," exclaimed Phillips, "that those pictured lips would have broken into voice to rebuke the recreant American—the slanderer of the dead. . . . In the sentiments he has uttered, on soil consecrated by the prayers of Puritans and the blood of patriots, the earth should have yawned and swallowed him up."[26] Phillips had just given a stunning demonstration of what Henry Adams meant when he recalled that "we lived in the atmosphere of the Stamp Act, the Tea Act and the Sons of Liberty." As the silenced crowd departed, it was clear, at least for the moment, that Faneuil Hall, and Boston's history, belonged to the abolitionists.

Events such as these, though usually not as dramatic, punctuated the abolitionists' struggle throughout the 1840s and 1850s for the ownership of both

Orator Wendell Phillips, called the "golden trumpet of abolitionism," in a carte de visite made about 1861. The Boston Athenæum.

history and the future in Boston. Abolitionist speeches, editorials, handbills, and private correspondence documenting fugitive slave rescue attempts in those two decades are rich with comparisons to the days of the Sons of Liberty and other analogies with the days of revolution. During the same period, orators such as the white Phillips and the black Samuel Snowden developed provocative speeches on Crispus Attucks that transformed this black patriot into an exemplar of insurrection. To register their disgust for the proslavery aftermath of the revolution they so loved, Boston's abolitionists of both races preferred to celebrate on August 1, the date of British emancipation in the West Indies, rather than on July 4. When they did decide to commemorate the fourth, they always convened *just outside* Boston, in Framingham, testimony to their sense of their city's historical dereliction.

Many such examples could be given, but the point should be clear. The historical markers, edifices, traditions, myths, rituals, and memories that surrounded Boston's abolitionists on every walk through town imparted to them an intensely local sense of obligation to make citizenship in the present serve the imperatives of the revolutionary past. Thus the rancorous struggles between Bostonians over slavery, their city's posture toward the Atlantic world, and its evolving obligations to its history were always conducted on an intensely personal, even parochial, level, linked intimately to the daily transactions of ordinary life.

But at the same time, as we have seen, Boston's abolitionists, black no less than white, also lived their daily lives within a panoramic international perspective. As confident actors in the worldwide drama of emancipation, they continued not only to look to Great Britain, but also to submerge themselves increasingly in its culture of English Victorian reform. George Thompson, for example, reappeared in 1850 to resume his speaking career, and Garrison again visited England before the Civil War. The friendships made abroad, the gossip shared by letter, the exchanges of hospitality, the monies raised and gifts given—all made the international experiences of Boston abolitionists as tangible to them as a stroll through the Common or a visit to Faneuil Hall. So did the elaborate "antislavery fairs" put on annually by Boston's abolitionist women which offered for sale such donated items as "a set of lovely teacups and saucers, contributed by Lord and Lady Morpeth," or "the famous Wedgwood medallion depicting the supplicating slave sent to us by our friends in Dublin, the Webbs."[27]

The tie to Great Britain was at least as enriching for Boston's African Americans as it was for whites, just as David Walker had suggested. For highly prominent figures such as Frederick Douglass, William Wells Brown, William and Ellen Craft, and Charles Lenox Remond, extended stays in the British Isles fostered not only contacts and reputations but also sophisticated cross-cultural understanding of the dynamics of slavery and discrimination. As excellent research has recently demonstrated, the anglophile nature of American abolitionism enabled African American activists to construct an "antislavery wall" of truly international scope, a network of agitation, influence, and information not only spanning the Atlantic, but stretching to the Caribbean and West Africa as well.[28]

Thus it was perhaps the black activists of Boston who realized most fully Walker's and Garrison's earliest visions for abolition. Theirs became an abolitionism as intensely American in its devotion to a liberating past as it was cosmopolitan in its global concern for the presently enslaved. Like their white Bostonian counterparts, they had created a powerful reconciliation between their patriotic embrace of the values of Boston's revolutionary past and their moral judgments on their city's proper place in the Atlantic world. This, at least, is one meaning that might be read in *The Liberator*'s ringing motto: "Our Country Is the World—Our Countrymen All Mankind."

But at the same time, abolitionist Bostonians never did find adequate responses to the mounting economic problems of their poorer fellow citizens. With the exception of a few white immediatists who dabbled in utopian socialism, and despite an abortive attempt by Phillips, Garrison, and Remond to enlist the immigrant Irish in the cause of the slave, Boston's abolitionists and its white working class always remained estranged from one another. However, this is not an occasion for evaluating the complex theoretical literature that debates the possible relationships between abolitionism and the rise of modern capitalism. Yet it is essential to stress that Bostonians before the Civil War, no less than Bostonians today, found themselves bedeviled and deeply divided by problems of growing poverty and their relationships to racial injustice.[29]

But if the abolitionists helped make Boston an ever more deeply divided city, they also created some profound elements of unity, elements that are well worth remembering as debates continue over "multiculturalism" and the proper approach to the teaching of history. For the plain fact was that black Bostonians and white found in abolitionism a common sense of the past, specifically a shared understanding of the meaning of the American Revolution and its pertinence to their time, that helped them to transcend their racial differences. In the same fashion, abolitionists of both races also came to embrace a distinctive view of the world, anglophile in orientation, global in scope. In this sense, Boston's abolitionists discovered for their time an inspiring and sustaining communality of vision that allowed them to explore, as few other Americans have been able to explore, the possibilities of interracial cooperation. This accomplishment, more than any other, should ensure that their history will continue to challenge and instruct us, even as we approach the end of the twentieth century.

NOTES

1. Henry Adams, *The Education of Henry Adams* (Boston: Houghton Mifflin, 1918), p. 29.

2. Works that convey a sense of Boston's historical flavor in the antebellum years include Harold Kirker and James Kirker, *Bulfinch's Boston, 1787–1817* (New York: Oxford University Press, 1964); John Daniels, *In Freedom's Birthplace* (Boston: Houghton Mifflin, 1914); Samuel Eliot Morison, *Harrison Gray Otis, 1765–1848: Urbane Federalist* (Boston: Houghton Mifflin, 1969); James Brewer Stewart, *Wendell Phillips: Liberty's Hero* (Baton Rouge: Louisiana State University Press, 1986), pp. 1–18.

3. Adams, *Education,* p. 43.

4. Roland Story, *The Forging of an Aristocracy: Harvard and the Boston Upper Class, 1800–1870* (Middletown, Conn.: Wesleyan University Press, 1980); Andrew R. L. Cayton, "The Fragmentation of 'A Great Family': The Panic of 1819 and the Rise of the Middling Interest in Boston," *Journal of the Early Republic* 4 (June 1982): 143–67; Tamara P. Thornton, *Cultivating Gentlemen: The Meaning of Country Life among the Boston Elite, 1785–1860* (New Haven and London: Yale University Press, 1989).

5. For general discussions of the relationships between antebellum economic development and the fears it engendered about the purity of republicanism, see Marvin Meyers, *The Jacksonian Persuasion: Politics and Belief* (Palo Alto, Calif.: Stanford University Press, 1957); Joyce Appleby, *Capitalism and a New Social Order* (New York: New York University Press, 1977); Lance Banning, *The Jeffersonian Persuasion* (Ithaca, N.Y.: Cornell University Press, 1978).

6. Thomas O'Connor, *The Lords of the Loom: The Cotton Whigs and the Coming of the Civil War* (New York: Scribner's, 1968).

7. For excellent discussions of these developments, see David B. Davis, *The Problem of Slavery in the Age of Revolution, 1770–1823* (New Haven: Yale University Press, 1974).

8. James O. and Lois E. Horton, *Black Bostonians: Black Life and Community Struggle in the Antebellum North* (New York: Holmes and Meier, 1979).

9. David Walker, *Appeal to the Colored Citizens of the World,* ed. Charles M. Wiltse (New York: Hill and Wang, 1965), p. 16.

10. Ibid., p. 41.

11. For biographical studies of Garrison, see John L. Thomas, *The Liberator: William Lloyd Garrison, A Biography* (Boston: Little Brown, 1963); James Brewer Stewart, *William Lloyd Garrison and the Challenge of Emancipation* (Homewood, Ill.: Harlan Davidson, 1991).

12. Stewart, *Garrison,* pp. 65–67.

13. Ibid., pp. 84–87.

14. Leonard Richards, *"Gentlemen of Property and Standing": Antiabolitionist Mobs in Jacksonian America* (New York: Oxford University Press, 1970).

15. In addition to the biographies listed in earlier notes, see Donald Yacavone, *Samuel Joseph May and the Dilemma of the Liberal Persuasion* (Philadelphia: Temple University Press, 1991); William and Jane Pease, *Bound with Them in Chains: A Biographical History of the Antislavery Movement in America* (Westport, Conn.: Greenwood Press, 1972), pp. 28–60, 191–218, 276–308; Dorothy Sterling, *"Ahead of Her Time": A Biography of Abby Kelly Foster* (New York: W. W. Norton, 1991).

16. Stewart, *Phillips,* pp. 2–54; Mary Beth Norton, *Liberty's Daughters: The Revolutionary Expression of American Women, 1750–1800* (New York: Little Brown, 1980), pp. 256–99.

17. *The Liberator,* July 10, 1857.

18. Boston *Courier,* quoted in Richards, *"Gentlemen of Property and Standing,"* p. 59.

19. Ibid., p. 58.

20. Ibid.

21. The historical literature bearing on these developments is quite extensive. For a good introduction, see Paul Faler, *Mechanics and Manufacturers in the Early Industrial Revolution: Lynn, Massachusetts, 1780–1860* (Albany: State University of New York Press, 1981).

22. Robert V. Sparks, "Abolitionism in Silver Slippers: A Biography of Edmund Quincy" (unpublished Ph.D. dissertation, Boston University, 1978), p. 143; Stewart, *Phillips,* p. 129.

23. Garrison, quoted in Jonathan Glickstein, "Poverty Is Not Slavery: Abolitionists and the Labor Movement," in Lewis Perry and Michael Fellman, eds., *Antislavery Reconsidered: New Perspectives on the Abolitionists* (Baton Rouge: Louisiana State University Press, 1979), pp. 203–204.

24. See especially Carleton Mabee, *Black Freedom: The Non-Violent Abolitionists from 1830 through the Civil War* (New York: Macmillan, 1970).

25. Horton and Horton, *Black Bostonians,* pp. 53–66.

26. Stewart, *Phillips,* pp. 54–65.

27. *The Liberator,* May 16, 1851.

28. Richard J. M. Blackett, *Building an Antislavery Wall: Black Americans in the Transatlantic Abolitionist Movement, 1830–1860* (Baton Rouge: Louisiana State University Press, 1983).

29. See, for example, Thomas Haskell, "Capitalism and the Origins of Humanitarian Sensibility," pts. 1 and 2, *American Historical Review* 90 (May 1985): 339–61 and 91 (August 1985): 952–83.

CHAPTER SIX

James Oliver Horton and Lois E. Horton

The Affirmation of Manhood

Black Garrisonians in Antebellum Boston

Although not denying the special relationship that existed between William Lloyd Garrison and Boston's black community, James and Lois Horton feel that certain of Garrison's ideas did not always sit well with the group historians have labeled "black Garrisonians." The Hortons contend that some of the strongest disagreements arose over issues related to political participation (which Garrison for the most part opposed) and nonviolence (which Garrison doggedly supported).

Critical to any understanding of the stance taken by Boston's blacks, the Hortons argue, is the blacks' interpretation of the notion of manhood. Manhood implied the willingness to take a strong, possibly militant, perhaps even violent stand against one's detractors, whether they be slaveholders or slave hunters. Garrisonian moral suasion did not satisfy this need; physical resistance did, becoming all the more necessary after passage of the 1850 Fugitive Slave Act.

Yet the Hortons are quick to point out that in spite of all of these difficulties that often severely tested the ties that bound Boston's blacks to Garrison, the alliance held, largely because Garrison, "understanding [the] increasing anger and frustration" of blacks, never required continuing and strict adherence to his "nonresistant and nonviolent" principles. In fact, as the Civil War drew near, Garrison even began to give strong support to the movement by blacks to gain membership in the all-white militia companies of Massachusetts. And while this effort did not succeed, he was present when the state's 54th Volunteer Infantry Regiment passed in review before heading south to participate in the Union effort to win the Civil War, accepting the necessity of using even violent means to bring freedom before peace could at last become a reality.

On Monday afternoon, the day after the beginning of the New Year in 1854, a group of black men gathered in the vestry of the Twelfth Baptist Church on Southac Street in Boston. In attendance were many of the best-known and most well-respected reformers of black Boston: clothing dealer Lewis Hayden, boardinghouse owner Joel Lewis, lawyer Robert Morris, and the minister of the Twelfth Baptist Church, Leonard A. Grimes. This convention of the State Council of Colored People of Massachusetts was called to order at 2:00 P.M. by William Cooper Nell. Nell was a community historian and Massachusetts' delegate to the National Convention of Colored People of the United States, an organization of free blacks dedicated to the eradication of slavery and the improvement of the rights and status of African Americans.

The meeting began with a tribute to William Lloyd Garrison as leader of the antislavery cause, recognizing the accomplishments of the abolition movement in "breaking down prejudice against the colored man" and "securing the acknowledgment of his manhood." All African Americans should honor and show appropriate gratitude to their allies in the struggle, they said, but the fate of black America was in the hands of black people, and they must demand and pursue the advantages of truly free men which "none can supply but themselves." Among these advantages were "self-dependence," education in intellectual and manual skills, and the development of those traits that would prepare them for greater "competition in every department of human effort."[1]

Black abolitionists' respect for Garrison coexisted with an insistence on black-directed action and institutions, expressing the complex relationship that had developed between them over the more than twenty years of their association. Since Garrison had begun publishing his *Liberator* in Boston in 1831, he had proven tenacious in his demands for the immediate abolition of slavery and for equal rights for black Americans. His actions and his words had earned him the admiration and trust of African Americans and, in Boston especially, a loyal group of black abolitionists who have come to be known as black Garrisonians.

Yet, even among Boston's blacks, Garrison's ideology received varying degrees of acceptance. Nor did Garrison himself demand agreement. He was strong in his beliefs but open to discussion on many issues. Over time he had revised some of his views in response to arguments made by his black associates, as he had earlier on African colonization, for example. Aileen Kraditor saw Garrison's changing perspective as the logical development of his philosophy, and found him to be far less dogmatic and unyielding than historians had previously asserted. As Blanche G. Hersh observed of his followers, "Garrisonians exhibited the righteousness of true believers by claiming a monopoly on the truth, [but] in practice their philosophy often meant that they were open to new ideas and supported a variety of reforms like women's rights, believing 'all good causes help one another.'"[2] Throughout the antebellum years, there was a continuing debate over antislavery means and a continuous process of mutual accommodation within the black abolitionist community in Boston, between blacks and white abolitionists, and between black Garrisonians and Garrison.

William Lloyd Garrison, in a carte de visite taken by J. W. Black between 1864 and 1873. The Boston Athenæum.

By the 1850s the most fundamental disagreements were clear, but political events in the fifties had only brought already existing points of contention into stark relief. The most serious disagreements among black Garrisonians centered on the questions of political participation and nonviolence.

The relationship between Boston's black community and William Lloyd Garrison actually started before the white reformer and newspaper editor came to live and work permanently in the city. On July 4, 1829, just eighteen months before he commenced publication of his abolitionist newspaper, Garrison came to Boston's Park Street Church to deliver the first of many antislavery lectures. He was then a colonizationist, believing that abolition would come by removing blacks from America and colonizing them on the shores of their "homeland" in West Africa. Garrison's support for colonization was part of a general devotion to moral reform which led to his involvement in many of the progressive causes of his day.

Garrison's early Baptist fundamentalism also led logically to his conviction that alcohol degraded men, prompting his commitment to the cause of temperance. In 1828, at the age of twenty-three, Garrison became editor of the *National Philanthropist*, a small temperance newspaper in Boston. The following year he established a newspaper in Bennington, Vermont, opposing slavery and organizing a petition drive for its abolition in the District of Columbia.

When he went to Baltimore in the fall of 1829 to work with fellow colonizationist Benjamin Lundy on the *Genius of Universal Emancipation*, Lundy's Quaker principles reinforced Garrison's belief that all war was wrong. In Baltimore he saw slavery firsthand and came to know several of the city's blacks. The counsel of many of his "colored friends" persuaded him that colonization was not the answer to slavery. By the time he returned to Boston in 1830, perhaps anticipating his need for black support for the newspaper he was planning to publish, Garrison had abandoned colonization and gradualism and had become committed to the immediate abolition of slavery—he had become a militant abolitionist.

Garrison's support for the immediate emancipation of all slaves and civil rights for all free blacks was popular among Boston's African Americans who had worked toward these ends for decades with only marginal assistance from white reformers. Yet blacks did not always find it easy to rally behind his brand of pacifism. Garrison opposed any government which forced its citizens to participate directly or indirectly in violence of any kind. This led him to question any governmental institution that gave its support to slavery, a stand which many blacks favored. On the other hand, he condemned the use of violence even in the cause of freedom, a view that many blacks found hard to accept.

Although some black abolitionists, such as Frederick Douglass and Charles Lenox Remond, initially agreed with Garrison, other blacks found it difficult to accept Garrison's principled opposition to the American government. Many were especially skeptical of his contention that the American Constitution was a slaveholder's document irredeemably flawed by its protection of slavery. Since the Revolution, many African Americans had been proud of their role in a war that had established a nation founded on the principles of liberty. Their disaffection focused on the failure of the country to live up to its principles. Boston slaves had petitioned for their freedom, citing the principles of the Declaration of Independence and the Revolution. Free blacks had demanded the right to vote under the Revolutionary slogan "No taxation without representation," and black revolutionaries such as Crispus Attucks, Peter Salem, and Salem Poor had become the mainstays of black Boston's proud heritage.

Charles Lenox Remond, abolitionist. Daguerreotype from 1848–1858. Trustees of the Public Library of the City of Boston.

Black children repeatedly listened to their elders recite the exploits of black Revolutionary heroes. One man recalled how the stories told by black Revolutionary veterans when he was a child had convinced him that "I had more right [as an American citizen] than any white man in the town . . . . Why should you [white Americans] be the chosen people more than me?" he asked rhetorically. Most African Americans found it difficult to renounce war when they were convinced that it was precisely their role in the Revolution and the Battle of New Orleans during the War of 1812 that entitled them to full American citizenship. While they agreed that the American government was not living up to its promises, they could not support the total rejection of that government.[3]

Many blacks in the 1830s believed that they could prove their worth and loyalty as Americans by accepting and obeying the government. Massachusetts blacks especially made it clear that they did not intend to obey unjust laws such as the Fugitive Slave Act of 1793, but pledged to obey all just laws because they were "true and faithful citizens of the Commonwealth." With this caveat, the bylaws of the mutual aid organization called the African Society promised to "take no one into the society who shall commit any injustice or outrage against the laws of our country."[4]

In his seventy-six-page *Appeal* published in 1829, Bostonian David Walker, using a common tactic, assailed America's failure to live up to the principles of its founding documents. Walker challenged white Americans to "compare your own language . . . extracted from your own Declaration of Independence, with your cruelties and murders inflicted by your cruel unmerciful fathers and your-selves on our fathers and on us."[5]

Walker claimed that American hypocrisy had subverted the goals of the Revolution and robbed black men of their rights. The most blatant transgression was slavery, and he emphasized physical aggression and even violence as a route to freedom for slaves and manhood for all black men. Walker wrote before the establishment of *The Liberator*, but his message bore directly on the impact of Garrisonianism among Boston blacks. His controversial publication gained national attention and raised southern fears by urging slaves to prove their manhood, to rise up and take their freedom by force if necessary.

Walker's call to arms was issued in partial answer to suggestions of African Americans' innate inferiority. Many whites believed that black men were not men at all, but brutes—uncivilizable savages, prone to violence, restrained only by slavery. Conceding that there was much yet unknown about the nature and capabilities of Africans, Thomas Jefferson nevertheless strongly suggested that "blacks, whether originally a distinct race, or made distinct by time and circumstances, are inferior to whites both in body and mind." Further, he feared the consequences of the abolition of slavery for America because he believed that blacks were a volatile race of people, unrestrained by the reason of civilized men. He had practical political fears as well. Once free, Jefferson argued, "ten thousand recollections by the blacks of the injuries they have sustained" at the hands of white Americans would push them inevitably toward revolution.[6]

Walker retorted that blacks were not brutes and could not be domesticated like animals. He goaded black men to action by rhetorically wondering how so many could be enslaved. "Are we Men!! How we could be so submissive to a gang of men, whom we cannot tell whether they are as good as ourselves or not, I never could conceive," he wrote. Blacks must not wait for either God or slaveholders to end slavery. "The man who would not fight . . . to be delivered from the most wretched, abject and servile slavery, that ever a people was afflicted with since the foundation of the world . . . ought to be kept with all his children or family, in slavery or in chains to be butchered by his cruel enemies."[7]

In his call to action, Walker claimed the physical superiority of black men. "I do declare," he wrote, "that one good black can put to death six white men." The assertion that slaves were stronger and better in combat than their masters was not new. It was part of the racial folklore of the period and was often cited in conjunction with rumors of slave uprisings. Yet, this declaration posed problems for African Americans. The use of violence to assert manhood tended to reinforce white stereotypes of the "brutish African nature" restrained only by slavery.[8]

Walker's advocacy of the use of violence as an acceptable tactic for the acquisition of freedom and equality remained an important position among Boston blacks throughout the antebellum period. At the time that Walker wrote, the imagination of many Americans had been captured by Greek revolutionaries seeking independence from Turkey, by the Poles' rising discontent with their Russian masters, and by the revolutions in Latin America which by 1826 had brought an end to slavery in many of the former Spanish colonies. Thus he drew on more than the distant models of the American Revolution or the successful Haitian rebellion against France which had led to the establishment of the free nation of Haiti in 1804. As he wrote, he was undoubtedly aware that freedom was being sought by means of force, and that revolutionary armies in Latin America had included black soldiers bearing arms supplied by the Haitian government.

Garrison's reaction to Walker's *Appeal* provides an important clue to the accommodation he would eventually work out with his black followers. He was in Baltimore working with Lundy when he first read Walker's angry pamphlet, but he delayed issuing a published response. However, as southern reaction became more strident and the *Appeal* became the center of controversy in the North as well, Garrison felt compelled to take a public stand. Although he rejected Walker's call for slave revolt, he praised Walker personally.

Later in Boston, in the pages of *The Liberator*, Garrison made his disagreement clear, stating, "We do not preach rebellion—no, but submission and peace." Garrison's stand on the use of violence by slaves was complex. He did consider slaves, "more than any people on the face of the earth," justified in the use of force. He even considered a slave revolt equal to the American Revolution in the justice of its cause; nonetheless, for Garrison, not even a cause such as this justified violence. These differences probably did not prevent the two men from sharing a mutual respect, and from seeing each other as important participants in the fight against slavery. Significantly, some years later, Walker's widow named her son Edward Garrison Walker.[9]

To those who argued that blacks generally and slaves in particular must assert themselves even to the point of violence to break the bonds of slavery and prove themselves men, Garrison answered that the route to manhood was through strength of character and principled action. In fact, it was on this issue, the achievement and assertion of manhood, that the greatest incompatibility between Garrison and the black Garrisonians rested. Virtually all abolitionists saw slavery as an attack on the manhood of male slaves. Most agreed that dignity and self-respect demanded resistance, but disagreements over the nature of the resistance required led to divergent opinions on the issue of the use of violence in the fight against slavery.

These issues were complicated by the prevailing gender ideals in nineteenth-century American society which associated manhood with power, physical strength, and self-determination. Surely the fight for freedom was carried on by black women as well as men, and just as surely black women were willing to use violence in their effort to maintain their dignity as women and as black people. Yet, in the discussion of these issues, men, and even most black women, concentrated on slavery as an assault on manhood. The institution was also seen as an attack on the gender roles and expectations of black women, but generally these expectations revolved around women's roles as mothers and good wives. Abolitionists' concern for women under slavery was less for their inability to be independent and assertive individuals than for the horror of the sexual abuse that they suffered and for their inability to care for their children. In their calls for racial progress, black leaders were likely to see freedom, equality, and citizenship as synonymous with "manhood." Slavery was the deprivation of manhood, and racially discriminatory laws and customs withheld "manhood rights."

Black activist Maria Stewart's speeches and writing provided a bridge between Walker's *Appeal* and Garrison's principles. She echoed Walker's sentiments, but without the appeal to violent means. Speaking to a gathering of black Bostonians in 1831, she did not call for slave rebellion, but issued her own call for black men to assert themselves. "O ye fearful ones, throw off your fearfulness. . . . If you are men, convince [whites] that you possess the spirit of men." She called forth the "Sons of Africa" to show their bravery, their intelligence, and their commitment to serving their community. "But give the man of color an equal opportunity . . . from the cradle to manhood, and from manhood to grave, and you would discover a dignified statesman, the man of science, and the philosopher."[10] Successful black men became assets to the black community, contributed to the struggle of black people, and were living refutations of ideas of racial inferiority. Although she did not call for violence, she did call for action. The heroes she convened to inspire black men to the competition included the black soldiers of the Revolution and the War of 1812 and David Walker.

Stewart's devotion to Walker did not prevent her from becoming a true Garrisonian. In the fight against slavery, she urged moral uplift, dedication to family and community, virtue, piety, and the cultivation of knowledge as the most effective weapons. She reminded blacks that "God has raised you up a Walker and a Garrison" for leadership and inspiration in the struggle. Much of Stewart's work was published in *The Liberator* beginning in 1831.[11]

Although Stewart's admiration for both Garrison and Walker may seem contradictory, it became an increasingly common pattern among Boston blacks. Especially after 1840 (but even in the 1830s) the two approaches to antislavery coexisted, though the principled belief in nonviolence seemed to have been the minority position. Domestic servant, author, and activist Robert Roberts, for example, was strongly committed to Garrisonian pacifist principles. He viewed violence as evil, the common root of war and slavery. He endorsed the notion that "the practice of non-resistance to physical aggression, is not only consistent with reason, but the surest method of obtaining a speedy triumph of the principles of universal peace."[12]

Yet black Garrisonians did not shrink from potentially violent action. In 1831 Georgia offered to pay five thousand dollars to anyone who would deliver Garrison to state officials. In the next few years, South Carolina and Virginia offered similar rewards. Realizing the vulnerability of their esteemed ally, several black Garrisonians armed themselves with clubs to provide Garrison with a clandestine bodyguard. Nor were they prevented from acting when violence seemed necessary to secure the freedom of fugitives threatened with recapture. This was dramatically illustrated in the "abolitionist riot" of 1836. When Eliza Small and Polly Ann Bates, fugitive slaves from Baltimore, were captured by slavecatchers, a group of black women descended upon the courtroom where the fugitives were being held, physically subdued court officials, and effected their rescue.

Black abolitionists' views on antislavery principles and tactics were based on their understanding of slavery. The institution demanded obedience, passivity, and deference from slaves. Ideally, the slave was to exhibit no independent spirit, strength of character, or physical prowess except under the master's direction. These demands were placed on both men and women. As a result, the rhetoric of black and white abolitionists generally saw slavery as preventing blacks from fulfilling their appropriate and natural gender roles. Slavery deprived black women of their morality and prevented them from being good wives and mothers, they argued. When Massachusetts slaves had petitioned the colonial governor for freedom in 1774, they had expressed the contradiction between slavery and the social responsibilities ordained by God for men and women. "How can a slave perform the duties of a husband to a wife or a parent to his child? . . . How can [wives] submit themselves to there [*sic*] husbands in all things?" they asked.[13] Slave men could not exercise their power as men to protect their families and to assert their own dignity, abilities inherent in the very definition of manhood. One former slave who escaped from Georgia to Boston observed that the slave master's habit of referring to male slaves as "boys" voiced slavery's denial of manhood.

In his autobiography, black abolitionist Frederick Douglass recalled his confrontation with the slave breaker Covey as the event that had signaled the achievement of his manhood and his first step toward freedom. After regular beatings from Covey, Douglass had run away. Later he returned and faced certain and severe punishment, but this time the young slave resisted. The two-hour struggle which ensued left both exhausted. But Frederick Douglass was not subdued, and Covey never beat him again. "My dear reader this battle with

A fugitive slave, illustration from *The Anti-Slavery Record* (1837). The Boston Athenæum.

THE
ANTI-SLAVERY RECORD.

Vol. III. No. VII.   JULY, 1837.   Whole No. 31.

This picture of a poor fugitive is from one of the stereotype cuts manufactured in this city for the southern market, and used on handbills offering rewards for runaway slaves.

THE RUNAWAY.

To escape from a powerful enemy, often requires as much courage and generalship as to conquer. One of the most celebrated military exploits on record, is the *retreat* of the ten thousand Greeks under

Mr. Covey," Douglass reported, " . . . was the turning point in my life as a slave. . . . I was nothing before; I was a man now." The contradiction between slavery and manhood was powerfully expressed in the ubiquitous antislavery emblem picturing a kneeling, manacled slave asking, "Am I not a man and brother?"[14]

As Douglass discovered, physical resistance could be a clear declaration of manhood. Slave men found many ways to assert themselves; even the threat of self-assertion could be effective. One man reported that he avoided being sold at auction by meeting the gaze of prospective buyers directly as they inspected him, an obvious sign of a willful slave. Another stopped his master from beating slave children by standing beside them and glaring at the master when he began to punish them. Among the slaves, men who refused to submit to the master's authority were accorded respect, and those who submitted too easily lost respect. "Them as won't fight," reported Lewis Clarke, "is called Poke-easy."[15]

When David Walker called for slave resistance, he was appealing to black men not merely to resist slavery but also to proclaim themselves men. In his *Appeal* Walker called upon the memory of the successful Haitian revolution as proof of the power of unity and manliness. "One thing which gives me joy," he wrote of the Haitians, "is, that they are men who would be cut off to a man before they would yield to the combined forces of the whole world." Black men demonstrated in Haiti, Walker contended, that "a groveling, servile and abject submission to the lash of tyrants" is not the African man's natural state. Walker believed that slaves could transform themselves into men through aggressive action. "If ever we become men," he said, "we must assert ourselves to the full."[16]

Here was a major dilemma for African Americans. The nonresistance message of "submission and peace" sounded uncomfortably close to the injunctions of slavery. Garrison did not counsel acquiescence to slavery, nor did he call for slaves to submit passively to the institution. His was a call for nonviolence, not inaction. Yet from the standpoint of African Americans, there was no clear distinction. How could a black man stand up like a man if he could not defend himself and his family from physical attacks by overseers and slave masters, anti-abolitionist mobs, or slavecatchers and kidnappers?

Some Garrisonians answered that the most effective way to establish black manhood was to prove white prejudices wrong. Maria Stewart had argued, and many blacks believed, that racial prejudice would be overcome as black men proved their worth. As she urged black men to strive for autonomy and achievement in the marketplace, the object of their success was to prove black men the equal of other men. Some black Garrisonians even argued that slavery and discrimination were not based on race at all, but were the result of the degraded condition of black people. They believed that improving the economic and social position of free blacks would destroy the basis for slavery. Many temperance men such as Robert Roberts, Joel Lewis, and William Whipper asserted that to resort to violence only reinforced white stereotypes, playing into the hands of those eager to see blacks as savage brutes.

There was legitimate cause for concern. The proslavery forces of the South, building on Jefferson's earlier speculations, mounted a powerful justification of slavery based on the contention that Africans were savages. In 1831 Thomas R. Dew argued that the civilizing influence of slavery restrained the Africans' brutish nature. According to William Drayton in 1836, only slavery checked the "wild frenzy of revenge, and the savage lust for blood" natural to the African and dramatically apparent in the Haitian revolution. Georgian Thomas R. R. Cobb alleged that once removed from the domesticating influence of slavery, Haitian blacks "relapsed into barbarism."[17]

Many northerners as well as southerners accepted these beliefs. Calvin Colton, a Massachusetts native and graduate of Andover Theological Seminary, believed that slavery was the natural state for African Americans, and that under slavery they were "as a body, the happiest in the world." Mercurial Boston minister Orestes Brownson agreed that slavery elevated blacks, and Harvard naturalist Louis Agassiz lent his prestige to the theory that the African brain was much smaller than the European, limiting the capacity of blacks to learn and to absorb the complexities of civilization. These and other theorists doubted that blacks would ever be ready to shoulder the responsibilities of free men.[18]

Faced with the development and increasing respectability of such theories, many black reformers began to despair of ever abolishing slavery and proving their manhood through the slow process of moral suasion and elevation. Men must assert themselves through direct action, they concluded. Peter Paul Simons spoke for a growing minority in 1839 when he challenged the efficacy of moral reform. Instead of lessening the hold of slavery and prejudice on blacks, he believed, it had encouraged timidity and self-doubt. African Americans do not suffer from lack of moral elevation, he argued. "There is no nation of people under the canopy of heaven, who are given more to good morals and piety than we are." He contended that blacks suffered from a lack of direct "physical and political" action. They lacked confidence in one another, he said, and were thus likely to depend on the leadership of whites, a not-so-subtle reference to the willingness of many blacks to follow Garrison's lead. Simons also charged that black children all too often learned passive acceptance, not manly action and leadership, through parental example. Action must be the watchword: "this we must physically practice, and we will be in truth an independent people."[19]

Other questions about the most effective approach to antislavery soon resulted in several serious splits in the abolitionist movement. In the fall of 1837, members of the clergy attacked Garrison for his opposition to the church. Garrison had indeed been extremely critical of the clergy for failing to stand unequivocally against slavery, but this did not prevent him from maintaining a close relationship with the black church. This dispute became part of a more general break between Garrisonians and other abolitionists two years later. The broader points of contention included the role of women in abolitionist organizations, the degree and type of political participation desirable, and the relationship of other reforms to antislavery. A split was avoided on yet another issue when Garrison agreed that it was probably necessary for African Americans to control their own affairs.

The establishment of the antislavery Liberty party in 1839 provided an organized outlet for those who favored following the political route to change. Garrison, always suspicious of organized politics, rejected the call for an antislavery third party, seeing it as a compromise with a thoroughly corrupt American political system. At the annual meeting of the Massachusetts Anti-Slavery Society in 1840, disagreements focused on the role of women in the organization, with

Theodore Parker, transcendental theologian and abolition activist. From a daguerreotype taken about 1843. His outspoken support for Anthony Burns helped to incite the attack upon the Boston Court House that ultimately failed to rescue the fugitive slave. The Boston Athenæum.

Garrisonians championing the right of women to equal participation. The attempt by the political abolitionists to prevent women from casting ballots at organizational sessions was voted down. They claimed they were not opposed to women's rights, but that they feared that linking women's rights to antislavery would weaken their efforts to propagate the abolitionist message. After losing the vote on this issue by a substantial margin, the political abolitionists walked out and established a rival state organization, the Massachusetts Abolition Society.

Although a few black leaders did join the new organizations which opposed Garrison and vocally denied public roles for women, most blacks supported the

Garrisonian stand on women's participation. When female delegates were refused seats at the London World Anti-Slavery Convention in 1840, Charles Lenox Remond voiced his objection and stood with Garrison and the women as they walked out in protest.

The Massachusetts Abolition Society, formed in Boston to challenge the power of Garrisonian abolition, condemned Garrison and nonresistance in its paper, the *Massachusetts Abolitionist*. One letter, signed by "A Colored Man" who claimed to speak for the majority of Boston's black citizens, charged that Garrison's leadership was outdated and endorsed the program and strategy of the new organization. Boston's black Garrisonians reacted swiftly and sharply. A large crowd gathered at the African Meeting House on Beacon Hill to show their support for Garrison. They declared that any charge that large numbers of blacks in the city were disciples of the counter organization was false. John T. Hilton, Joel W. Lewis, James G. Barbadoes, Joshua B. Smith, Christopher Weeden, John P. Coburn, George Washington, William Cooper Nell, and others discussed and unanimously adopted a resolution repudiating these contentions made by "A Colored Man."

They resolved "to register our united and unqualified denial of the truth of these unwarranted assertions." They went on to make clear that the new abolitionist organization did not have the support of Boston's black community, that not only did Garrison have their admiration, but to slander him "was certainly the most unkind and ungrateful expression that could ever escape the lips of a colored man," and that "we will, while life remains, prove steadfast and true to the old Massachusetts Anti-Slavery Society." They also determined to attempt to discover the identity of the writer who called himself "A Colored Man." Finally the meeting ended by listing the many gains and successes brought about by Garrison, the New England Anti-Slavery Society, and the American Anti-Slavery Society.[20]

Although the meeting was firmly in Garrison's camp and was squarely behind the wing of abolition that he dominated, the support given was clearly personal. Garrison and his devotion to the cause were praised; the progress made over the decade was lauded, but Garrisonian philosophy was not mentioned. They did not state their faith in his antigovernment views; nor was there any pledge of continued loyalty to its tenets. Thus, the overwhelming commitment to Garrison the man without any mention of his methods is instructive. Perhaps Boston blacks were saying exactly what they meant—they were deeply devoted to Garrison but ambivalent about his philosophies. During the next few years their ambivalence grew, but their devotion never wavered. Despite disagreements, Garrison and most black Garrisonians were able to accommodate their differences and maintain their alliance.

Their defense of Garrison set blacks in Boston and Philadelphia against black abolitionists in New York, where political abolition attracted a sizable following. Yet even among those open to political activism, there was concern that the increasingly bitter disputes within the antislavery movement would weaken the

"Remember your weekly pledge to the Massachusetts Anti-Slavery Society." Poster or broadside from about 1850. Trustees of the Public Library of the City of Boston.

cause. Writing from Pittsburgh, Lewis Woodson acknowledged that "abolitionists must resort ultimately to political action . . . because slavery has been sanctioned and regulated by law." He then went on to add, "Moral action must first be had on this question, then political action." Then, addressing his remarks to "our brethren in the East," Woodson warned against destructive divisions within the ranks of black abolitionists, asking, "Do our numbers and strength give such an assurance of victory, that we may turn from combating the common enemy to fight among ourselves?"[21] Charles B. Ray, publisher of the New York *Colored American*, was concerned that such disputes might destroy some of the gains already made by the abolition movement, which had awakened, he thought, "our guilty nation to its sins and danger" and brought a "dispirited people to the dignity of manhood and to the energy and enterprize [*sic*] of freemen."[22]

Black abolitionists were generally reluctant to choose sides in the debate over political participation, but there was great enthusiasm for the Liberty party, which ran its first presidential candidate in 1840. Ironically, this hopeful political development came at a time when blacks in several northern states faced the curtailment or loss of their voting rights. The vote was an instrument of male political power, and thus blacks viewed disenfranchisement as an attack on their rights both as blacks and as men. Garrison himself conceded that where rights were in jeopardy, black voters should cast their ballots in self-defense.

The debate about whether to participate in politics was short-lived among blacks, and even Boston blacks were openly taking part in electoral politics by the mid-1840s. There were Liberty party announcements inserted in the pages of *The Liberator*, and by 1848 the paper reported on meetings at which African Americans in Boston discussed the formation of an auxiliary to the Liberty party. Even William Cooper Nell, one of the most loyal of the black Garrisonians, in 1850 allowed his name to be put into nomination as Free Soil party candidate for the Massachusetts legislature.

Strident voices in the 1840s also challenged Garrison's stand on nonviolence. A speech in 1841 by New York black abolitionist David Ruggles was indicative of the changes taking place in the debate over antislavery strategy. That summer Ruggles addressed a meeting of the American Reform Board of Disfranchised Commissioners, a New York protest group of which he was a founding member. In blunt language he rallied the group to action and explained that "in our cause" words alone would not suffice. "Rise brethren rise!" he urged the distant slaves. "Strike for freedom or die slaves!"[23]

An equally direct message was delivered two years later by Henry Highland Garnet. A young minister from New York State, Garnet was one of the most active black leaders urging political participation in support of the antislavery cause. Although he received training in Garrisonian reform at the Oneida Institute, Garnet was an early supporter of the idea of a third party which would bring opposition to slavery directly into the political arena. Moreover, he was militant in his outlook and willing to depart from other Garrisonian antislavery

Patriotic covers indicating the political sentiments of their senders were used by both the North and the South in the years preceding the Civil War. The Boston Athenæum.

positions. His address in 1843 to the Buffalo meeting of the National Negro Convention took up Ruggles's theme and was reminiscent of David Walker's earlier exhortations, once again linking slave rebellion to manhood.

Addressing himself to the slaves, Garnet used provocative and incendiary language. "It is sinful in the extreme," he admonished, "for you to make voluntary submission." As Walker had accepted the necessity for a man to use violence in the assertion of his manhood, so Garnet concluded that "there is not much hope of Redemption without the shedding of blood." Black men must not shrink from bloody confrontation—there was no escape. A mass exodus was not an option for African Americans, he argued. The solution must be found in America, and it might well be violent. "If you must bleed, let it come at once, rather, die freemen than live to be slaves." Garnet did not urge a revolution: "Your numbers are too small," he observed. But all slaves should immediately "cease to labor for tyrants who will not remunerate you." He assumed, however, that violence would be the inevitable result of this tactic. And when it comes, he instructed, "Remember that you are THREE MILLIONS."[24]

Condemning passivity, Garnet cut to the heart of masculine pride. "You act as though your daughters were born to pamper the lusts of your masters and overseers," he charged.

> And worst of all, you timidly submit while your lords tear your wives from your embraces and defile them before your eyes. In the name of God, we ask, are you men? Where is the blood of your fathers? Has it all run out of your veins?[25]

Here Garnet drew upon one of the most powerful justifications for the link between physical prowess and masculinity in American gender ideals—the responsibility of men to protect their families. This responsibility was an important part of all male ideals in the society. Even the most fervent black supporters of nonresistance had great difficulty arguing that nonviolence was the only recourse when one's family was in physical danger.

Garnet's speech split the convention; debate was heated. Ardent Garrisonians Frederick Douglass, William Wells Brown, and Charles Lenox Remond spoke against the convention endorsing his sentiments. They pointed to the bloody retribution slaves and free blacks, especially those in the border states, would suffer should the convention support such a radical call to violence. Although there was substantial backing for Garnet's message, by a very narrow margin the convention refused to endorse his demands. For the time being, the black Garrisonians had blocked the call to slave rebellion.

Although they may not have been ready to endorse open slave rebellion, Boston blacks had already supported potentially violent actions in defense of fugitives. One year before Garnet's speech, they had joined other blacks from New England to form the Freedom Association to aid, protect, and ensure the safety and well-being of fugitives. William Cooper Nell and Henry Weeden, two of Garrison's strongest supporters in Boston, were among the founding members of this organization, which included women as well as men. Shortly thereafter, George Latimer, a fugitive from Norfolk, Virginia, was captured in Boston. The city's blacks were already angered by the decision of the U.S. Supreme Court in the case of *Prigg v. Pennsylvania* strengthening the existing fugitive slave law. At a mass meeting, they called on the memory of their Revolutionary ancestors and pledged to use violence if necessary to prevent the "perversion of right and justice."[26]

All legal efforts to save Latimer failed, but blacks were determined to prevent his being returned to slavery. In the incident Douglass, who in 1843 at Buffalo voted against endorsing Garnet's call for slave rebellion, seemed to support the use of force to free a fugitive. "Make up your minds to what your duty is to

THE

ANTI-SLAVERY RECORD.

VOL. II. No. I.   JANUARY, 1836.   WHOLE No. 13

A FACT WITH A SHORT COMMENTARY.

NOT many years ago, a slave was murdered near Woodville, Mississippi, under the following circumstances. The master's child went into the slave's hut and took a stool which belonged to the slave's child. The slave took away the stool and sent the white child home. The child ran crying to his father, and complained bitterly of the ill-treatment he had received in the hut. The father, in a passion, proceeded to the hut, threw the stool out of doors, and severely reprimanded the slave, threatening to flog him. The slave, who had never been flogged, declared he would not be, and fled. After being gone beyond reach, for a day or two, he returned to his master's door, and offered to work faithfully, as he ever had done, if he might not be flogged. His master refused this condition, and repeated his threat. "I have heard," said the slave, "that you have threatened to shoot me. If you do it, you must do it soon." On this, he turned upon his heel and ran. The master took down his double-barrelled fowling-piece, and pursued. He presently discharged a load of shot from one barrel, which wounded the negro in the thigh, and brought him to the ground. He then walked deliberately up, and lodged the contents of the other barrel in his head, producing instant death. Of this crime there

An illustrated tale from *The Anti-Slavery Record* (1836). The Boston Athenæum.

Latimer," he urged, then do what must be done, and "I have no fears of George Latimer going back." Historians Jane and William Pease suggest that only the willingness of Latimer's master to sell the slave forestalled violence.[27]

Douglass's expressed opposition to slave rebellion at Buffalo thereafter may not have been a general stand against the use of all physical force in defense of freedom. Regardless of their position on nonviolence, most blacks understood the dangers the relatively powerless slaves faced and the probable consequences of slave rebellion. This knowledge obviously prevented them from urging slaves to foment a revolution which would mean sure death for many. Admonitions to "die men" were important rallying cries, but many black abolitionists had been slaves and were intimately familiar with the dangers involved. Douglass printed a story in his newspaper, the *North Star*, in the late 1840s which illustrated the horrors of slavery, making painfully clear the point that resistance could be deadly:

Wm. A. Andrews, an overseer of J. W. Perkins, Mississippi attempted to chastise one of the negro boys who seized a stick and prepared to do battle. The overseer told the boy to lay the stick down or he would shoot him; he refused, and the overseer then fired his pistol, and shot the boy in the face, killing him instantly.

The jury of inquest found the verdict, "that the said Wm. A. Andrews committed the killing in self-defense."[28]

During the 1840s, black Bostonians continued to aid fugitives and even used violence in their defense, but they generally remained reluctant to advocate slave rebellion. Events in the 1850s, however, escalated the conflicts and seemed increasingly to demand the use of force. Even those who still called themselves Garrisonians regularly breached the principle of nonresistance. Remaining black reservations about the appropriateness of violence in the struggle against slavery were all but destroyed by the passage of the new federal Fugitive Slave Act of 1850, which made it easier for fugitives to be captured and for free blacks to be kidnapped into slavery. Seen as a direct blow to all African Americans, this measure generated a strongly militant reaction even among those who had favored nonviolence.

Charles Lenox Remond, who had opposed Garnet's call to arms in the early 1840s, demanded defiance of the Fugitive Slave Act, protection of all fugitives, and the withholding of federal troops should the southern slaves rise against their masters. At a community meeting in Boston in 1850, William Cooper Nell cautioned African Americans to be watchful for kidnappers. If confronted, he urged them to defend themselves, acting as they would to "rid themselves of any wild beast."[29] Douglass again gave indirect sanction to violence when he published a novella in 1853 in which slaves rose up and killed the captain of a slave ship and a slave owner.

New vigilance committees were formed to protect fugitives, and committees already established redoubled their efforts, publicly vowing that no fugitive would be returned to slavery. Not simply action but violent action in the fugitives' defense was identified as a manly pursuit—every "slavehunter who meets a bloody death in his infernal business," it was said, "is an argument in favor of the manhood of our race." Since some slave hunters did not discriminate between fugitive slaves and free blacks, all African Americans were in greater danger of being kidnapped. The sons of black Methodist minister Samuel Snowden were arrested on the Boston Common for carrying guns. When stopped and questioned by police, they proclaimed their intention to defend their freedom against kidnappers. They were arrested. Boston clothing dealer Lewis Hayden, himself an escaped slave, regularly sheltered fugitives. At one point he and several armed men barricaded his home and when confronted by slavecatchers threatened to ignite two kegs of gunpowder rather than allow the fugitives to be taken back to slavery.[30]

In 1854, in one of the most celebrated rescue attempts in Boston, black activists were joined by white allies in storming the federal courthouse where fugitive slave Anthony Burns was being held. Before the melee ended, the mob had

Daniel Webster, in a daguerreotype taken about 1850, the year he supported the compromise Fugitive Slave Bill. The Boston Athenæum.

battered down the courthouse door and killed a deputy marshal. Only the presence of local militia, and later federal troops, prevented Burns's escape. Attempts to rescue Burns by large numbers of abolitionists from Boston and the surrounding area indicate that in spite of the threat of intervention by the federal government and the possible use of troops, violence was becoming a more acceptable tactic in the fight to maintain the freedom of fugitive slaves. Frederick Douglass was forthright in his defense of violence in the Burns affair. In an editorial entitled "Is It Right and Wise to Kill a Kidnapper?" published in *Frederick Douglass' Paper*, he declared that violence, even deadly violence, was justifiable when used to protect oneself, one's family, or one's community.[31]

Landing a fugitive slave in South Boston about 1853, illustration from Austin Bearse's *Reminiscences of Fugitive Slave Days in Boston* (1880). The Boston Athenæum.

In a Fourth of July speech in Framingham, Massachusetts, shortly after Burns's return to slavery, William Lloyd Garrison excoriated the government in his typically dramatic fashion for its part in the kidnapping of Anthony Burns. To the cheering response of his abolitionist audience, Garrison burned copies of the Fugitive Slave Act, official papers associated with Burns's rendition, and the Constitution of the United States. Although black Bostonians were still not willing to concede that the document itself was sinful, they surely agreed with Garrison that it was being used to evil effect.

The rising anger over this attack by the "slave power," demonstrating again its influence over the federal government, led many blacks to express support for military preparedness. The Negro Convention in Rochester in 1853 called for the removal of all restrictions on black enlistment in state militia. Sixty-five Massachusetts blacks led by Remond and black Boston lawyer Robert Morris petitioned their state legislature, demanding that a black military company be chartered. The right to bear arms for their state, they contended, was one of their "rights as men." Their petition was rejected, but with the assistance of Nell and other black Garrisonians, a black military company called the Massasoit Guard was formed in Boston in 1854. The unit took its name from a pow-

The Rendition of Anthony Burns, from Bryant and Gay's *Popular History of the United States* (1881). An illustration depicting federal troops gathered to escort captured slave Anthony Burns to a ship that was to return him to servitude in Virginia, June 1854. The plight of Burns provoked such outrage in Boston that after him no other fugitive slave was ever again returned to the South. The Boston Athenæum.

Portrait of fugitive slave Anthony Burns surrounded by scenes from his life (1855). The Library of Congress.

erful seventeenth-century Indian chief. Most would have preferred the name Attucks in honor of the black Revolutionary War hero Crispus Attucks, but that name had already been taken by two other black military companies, the Attucks Guards of New York and the Attucks Blues of Cincinnati. Before the decade ended, there were several black military units in northern cities. Thus during the 1850s, Boston's black men moved to arm themselves, poised to strike against slavery.

The Supreme Court opinion in the *Dred Scott* decision in 1857 declaring that African Americans were not citizens of the United States further inflamed antigovernment sentiment, since it placed African Americans in an even more perilous position. Black Bostonians felt under attack from the federal government as never before. Remond spoke for many in his community when he questioned the allegiance blacks owed to a government which "treats us like dogs. The time has gone by," he argued, "for colored people to talk of patriotism."[32]

Increasing militancy and the continuing formation of black military companies led white abolitionist John Brown to believe that substantial numbers of northern free blacks might join a military attack on slavery. Brown and his sons had been Lewis Hayden's guests on their frequent trips to Boston in the 1850s, speaking to the community and raising money. But when Brown led a band of sixteen whites and five blacks in an unsuccessful attack on the federal arsenal at Harpers Ferry, Virginia in 1859, none of Boston's blacks showed a willingness to join him. Despite their anger and frustration and depth of antislavery feeling, most African Americans were not ready to join a private venture which seemed doomed to failure. The capture and execution of Brown and nearly all of his followers confirmed their fears.

In the midst of this growing militancy, Garrison and the black Garrisonians continued to maintain their alliance, accommodating themselves to the changing situation and to each other's shifting views. Although Garrison remained both nonresistant and nonviolent, he did not require adherence to these principles from his black allies, and he understood their increasing anger and frustration. Without endorsing either violence or slave rebellion, Garrison called upon Americans who celebrated the exploits of Revolutionary War heroes to recognize the equal justice of the cause of antislavery. He accused the man "who in one breath exalts the deeds of Washington . . . and in the next denounces Nat Turner as a monster for refusing longer to wear the yoke and be driven under the lash" of being a "hypocrite and dastard."[33]

Within two years, John Brown's private war assumed national proportions. Although Lincoln firmly proclaimed preservation of the Union as his sole Civil War aim, northern blacks were convinced that abolition would be its outcome. Their immediate offer of service was refused, even though more than 8,500 men had joined black militia units by the fall of 1861. Two years later, however, with casualties mounting and the nation bogged down in a protracted war, the government reversed itself and began active recruitment of African American troops. Lincoln's issuance of the Emancipation Proclamation in January of

John Brown. From a daguerreotype taken about 1856. The Boston Athenæum.

1863 encouraged the effort. Still, with discrimination in both pay and equipment and the refusal to commission black officers, there were disagreements about whether African Americans should serve. After initial consideration and protest, black Garrisonians took a central role in recruiting soldiers to fill the ranks of a Massachusetts black regiment. By February, Remond, Nell, and William Wells Brown had joined Garnet and more than one hundred other blacks to form the Black Committee, recruiting African Americans to serve the cause of freedom. Black men came to Boston from all over the North, and in less than one month the ranks of the Massachusetts 54th Colored Regiment were filled and a second regiment was begun.

Even Garrison, who never abandoned his own pacifist principles, felt the strength of black opinion. He understood the passionate belief in freedom which impelled blacks to fight for the end of slavery. Black Garrisonians with whom he had worked for over a generation were actively involved in raising support for the military effort. When the first black Union army regiment established in the North, the 54th Massachusetts, was organized and marched eagerly from Boston, Garrison was there to review the troops. If men must fight, he thought, they should at least fight for a good cause, and what better cause than freedom. Writing in *The Liberator*, he expressed his acquiescence:

> What would peace gain if men who will fight for other things would not fight for liberty? . . . When we get . . . liberty, we shall have peace. . . . I am glad to see the men of the north who will not accept my peace-views acting earnestly . . . in support of my liberty-views.[34]

When Americans fought for their independence from Britain in the Revolution, they rallied support with calls for freedom from tyranny and a refusal to be enslaved. As blacks enlisted in the Civil War, they recalled their own Revolutionary War heroes and their willingness to give their lives for liberty. One newspaper said what they already knew: "The eyes of the whole world are upon you, civilized man everywhere waits to see if you will prove yourselves. . . . Will you vindicate your manhood?"[35] Fighting the war was a test and assertion of a soldier's manhood; for African Americans in Boston, in Massachusetts, and all across the North, fighting for the abolition of slavery was a clear assertion of the manhood of the race.

NOTES

1. *Proceedings of the Black State Conventions, 1840–1865,* ed. Philip S. Foner and George E. Walker (Philadelphia: Temple University Press, 1980), vol. 2, p. 88.

2. Blanche Glassman Hersh, " 'Am I Not a Woman and a Sister?': Abolitionist Beginnings of Nineteenth-Century Feminism," in Lewis Perry and Michael Fellman, eds., *Antislavery Reconsidered* (Baton Rouge: Louisiana State University Press, 1979), pp. 252–83.

3. Leonard I. Sweet, *Black Images of America, 1784–1870* (New York: W. W. Norton and Co., 1976), p. 45.

4. James Oliver Horton and Lois E. Horton, *Black Bostonians: Family Life and Community Struggle in the Antebellum North* (New York: Holmes and Meier Publishers, 1979), p. 29.

5. Quoted in Benjamin Quarles, *Black Mosaic* (Amherst: The University of Massachusetts Press, 1988), p. 95.

6. Thomas Jefferson, "Notes on Virginia," in *The Life and Selected Writings of Thomas Jefferson,* ed. Adrienne Koch and William Peden (New York: Modern Library, 1944), pp. 256–62.

7. *David Walker's Appeal,* edited with an introduction by Charles M. Wiltse (3rd ed., June, 1830; New York: Hill and Wang, 1965), pp. 12–16. The official name of Walker's pamphlet was *David Walker's Appeal in Four Articles: Together with a Preamble to the Coloured Citizens of the World, but in Particular, and Very Expressly to Those of the United States of America.*

8. Merton L. Dillon, *Slavery Attacked* (Baton Rouge: Louisiana State University Press, 1990), pp. 146–47.

9. *Liberator*, January 8 and September 3, 1831.

10. *Maria W. Stewart, America's First Black Woman Political Writer: Essays and Speeches*, ed. Marilyn Richardson (Bloomington: Indiana University Press, 1987), p. 57.

11. Maria W. Stewart, *Religion and the Pure Principles of Morality: The Sure Foundation on Which We Must Build* (Boston: Garrison and Knapp, 1831), quoted in Richardson, *Maria W. Stewart*, p. 40.

12. "Speech by William Whipper," August 16, 1837, *Colored American*, September 9, 16, 23, and 30, 1837, in C. Ripley et al., eds., *Black Abolitionist Papers* (Chapel Hill: The University of North Carolina Press, 1991), vol. 3, pp. 238–51.

13. "To His Excellency Thomas Gage Esq . . . ," *Collections,* Massachusetts Historical Society, 5th Series 3 (Boston, 1877), pp. 432–37, quoted in *Documentary History of Negro People in the United States* (New York: Citadel Press, 1951), vol. 1, p. 9.

14. Frederick Douglass, *Life and Times of Frederick Douglass* (London: Collier-Macmillan Ltd., 1962), p. 143.

15. *Slave Testimony*, ed. John W. Blassingame (Baton Rouge: Louisiana State University Press, 1977), p. 157.

16. *David Walker's Appeal*, pp. 21, 62.

17. William Drayton, *The South Vindicated from the Treason and Fanaticism of the Northern Abolitionists* (Philadelphia, 1836), p. 246; Thomas R. R. Cobb, *An Inquiry into the Law of Negro Slavery in the United States of America* (Philadelphia, 1858), quoted in George M. Fredrickson, *The Black Image in the White Mind* (New York: Harper and Row, 1971), p. 54.

18. Philip S. Foner, *History of Black Americans* (Westport, Conn.: Greenwood Press, 1983), vol. 2, pp. 374–75.

19. Peter Paul Simons, "Speech Delivered before the African Clarkson Association" (New York, April 23, 1839), reprinted in *Black Abolitionist Papers*, vol. 3, pp. 288–93.

20. "Resolutions by a Committee of Boston Blacks Presented at the First Independent Baptist Church" (March 19, 1840), ibid., pp. 298–310, 300, 301.

21. *Colored American*, March 14, 1840, ibid., pp. 323–25.

22. *Colored American*, July 13, 1839, ibid., pp. 311–13.

23. *Liberator*, August 13, 1841.

24. "Speech by Henry Highland Garnet delivered before the National Convention of Colored Citizens, Buffalo, New York, August 16, 1843," reprinted in *Black Abolitionist Papers*, vol. 3, pp. 403–12, quotes pp. 408–10.

25. Ibid., pp. 407 and 410.

26. *Liberator*, December 23, 1842.

27. *Liberator*, November 18, 1842.

28. *North Star*, May 12, 1848.

29. William Cooper Nell, *The Colored Patriots of the American Revolution* (Boston: R. F. Wallcut, 1855; reprint, New York: Arno Press, 1968), p. 393.

30. *Liberator*, July 7, 1854.

31. *Frederick Douglass' Paper*, June 2, 1854.

32. *Liberator*, April 10, 1857.

33. *Liberator*, December 9, 1859.

34. Quoted in Donald Jacobs, "William Lloyd Garrison's *Liberator* and Boston's Blacks, 1830–1865," *New England Quarterly* (June 1971): 274.

35. *Weekly Anglo-African*, January 31, 1863.

CHAPTER SEVEN

Adelaide M. Cromwell

The Black Presence in the West End of Boston, 1800–1864

A Demographic Map

As we continue to examine Boston's black community, we find that its uniqueness is at least in part influenced by demographic considerations related to population and location. In the discussion and map that follow, Adelaide Cromwell keys in on the statistically most significant group within Boston's antebellum black population, the more than 60 percent who resided in the West End section of the city.

Cromwell notes the difficulty of identifying the exact locations where the city's blacks lived, including those who resided in the West End. Nonetheless, she is able to offer some valuable insights into those elements of Boston's black community that lived on the north slope of Beacon Hill, barely a stone's throw from the State House, close by City Hall, and near to the headquarters of their closest supporters and allies, whose numbers many of them joined, the Garrisonian abolitionists.

Cromwell also takes note of the occupational diversity of Boston's West End black community, leavening some of the earlier emphasis on black Bostonians as little more than laborers. What begins to emerge, in both the descriptive essay and the accompanying map, is a sense of the significant distinctiveness of Boston's blacks as evidenced by their many and various accomplishments during the years preceding the Civil War.

The first blacks were brought to Boston in 1638 on a trading vessel, the *Desire*, directly from New Providence, a Puritan colony belonging to England located in the Bahamas. They came as slaves and settled at Noddles Island, an area that is now East Boston. While most of the blacks that came during the ensuing years retained their slave status, by the latter part of the seventeenth century there were free blacks living on their own in the North End of the town.

But eventually, by the beginning of the nineteenth century, some twenty years after slavery had ended in Massachusetts (the first federal census, in 1790, lists no blacks in Massachusetts as slaves), most of the blacks who lived in that area began to leave because of the North End's growing reputation for crime and vice. Many chose to move to the West End on the north side of Beacon Hill. This population shift helped accelerate the establishment of black institutions in this area, most notably the First African Baptist Church, which was organized in 1805. This institution, led by the Reverend Thomas Paul, together with the other black churches that were soon to follow, became the focal points for the community's development.

The borders of this growing black community were Charles Street on the west, Myrtle and Revere streets to the south, Bowdoin Street on the east, and Cambridge Street to the north. Some members of the West End community also lived across Cambridge Street on Blossom and Bridge streets, on the present site of the Massachusetts General Hospital, or farther northeast on Fruit, Vine, Poplar, Second, Spring, and Kennard streets.

Prior to 1830, based on information provided by the earliest city directories, black Bostonians lived on eighty-four streets throughout the city, often without a specific residence identified. The exceptions were residences on Ann, Belknap, Broad, Court, Elm, Fish, Prince, Warren, Washington, and Water streets. At that time the largest number of specific black residences about which we are aware were located on Fish Street, where there were eight. Although usually in unnumbered residences, large clusters of black persons eventually came to live on Belknap (later Joy) Street (171), followed by May Street (43), Robinson Lane (31), Gibbon Court (24), Fish Street (21), and Botolph Street (16).

By 1830 the largest number of recorded addresses also appear on Belknap Street (16 of 32). At this time some important names also begin to appear: Methodist minister Samuel Snowden at number 5, abolitionist and Masonic leader John T. Hilton at number 12, the Reverend Stephen Dalton at number 20, and George Washington, a deacon of the African Baptist Church, at number 29. And although abolitionist leader David Walker is enumerated, it is his place of business at 42 Brattle Street that is listed rather than his residence on Bridge Street. Thomas Paul during this period lived at 26 George Street.

In 1830 there were a total of 1,875 blacks living in Boston, constituting 3.1 percent of the city's total population. Most of them were located in what were then wards six and seven in the West End. However, all through the 1830s, significant numbers of blacks continued to reside in the North End in ward two. During the height of abolition activity, the black population of the city remained clustered in and around ward six, where by 1860, 1,395, or more than 60 percent, were living out of a total black population in Boston of 2,261.[1]

The Boston City Directory of 1849, the last one to list "People of Color" separately from other residents, continues to reveal a substantial number of blacks living in other parts of the city, mainly the North End. However, it also documents even more fully the presence of blacks in the West End, noting specific residences. Belknap and Southac (later Phillips) are the most heavily populated streets, and are where the largest number of different residences are identified—forty-three out of forty-seven residences on Belknap, and nineteen residences for forty-seven persons on Southac Place. A significant number of blacks also lived on West Cedar, West Centre, Grove, and May streets, as well as on Wilberforce Place, Holden Place, and Botolph Street.

Although the black community in the West End had begun to solidify by 1830, its economic base was so fragile that William Lloyd Garrison, in one of the early issues of *The Liberator*, described it as follows:

> In Boston where there are near 2000 people of color it does not appear that there is among them one merchant, broker, physician, lawyer, blacksmith, shipwright, tin-man, caulker and graver, rigger, sail maker, coppersmith, silversmith, brass founder, mason, cooper . . . glazier, printer, bookbinder, cabinet maker, truckman, baker or stone cutter or [anyone involved in] any trade in any article except clothes![2]

In spite of the fact that the economic position of blacks in the North was quite unfavorable when compared with that of free blacks in the South,[3] Garrison's assessment is not entirely correct, because it clearly reveals a lack of understanding of the economic potential of Boston's blacks. A survey of the tax records for the city of Boston from 1828 to 1860, together with an examination of certain city directories, reveals a more positive picture.[4]

While it is true that most of the black males during this period were either seamen or laborers, quite a few were also barbers, hairdressers, and waiters. And there is ample documentation showing that many improved their status over the years, especially those who progressed from laborer to waiter. In addition there were cooks, carpenters, shoemakers, caterers, musicians, tailors, clothes cleaners, house servants, printers, an engineer, and a student. Some of these were owners of small shops. A variety of semiskilled occupations that involved blacks are also noted, such as rope maker, cordwainer, grain measurer, and cigar maker.

Interestingly enough, six persons were identified as belonging to the medical profession: Robert Johnson, a physician, on Southac Street (1835); Lenea Stewart, a "doctress," on South Russell Street (1836); Rachaell Bell, a physician, at 31 Garden Street (1849); Paschall B. Randolph, a doctor, at 18 Irving Street (1860); John S. Rock, a physician, at 83 Southac Street (1860); and John De Grasse, a physician, at 31 Charles Street (1860).[5]

Rock came to Boston in 1853 from Pennsylvania, where he had been a den-

Lewis Hayden, one of the most active of Boston abolitionists. His house on Southac (now Phillips) Street was a well-known stop on the Underground Railroad. The Boston Athenæum.

tist, and eventually turned to studying the law. Just before his death in 1866, he was sworn in as the first black lawyer qualified to try a case before the United States Supreme Court. Rock lived in Boston for only a short time, dying at the age of forty-one. Nonetheless he became one of the outstanding black activists in the West End, leading the unsuccessful fight for integrated militia companies in Massachusetts.[6]

Born in New York in 1825, De Grasse received his M.D. degree in 1849 from Bowdoin College. After traveling in Europe, he practiced medicine in New York for two years. He then moved to Boston and in 1854 was admitted as a member of the Massachusetts Medical Society. De Grasse served in the Union army during the Civil War, becoming assistant surgeon with the 35th Colored Troops in 1863. He was among the first blacks to be commissioned as surgeons in the United States Army.[7] While it is not clear what type of medical education a doctor, "doctress," or physician might have received at this time, it is clear that both Rock and De Grasse were trained according to the professional requirements of the time.

According to the records, three persons were listed as "gentleman." The first was Jonathan Cash, who during the 1830s lived at 103 Chambers Street and worked as a handcartman. Cash owned the home in which he lived. Darby Vassall was listed in 1860 as an "Old Gentleman" living at 20 Grove Street. Robert Roberts, no doubt enjoying the profits from the sale of his book *The House Servant's Directory: or, A Monitor for Private Families, etc.,* in 1860 lived in his own home at 8 Napier Street.[8]

Leadership in the black community at this time stemmed from participation in various organizations and movements, but particularly from church activity. Thirteen black ministers appeared on the tax records over the years, the most prominent being Jehiel C. Beman, Leonard A. Grimes, J. Sella Martin, Thomas Paul, and Samuel Snowden. Also listed were Stephen Dutton, Thomas Freeman, Henry J. Johnson, James Lee, John H. Lewis, Jacob Matthews, George S. Spywood, and William Thompson.

Aside from making a living and establishing their churches, these church leaders were mainly concerned with their people's education, the abolition of slavery, the impact of colonization, and temperance. Indeed, when William Lloyd Garrison arrived in Boston, many in the black community had already become activists involved with many such issues. The African Society had been formed as a mutual aid and charity society in 1796, while thirty years later the Massachusetts General Colored Association was founded, taking a strong stand against colonization and for immediate emancipation. The offices of both *The Liberator* and the New England Anti-Slavery Society were located close by the black community in the West End, and during the early 1830s both began to provide meaningful support for the unique and very successful brand of militant activism that epitomized the way the city's blacks increasingly dealt with their concerns regarding freedom and equality.

Besides William Guion Nell and his son, William Cooper Nell, other important figures who were not clergymen included Joshua B. Smith, the successful caterer; John T. Hilton, hairdresser; and George L. Ruffin and John J. Smith, barbers. Ruffin in 1869 became the first black to graduate from the Harvard Law School. He had a successful career in politics, culminating in his appointment in 1886 as justice of the municipal court in Charlestown, Massachusetts, the highest judicial appointment for a black man. John J. Smith owned a barbershop located at the corner of Howard and Bulfinch streets, which was a center for black abolitionist activity and often a rendezvous for fugitive slaves.

Aside from the role played by the ministers, property ownership was usually more important than occupation as the basis for determining leadership within

John J. Smith, owner of a barbershop on the north slope of Beacon Hill which was often used as a rendezvous for fugitive slaves. The Boston Athenæum.

the black community. John P. Coburn, a businessman dealing in clothing but later the owner of several properties, was an active abolitionist and cofounder of the Massasoit Guards (a military group the community organized to protect itself from slavecatchers).[9] While Coburn represented the convergence of wealth and activism, there were also men such as Thomas Dalton, a bootblack who lived on Flagg Alley and purchased with Dudley Tidd, a laborer, land from the estate of Thomas Paul. Dalton later became a waiter, a homeowner at 30 South Russell Street, and president of the Massachusetts General Colored Association.[10] The most frequently mentioned leaders of the period usually owned their own residences.

At times there are cases such as that of Joshua Bennett, who remains somewhat of a mystery. None of the records lists his occupation, but the 1850 city directory shows him living behind Belknap Street (perhaps on Smith Court). However, according to the tax records, Mr. Bennett eventually acquired extensive property holdings: 17 May Street, 241 Southac Street, 40 Bridge Street, 61 Joy Street, 168 and 170 Cambridge Street, 21 Belknap Street, 53 Revere Street,

A black-operated rooming house off Anderson Street (formerly West Centre Street), on the north slope of Beacon Hill (after 1861). The Boston Athenæum.

and 7 West Centre Street. Yet it is impossible to learn more about this enterprising and apparently affluent individual from the usual histories of the period.

Six women were listed as property owners—Mary Bates, Mary Brown, Alice Bush, Chloe Jackson, Chloe Russell, and Chloe Smith. These women, and most of the other ninety-three enumerated in the tax records or the directories, either had not listed an occupation or were laundresses.* However, there were some

*See Appendix A for a listing of African-American women who were heads of household in the West End of Boston during the three decades prior to the Civil War.

exceptions. Aside from Rachaell Bell and Lenea Stewart, listed above, Chloe Russell was a cook, while Theresa Turner, Catherine Barbadoes, and Susan Garrison were dressmakers. Mrs. Emma Gray appeared in 1852 as president of the Female Benevolent Firm and resided at 24 Phillips Street. In 1845 Miss Eliza Gardner was listed as treasurer of the United Daughters of Zion and lived at 20 North Anderson Street.

Perhaps the most unusual and little-known woman of this period was Christiana Carteaux, who was of Indian ancestry, a native of Kingston, Rhode Island, and a very successful businesswoman. She was known professionally as Madame Carteaux, Women's Hairdresser and Wigmaker.[11] From 1847 to 1871 she maintained several places of business at different Boston locations on Cambridge, Washington, and Winter streets.[12]

Madame Carteaux advertised frequently in *The Liberator* and was generally active in the abolition movement. In 1857 she married Edward Bannister, the eminent painter, apparently providing him with much of the strength and support that helped him attain success as an artist. In 1864, during the Civil War, she became chairperson of the Colored Ladies Sanitation Commission, an organization much concerned with the health and welfare of black soldiers.

In fact, as the Civil War approached, a more positive mood in general began to invigorate the black community. For this, they felt strongly, would be primarily a war to free the slaves. As a result, many volunteered to serve the Union cause, but at first they were turned aside. And when finally they were given their chance, to their great disappointment it would be in all-black regiments commanded by white officers serving under a commander-in-chief who saw the conflict as a war only to preserve the Union.

In spite of this, a recruiting station for blacks who wanted to volunteer to serve in the Civil War was established at the corner of North Russell and Cambridge streets. Eventually forty-seven blacks from Boston would serve in the Massachusetts 54th Volunteer Infantry Regiment, the first such regiment to be recruited in the North. Perhaps the Civil War would yet become what blacks everywhere thought it should be, not only a war to destroy slavery, but also a war whose end would signal the coming of a better day for blacks everywhere.

THE MAP AS A PORTRAYAL OF BOSTON'S WEST END BLACK COMMUNITY PRIOR TO THE CIVIL WAR

The map that follows attempts to represent as accurately as possible the presence and the impact of a select group of blacks who resided in the West End of Boston during the antebellum period. However, there are many difficulties that prevent these map materials from providing a complete picture of the black community during the years before the Civil War.

Many individuals did not give a precise street address, naming instead either a street (omitting a house number) or an intersection between streets, or a general vicinity or only a business address. In addition, the names of many streets

Christiana Carteaux Bannister (fl. 1847–1871). Wife of painter Edward Bannister, she was a women's hairdresser and wigmaker in Boston and an active abolitionist. Photo courtesy of the Bannister Nursing Care Center.

changed during this period.[13] In significant other cases, the streets themselves were paved over and thus are impossible to identify.

Finally, since few blacks actually owned their residences, there was considerable mobility within the community, and there were also many boardinghouses in the area. In spite of these limitations, it is still possible to define over time (1800–1864) the perimeters of the community and at least begin to identify within those perimeters some of the elements that made up the general population, as well as some of the more prominent personages.*

*See Appendix B for a listing of some of the more prominent black men of Boston who resided in the West End section of the city during the three decades prior to the Civil War.

SELECTED BLACK RESIDENTS

**Area of Black Concentration
The West End of Boston
1800-1864**

▲ Single Prominent Black Male (1828-1864)

▲ Address with 2 or more Prominent Black Males

◉ Single Registered Black Male Voter (1864)

● Address with 2 or more Registered Black Male Voters

■ Black Institution

☐ White Institution

▨ Street with Known Selected Black Residents

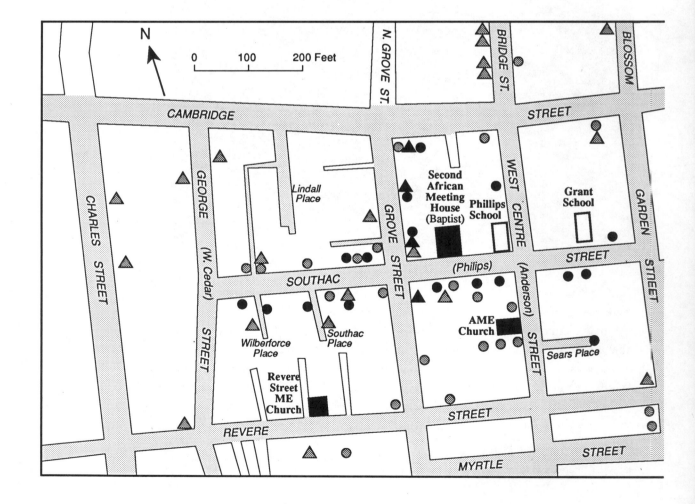

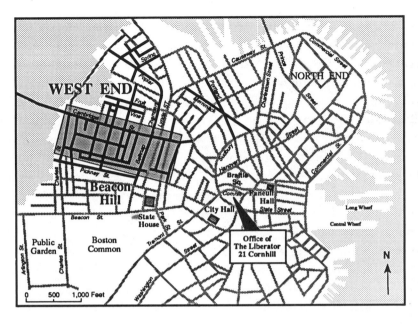

**Location of The West End
Boston - 1859**

Area of Black Concentration
Shown on Detailed Map
1800-1864

Street with Known Selected
Black Residents

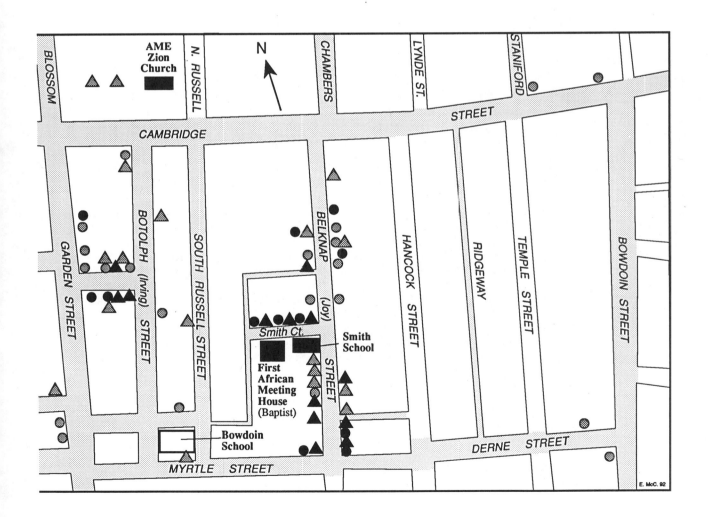

[△] Triangles have been placed on the map to mark the residences of black people of prominence in the community as identified by the available source materials for the period. Three persons are included because of their importance to the West End black community, even though no numbered address is provided for them by any of the sources. They are David Walker, Primus Hall, and James G. Barbadoes.

[○] Circles have been placed on the map to mark the residences of persons listed in "New and Old Voters, First List after Emancipation," for 1864.* This list, found among the papers of Judge George L. Ruffin at the Moorland Spingarn Research Library at Howard University, unfortunately is not complete. However, it does provide a useful measure of the civic responsibility demonstrated by numerous blacks living in the West End at the time.

Important community landmarks such as the various black churches, the all-black Smith School, and the two all-white schools located in the West End—the Bowdoin and the Phillips—from which blacks were barred prior to 1855, have also been designated. Also shown are the locations of the State House, City Hall, and the offices of *The Liberator* and the Massachusetts Anti-Slavery Society.

BIBLIOGRAPHICAL NOTE

Data for the preparation of this essay and map have been derived from selected Boston city directories from 1803 to 1860; from a partial voting list found in the papers of George L. Ruffin (former judge of the Charlestown, Massachusetts Court), now on deposit at the Moorland Spingarn Research Center at Howard University (Washington, D.C.); and tax records from the city of Boston (1828–1860).

Also quite helpful were three well-known books dealing with Boston and Boston's black community: John Daniels, *In Freedom's Birthplace: A Study of the Boston Negroes* (Boston: Houghton Mifflin, 1914); James and Lois Horton, *Black Bostonians: Family Life and Community Struggle in the Antebellum North* (New York: Holmes and Meier, 1979); and Peter R. Knights, *The Plain People of Boston, 1830–1860* (New York: Oxford University Press, 1971).

A particularly important bibliographical source was C. Peter Ripley et al., *The Black Abolitionist Papers in the United States, 1830–1846*, vol. 3 (Chapel Hill: University of North Carolina Press, 1991), as was "Supplementary Lists of Black Abolitionists and Participants in the Boston Temperance Movement from 1833 to 1840," graciously supplied by Roy E. Finkenbine, then associate editor of the *Black Abolitionist Papers* project.

George K. Lewis, Professor Emeritus, Boston University, and Robert Bellinger, instructor of history at Suffolk University, were of valuable assistance during the early stages of the preparation of the map.

*See Appendix C for a partial listing of those eligible black voters who cast ballots in the 1864 election.

NOTES

1. James Oliver Horton and Lois E. Horton, *Black Bostonians: Family Life and Community Struggle in the Antebellum North* (New York: Holmes and Meier, 1979), p. 4.

2. *The Liberator*, January 22, 1831, p. 14.

3. Michael Johnson and James L. Roark, *Black Masters: A Free Family of Color in the Old South* (New York: Norton, 1984). The authors, although focusing on the extraordinary success of William Ellison, a free black businessman in antebellum South Carolina, also provide documentation on the business opportunities of many other free blacks in Charleston.

4. City of Boston Tax Records, 1828–1860; Boston City Directories, 1803, 1805, 1810, 1813, 1816, 1818, 1823, 1830, 1834, 1845, 1849, 1860.

5. William Crowd was listed in 1832 as a physician on Peck Lane in the North End, and in 1849 as a practitioner of "Indian medicine" at 52 Commonwealth Avenue.

6. See Rayford W. Logan and Michael R. Winston, eds., *Dictionary of American Negro Biography* (New York and London: W. W. Norton and Co., 1982), pp. 529–31.

7. Ibid., p. 169.

8. Robert Roberts, *The House Servant's Directory: or, A Monitor for Private Families, etc.* (Boston: Munroe and Francis; New York: Charles S. Francis, 1827).

9. C. Peter Ripley et al., eds., *The Black Abolitionist Papers* (Chapel Hill and London: The University of North Carolina Press, 1991), vol. 3, pp. 308–309.

10. Land Records, City of Boston, Back of 131, Book 194, 1800–1899.

11. Logan and Winston, *Dictionary of American Negro Biography*, pp. 25–26.

12. 110/112 Cambridge Street; 191, 284, 323, and 365 Washington Street; and 12, 31, and 43 Winter Street.

13. Belknap Street changed to Joy Street (from Beacon to Myrtle, 1851; from Myrtle to Cambridge, 1855–56); Botolph or Butolph Street changed to Irving Street (1855); West Centre Street changed to Anderson Street (1861); George Street changed to West Cedar Street (1839); Southac Street changed to Phillips Street (1866); James Place was paved over in 1902; Sears Place was paved over in 1906.

CHAPTER EIGHT

Roy E. Finkenbine

Boston's Black Churches

Institutional Centers of the Antislavery Movement

Many would argue that Boston's brand of abolitionism was uniquely different from that of the antislavery organizations that evolved in other cities. Boston's blacks, in terms of tactics, strategies, and results, also differed when one compares their efforts to those of other antebellum blacks to destroy slavery and gain equality prevalent in other parts of the North. Significantly, these differences apparently led to their making more progress in their attempts to gain equal rights than did their more numerous counterparts in either New York or Philadelphia. If this be so, what role can then be ascribed to black religious institutions?

In the following essay, Roy Finkenbine closely examines Boston's black religious establishment during the period prior to the Civil War. He concludes that instead of "fostering an otherworldly preoccupation" and "diverting attention from the cruel realities of daily existence," an assessment frequently made regarding African-American congregations in general, during the antebellum period Boston's black churches became centers of antislavery activism, serving as "vigorous agencies of advocacy, resistance, and social change."

Centered in Baptist and Methodist denominations, Boston's black community prior to the Civil War established five churches to accommodate the approximately two thousand of their number that resided in the city during the antebellum period. According to Finkenbine, while the city's blacks became involved over the years in a wide variety of social and political issues, it was slavery that clearly "evoked the most widespread and sustained response from Boston's black Christians," likely spilling over into other concerns that helped significantly to shape the broad-based activism that became the hallmark of Boston's antebellum black community.

Writing to *The Liberator* in 1851, black abolitionist William J. Watkins complained that Boston blacks, although numbering a mere two thousand souls, supported five of their own churches. A committed integrationist, he saw no reason for such institutions to exist and argued:

> Were we compelled, on account of our complexion, to occupy the highest seat in the synagogue, or hide ourselves in some remote corner, and catch the crumbs as they fall from the white man's table; then there would be extenuating circumstances sufficient to justify us in worshipping God exclusively under our own vine and fig tree. But no such mitigating circumstances present themselves. Churches in which we can unite and worship God as men and brethren are thrown wide open for our reception, but few of us wend our way thither.[1]

A scant number of blacks shared Watkins's optimistic assessment of the racial climate in Boston's white churches.

Prior to the Civil War, nearly half of the local black community attended racially separate congregations. In 1853, an abolitionist journal estimated that on a typical Sunday, more than eight hundred of Boston's two thousand blacks worshipped in one of these churches.[2] Blacks chose to worship under their "own vine and fig tree" for several reasons. First, despite Watkins's assertions to the contrary, they were "expected to sit in the less desirable and least conspicuous seats" in most local houses of worship—consigned to an unobtrusive gallery or "Negro pew."[3] Some churches excluded them altogether. At several, whites were so incensed by the presence of blacks in the sanctuary that they forcibly barred or removed the offending parties.[4] Many blacks agreed with "Zelmire," an anonymous African-American woman who in 1832 argued in the pages of *The Liberator* that neither denominational preferences nor doctrinal distinctions were sufficient cause for blacks to stay in white churches where they were not wanted.

> There are places of worship where we can go and hear ministers of our own color; and is it not better to encourage them by attending upon their ministrations, if they preach the gospel of Christ, even if they differ from us in non-essential points, than to go where our feelings are injured by this "most foul, strange, and unnatural" prejudice, which exists among many white Christians towards us?[5]

A second reason for the existence of separate churches was the desire of some blacks to worship in a more demonstrative style than that permitted in most white congregations. Black churches at times originated with white encouragement, as in 1818, when whites in the Bromfield Street Methodist Church helped black members establish their own parish. They admitted to having been made uncomfortable by the "shouting" behavior of blacks during services.[6]

A third, but equally important, reason was the role played by separate churches in Boston's black community. As the city's African-American population clustered on Beacon Hill in the decades after 1800, black church buildings performed a growing variety of functions. They became much more than just religious institutions, housing schools and hosting political meetings, concerts, debates, benevolent and moral improvement societies, and other gatherings. Outside the family, they were the central institutions in black life.[7]

Founded for many reasons, Boston's black churches were established over more than four decades. The city's oldest black congregation, the First African Baptist Church, emerged at least in part from a desire to escape discriminatory treatment within the white Baptist churches. Local blacks had begun attending the First and Second Baptist congregations about the time of the American Revolution. Granted few of the membership privileges shared by whites, they found themselves assigned to seats in the galleries, where they could hear but not see the preacher and could not be seen by him or the white members of the congregation. Denied the privilege of voting or holding office in these congregations, they saw their participation in church life restricted to attendance at worship services and those rites connected with birth, baptism, marriage, and death.[8] Little wonder, then, that blacks soon felt the need for a separate and independent congregation.

Sometime in the late eighteenth century, disgruntled black Baptists began meeting in private homes and rented halls under the leadership of Thomas Paul, a young exhorter from New Hampshire. In 1805, with the cooperation of the First and Second Baptist congregations, the First African Baptist Church was organized under Paul's leadership with twenty members. A year later, they completed construction of the African Meeting House on Belknap Street (now Joy Street) on Beacon Hill. Ironically, when the building was dedicated, black members chose to sit in the gallery, reserving pews on the floor for whites "benevolently disposed to the Africans."[9] The structure, which still stands at its original location, now houses the Museum of Afro-American History and is a National Park Service site.

Paul used his pulpit to voice the concerns of the Boston black community during the first quarter of the nineteenth century. After his retirement in 1829, the fortunes of the church fluctuated. In 1838 the congregation changed its name to the First Independent Baptist Church, "for the very good reason that the term African is ill applied to a church composed of American citizens."[10] At the time, the members were becoming increasingly divided. Finally, in 1840, led by the Reverend George H. Black, forty-six of them broke away from the original fold. For several years, they continued to meet separately in the schoolroom of the African Meeting House. Although the reasons for the split are not completely clear, a few historians have suggested that it occurred because of differences over the church's involvement in the antislavery movement.[11]

Boston's first black Methodist congregation arose for a slightly different reason. As more and more blacks joined the Bromfield Street Methodist Church after 1796, white members grew increasingly uncomfortable with the emotional worship behavior of their darker brethren. Finally, in 1818, black members and white church officials agreed on a plan to establish a separate black

The Reverend Thomas Paul, organizer and first minister of the First African Baptist Church, later known as the First Independent Baptist Church. The Boston Athenæum.

chapel under the direction of the Bromfield Street congregation. Samuel Snowden, a black exhorter connected with a Methodist parish in Portland, Maine, was called to fill the pulpit of this new church. Members worshipped in private homes, rented halls, and vacant storefronts for another five years until the New England Conference of the Methodist Episcopal denomination purchased a building for the congregation on May Street (later Revere Street) in Boston's West End. Although the May Street Methodist Episcopal Church grew, moving into larger quarters in 1835, it remained under the control of the deacons of Bromfield until 1903.[12]

The subordinate status of the May Street church led black Bostonians to establish two other separate churches during the 1830s. The first began when disgruntled members of the May Street congregation, bristling at white control, started to meet separately in individual homes in the late 1820s. By 1833 the group had grown sufficiently large to organize as the First Independent Methodist Church (or Bethel Society). Five years later, the congregation placed itself under the discipline of the African Methodist Episcopal (AME) denomination. Unable to support a pastor until 1843, it was served for several years by itinerant AME clergymen from Providence. Finally, in 1844, a permanent building was purchased on West Centre Street (now Anderson) on Beacon Hill. The congregation remained in this location until 1876.[13]

In 1838 a second group broke away from the May Street congregation and formed the First African Methodist Episcopal Zion church (AMEZ). These separatists sought black control of local church affairs and membership in an all-black denomination. They also wanted to break organizational ties with pro-slavery Methodists in the South. Shortly after organizing, members called Jehiel C. Beman of Middletown, Connecticut, to become their pastor. He stayed for seven years, increasing the membership to nearly two hundred and making his leadership felt throughout the city. In 1841 the congregation moved to a small structure (sometimes known as "Rush Chapel") on West Centre Street. It remained on that site until after the Civil War.[14]

Boston's fifth (and last) black congregation to be founded before the war, the Twelfth Baptist Church, was established in 1848 by the group of separatists who had followed the Reverend George Black out of the First Independent Baptist Church eight years earlier. Members selected Leonard A. Grimes as their first pastor; he would serve in that capacity until his death in 1874. Under his guiding hand, the church experienced rapid growth. Land was purchased on Southac Street (now Phillips) in 1849, and construction began on a building the following year. Although passage of the Fugitive Slave Act of 1850 interrupted this process, by 1855 construction had been completed. The new building met the physical needs of a growing congregation.[15]

An assortment of concerns vied for the attention of both clergy and lay people in these churches. Foremost were the transcendent questions of worshipping God, seeking spiritual guidance, and imploring divine assistance for daily living. But there were also the more mundane matters of paying the pastor, heating and lighting the edifice, and disciplining wayward members. Each of these congregations was inspired by waves of revivalism or unsettled by the winds of religious doctrine. At different periods, all underwent dramatic growth as a result of gains in membership among the recently converted.

During 1841–42, more than three hundred blacks joined Boston's four existing separate churches, largely as a result of revivals within these congregations. Opposing views of the millennialist teachings of William Miller divided the May Street congregation in the early 1840s. Some members believed Miller's prediction that the second coming of Christ would occur in October 1843; others flatly rejected the claim. At about the same time, the conversion of

The Twelfth Baptist Church, Boston, also known as the Church of the Fugitive Slaves. The Boston Athenæum.

CHURCH OF THE FUGITIVE SLAVES IN BOSTON

This church once stood near the house of Lewis Hayden, 66 Phillips Street, Boston, Massachusetts.

(From an old engraving.)

member Julia Foote to holiness beliefs in Christian perfectionism had a similar effect on Jehiel C. Beman's flock. Beman and his church council refused to permit this effrontery to AMEZ doctrine.[16]

Members of these churches were also called upon to consider a wide range of social issues, including colonization, the causes of white racism, civil rights, education, the gospel of moral improvement, temperance, and the value of politics for racial uplift. Even those on the periphery of Boston's separate congregations found it difficult to escape such concerns. For many blacks, the best argument for the existence of separate churches was the opportunity they provided to discuss and confront these social issues among themselves, away from the controlling influence of whites.

Not surprisingly, of all the major social issues, slavery evoked the most widespread and sustained response from Boston's black Christians. It touched individual lives, penetrated deep into the fabric of congregations, and influenced virtually every aspect of black religious life. Because of slavery's importance, black churches functioned as institutional centers for the antislavery movement

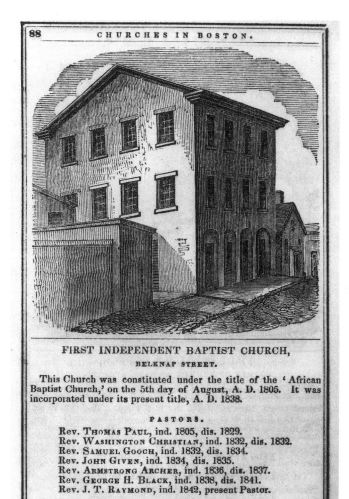

The First Independent Baptist Church (later the African Meeting House), Boston (1843). The Boston Athenæum.

throughout the antebellum decades.[17] Although the city's five black congregations varied in the degree of their involvement, each participated at some level, serving as a hub for abolitionism within the broader black community. They provided the movement with willing workers, sources of funds, meeting places where tactics and strategies could be planned, forums where issues could be discussed, and a shared world of belief where black activists could collectively commit (and recommit) themselves to the antislavery struggle.

Significantly, black churches were gathering places for abolitionists of both races in Boston. Foremost among them was the African Meeting House, which accommodated antislavery assemblies for nearly four decades, becoming known to many as "the abolition church." Local blacks met in the church regularly to discuss the subject of slavery. Every August 1, the building hosted city-wide festivities marking the end of bondage in the British Empire. Both the all-black New England Freedom Association and the biracial Boston Vigilance Committee, groups dedicated to the defense and protection of fugitive slaves in the city, held strategy sessions there. Crowds filled the church on hundreds of occasions to hear antislavery lecturers ranging from unlettered fugitives to celebrities such as William Lloyd Garrison and Frederick Douglass. The Twelfth Baptist Church performed similar functions in the 1850s. These two structures were natural locations for conclaves of Boston abolitionists. Each could hold an audience of close to six hundred people. Even the three black Methodist churches in the city, although considerably smaller, were home to numerous antislavery gatherings.[18]

When white antislavery activists found it difficult to obtain a meeting hall in Boston during the early 1830s, black congregations were often the only institutions willing to open their doors. Reform journalist Oliver Johnson told of wandering from church to church in Boston "in a vain effort to persuade some one among a dozen white clergymen" to permit an antislavery meeting to be held in his sanctuary, before having "to accept the services of a 'nigger' preacher from 'nigger' hill!"—Methodist Samuel Snowden.[19] In January 1832, a dozen white abolitionists formed the New England Anti-Slavery Society at the African Meeting House.[20]

Because of their well-deserved reputation as centers of antislavery activity, Boston's black churches sometimes faced the very real possibility of mob violence. Abolitionism was not popular among many segments of the local society, and as a result, black churches became convenient targets. Such was the case when controversial feminist-abolitionist Angelina Grimké lectured at the African Meeting House in March 1838. Sympathetic whites were urged to stay away out of fear that a gender-mixed, interracial audience would provoke a racist attack. A similar problem arose in December 1860, when an antislavery audience gathered at the Meeting House after a mob broke up a John Brown memorial meeting at the Tremont Temple. Fearful that the howling multitude outside would rush the building, church members armed themselves in preparation for a possible attack.[21]

A major reason that Boston's black congregations inclined toward abolitionism was the conspicuous efforts of their pastors to speak out and work against slavery.[22] Thomas Paul and Samuel Snowden first introduced Garrison to local blacks and gained him a fair hearing. Snowden later served as a counselor in the New England Anti-Slavery Society, a Garrisonian group. Jehiel C. Beman gained renown, and engendered some controversy, as an agent for political antislavery organizations in Massachusetts. Leonard Grimes was a key figure in the local operation of the Underground Railroad. Several black clergymen became skilled antislavery speakers. J. Sella Martin of the First Independent Bap-

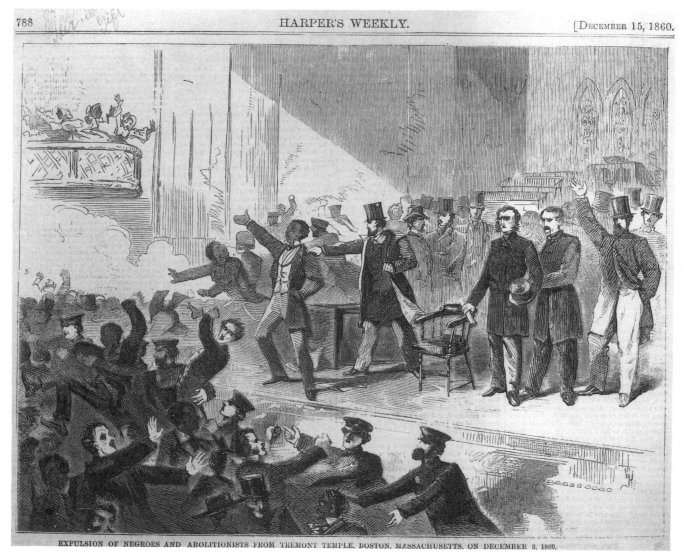

HARPER'S WEEKLY. [December 15, 1860.

EXPULSION OF NEGROES AND ABOLITIONISTS FROM TREMONT TEMPLE, BOSTON, MASSACHUSETTS, ON DECEMBER 8, 1860.

Illustration from *Harper's Weekly* depicting the riot at Tremont Temple during the John Brown Memorial Meeting, December 3, 1860. The Boston Athenæum.

tist Church, whose oratorical skills were favorably compared to those of Frederick Douglass, toured for the cause on both sides of the Atlantic.[23]

Because of differences between Baptist and Methodist church organization, black Baptist ministers were often far more visible in the antislavery movement than their Methodist brethren. Baptists permitted charismatic clergymen to have lengthy tenures in the same pulpit, giving leaders such as Paul (1805–29) and Grimes (1848–74) the time to construct personal power bases and to cultivate the social consciences of their flocks. But Baptist pastors who served shorter terms in Boston—most notably George H. Black (1838–40), John T. Raymond (1841–45), Thomas Henson (1855–58), and Martin (1859–63) at the First Independent Baptist church—also participated in local antislavery efforts.[24]

Methodists (including the AME and AMEZ) tended to restrict their pastoral leaders to briefer periods at the same church, usually no more than four or five years. Only AMEZ pastor Beman (1838–45), Snowden (1818–50), and Elijah Grissom (1850–57) at the May Street Methodist Church were exceptions to this rule. Yet, even with the limitations that the Methodist organization imposed, black clergy involvement in the fight against slavery crossed denominational lines. Noah W. C. Cannon and Jabez P. Campbell, itinerant ministers who served Boston's AME congregation during the 1830s and early 1840s, were active abolitionists. The Reverend Thomas James, an AMEZ clergyman loosely affiliated with Beman's congregation, in the 1840s conducted antislavery speaking tours and participated in several slave rescues, including the attempt to free Anthony Burns. Local lay exhorters Charles V. Caples (May Street Methodist Church) and Solomon R. Alexander (AMEZ) also achieved prominence as a result of their antislavery work.[25]

Of course, several members of the city's black clergy were personally acquainted with the "peculiar institution." Grimes, a free black native of Virginia and Washington, D.C., had seen slavery at close range and had helped dozens of blacks escape from bondage in the upper South. A few had felt the lash themselves. Martin had served eight different masters throughout the lower South before fleeing to freedom in 1856. Grissom had been a slave preacher in Maryland. In 1846, believing that he could be a more effective minister as a free man, he came northward "as fast as the cars could carry him." Lunsford Lane and Peter Randolph, lay preachers in the city's black Baptist congregations, were both former bondsmen. All of these men drew on their slave background to further the objectives of the antislavery movement.[26]

One free black clergyman, Jehiel Beman, visited the upper South to observe the effects of slavery firsthand. In July 1844 he traveled by train to Maryland and the nation's capital, enduring the humiliation of the pass system and Jim Crow cars to investigate slave life. Although he had been an active abolitionist for over a decade by the time of this trip, neither his antislavery work nor frequent encounters with prejudice had prepared him for what he found. When he crossed the Mason-Dixon line, a feeling of powerlessness swept over him at the sight of his "sisters toiling, pitchfork and rake in hand, under the scorching rays of the sun." Beman recalled that he cried, then sat in silence as the cars rolled on.[27]

The careers of Grimes and Beman illustrate the differing ways that Boston's black pastors worked to further the goals of the antislavery movement. Grimes, the city's best-known clergy activist, preferred to labor alone or through institutions within the black community. After arriving in the city in 1848, he made his congregation a center of social protest and an important station on the Underground Railroad. He worked directly to secure the freedom of individual fugitive slaves, sometimes participating in attempts to rescue fugitives held by

REV. JEHIAL C. BEMAN.

Pastor of the Wesleyan Methodist Episcopal Zion Church. Boston Mass.

The Reverend Jehiel C. Beman, active abolitionist and pastor of the First African Methodist Episcopal Zion Church in Boston between 1838 and 1845. The Boston Athenæum.

federal authorities in Boston. On those occasions when other means failed, he worked with his congregation to purchase the freedom of individual slaves such as Anthony Burns.[28]

Unlike Grimes, Beman chose to work in mainstream antislavery organizations. After participating in American Anti-Slavery Society auxiliaries for most of the 1830s, he broke with William Lloyd Garrison near the end of the decade, preferring to fight slavery through political means. Beman worked as an office agent for the Massachusetts Abolition Society and as assistant secretary of the

American and Foreign Anti-Slavery Society in the early 1840s, two organizations strongly opposed by Garrison. This drew considerable criticism from local blacks, many of whom disagreed with Beman on tactics although respecting his commitment to the antislavery cause. Beman later campaigned for Liberty party candidates in black communities across New England, becoming further estranged from Garrison and his supporters in the process.[29]

Clergy activism provoked occasional clashes between pastors and parishioners. Although the evidence is unclear, it may have caused the split in the First Independent Baptist Church about 1840. J. Sella Martin encountered congregational hostility to his antislavery work on at least two occasions. In December 1860, when an anti-abolitionist mob broke up a meeting at the interracial Tremont Temple commemorating the first anniversary of the execution of John Brown, Martin invited the audience to reassemble at his Joy Street church. The congregation's trustees, fearing further violence, advised that they would bolt the doors against such a gathering. Only after Martin threatened to resign did they decide that "it were better that the house be pulled down than the colored people should surrender the right of free speech at the dictation of an unprincipled and lawless mob." Later, during the Civil War, Martin's efforts to raise funds in Britain for the contrabands in the American South so alienated some members of his congregation that this time his resignation was called for and willingly accepted.[30]

Despite occasional conflict with parishioners, Boston's black clergymen generally acted as catalysts, inspiring greater lay involvement in the struggle against slavery. As ministers, they were the natural leaders of the city's black community. And unlike many of the members of their congregations, they were relatively independent of white society and skilled in the art of managing people and resources. Through preaching, coaxing, and personal example, they encouraged church members to join antislavery societies, slave rescues, the Underground Railroad, vigilance committee work, petition campaigns for personal liberty laws, drives to purchase the freedom of individual slaves, and eventually the freedmen's aid effort. They also persuaded congregations to open their pocketbooks and contribute the funds necessary to carry out these projects.

Boston's best-known black abolitionists were also dominant figures in the black churches. This included a majority of the lay activists in the city. The list of delegates from the First Independent Baptist Church to annual conferences of the Boston Baptist Association includes key names such as John T. Hilton, Coffin Pitts, Peter M. Howard, Robert Johnson, Robert Roberts, and Robert Morris. Other prominent abolitionists—Maria W. Stewart, Susan Paul, Thomas Cole, Henry and Benjamin Weeden, and William G. Nell—were members of the congregation as well. Leading lights Christopher R. Weeden, John B. Cutler, Thomas Dalton, John J. Smith, Henry Watson, and Henry L. W. Thacker were trustees of the AMEZ church. During the 1850s, the Twelfth Baptist Church counted renowned Underground Railroad organizers Lewis and Harriet Hayden and antislavery lecturer John S. Rock among their own. Dozens of second-tier activists also belonged to these congregations.[31]

Although fewer abolitionists could be found within the May Street Methodist Church and its AME counterpart, this was largely a function of class. These congregations appealed to black seamen and other working-class folk, who had less time to devote to outside causes. Nevertheless, a sizable minority within these churches joined in antislavery work, particularly after the passage of the Fugitive Slave Act of 1850. David Walker, the city's most famous black abolitionist, was a member of the May Street congregation.[32] At any given period, a few outspoken abolitionists and dozens of others who toiled behind the scenes could be found within any one of the city's black churches.

As a rule, black abolitionists gravitated toward those congregations whose ministers were most visible in antislavery activities. During Thomas Paul's tenure at the African Meeting House, most of the city's black activists were members there. When he was followed by a succession of less outspoken ministers in the 1830s, many of them went elsewhere. Beman attracted dozens of prominent black abolitionists to his congregation after his arrival in the city in 1838. When he left seven years later, most of them also departed. Simpson H. Lewis is a case in point. A leading member of the AMEZ parish from its founding, he became disgruntled at the conservatism of the clergymen who followed Beman. In the late 1840s, he was attracted by Grimes's example, crossed denominational boundaries, and joined the Twelfth Baptist Church. Grimes's efforts to mobilize Boston blacks against enforcement of the Fugitive Slave Act of 1850 brought dozens of other activists to his church during the following decade.[33]

Black pastors and parishioners in Boston also raised thousands of dollars for the abolitionist movement. Collections taken up on a Sunday morning often supported antislavery activities throughout the week. This sometimes meant that the bills of the congregation went unpaid. On occasion, the plate was passed to generate income for various antislavery organizations. Samuel Snowden regularly pressed his congregation to donate to the work of the American Anti-Slavery Society in the 1830s. But more often, collections went to the work of the Underground Railroad. When emergencies demanded, special offerings were solicited to provide for the legal defense of fugitive slaves, to buy their freedom, or to resupply the coffers of local vigilance committees. Escaped slaves regularly lectured in the black churches as a way to accumulate the funds needed to buy their own or their family's freedom. When fugitive Thomas H. Jones arrived in the city in October 1849, he found all three black Methodist congregations willing to lend him their pulpits and to donate funds to free his wife and children and bring them north.[34]

In many different ways, the clergy and laity of Boston's black churches labored to advance the freedom of their race. Religious historian Will Gravely's assessment of the role and purpose of antebellum African-American churches accurately characterizes these congregations:

Always [they] stood as institutional symbols of human liberation. They did not often get the headlines which marked white abolitionist activity, but within their communities they carried on a continual struggle to defend, protect, extend, and expand black freedom. Unlike white Christians of the period, black churchfolk did not have a choice as to whether they would work for black freedom, for their own liberty was inescapably bound up with the liberation of their people.[35]

The area of antislavery activity attracting the greatest amount of church involvement was the protection of fugitive slaves. This was to be expected. Runaway bondsmen flocked to Boston after 1830, becoming a significant portion of the local black community. By 1850 a quarter of the city's adult blacks had been born in the South, and a majority of these were escaped slaves. Fugitives belonged to each of Boston's five black congregations, and most free black parishioners included at least one among their family or friends.[36]

The threat of slavecatchers posed a persistent problem for Boston's black congregations. Black churches were often key points of reconnaissance for southern slave hunters tracking fugitive slaves in the city, making it hazardous for runaway blacks to worship with their brethren. Escaped slave Moses Roper found this to be the case while living and working in Boston in the mid-1830s. After attending the African Baptist Church for a time, he became so alarmed by the presence of slavecatchers near the building that he began worshipping with a white Baptist congregation.[37]

Passage of the Fugitive Slave Act of 1850 further disrupted Boston's black churches. Congregations were rent as the threat of the slavecatcher prompted dozens of church members to flee to Canada West or the Maritime Provinces. Within Boston's AME body, some 30 to 40 of 106 parishioners took flight. So did 10 of the AMEZ congregation's leading members. The First Independent Baptist Church lost nearly 40 of its 124 members. The impact was greatest at the Twelfth Baptist Church, known as the "fugitive slave church" because its membership included so many escaped bondsmen. The Fugitive Slave Act "struck the church like a thunderbolt, and scattered the flock," compelling 60 members, including two deacons, to abandon the city. The crisis also forced the congregation to halt renovations to the building and to suspend services temporarily, depriving remaining members of much-needed spiritual sustenance.[38]

Labeling the Fugitive Slave Act an "unchristian" edict, Boston's black congregations quickly banded together to resist its enforcement. After a series of meetings at the May Street Methodist Church and the African Meeting House, most black abolitionists resolved to fight the law by any means, including violence. Joshua B. Smith, a respected black Baptist, expressed the views of many churchgoers when he displayed a dagger and a revolver from the meeting house pulpit. Such action was felt to be justified, since escaped bondsmen were being threatened with reenslavement. Two of these, Frederick "Shadrach" Wilkins, who was rescued in February 1851, and Anthony Burns, who was not, were members of the Twelfth Baptist Church. Leonard A. Grimes and his parishioner

'CONQUERING PREJUDICE,'
or
"Fulfilling a Constitutional duty with alacrity."

"My God!— My Child!—Will
no one help!— Is there no mercy!"

"Any man can perform an agreeable
duty— it is not every one that can perform a disagreeable duty."

"By Heaven! he exceeds my most sanguine
expectation—he marks his way so clearly &
treads so loyally on the track of the Constitution— It is more than great— it is sublime—
I feel a great sense of relief."

Conquering Prejudice (ca. 1850). Lithograph by P. Kramer satirizing Daniel Webster's support of the Fugitive Slave Law compromise in the name of the Constitution. Charles E. Goodspeed Collection, the Worcester Art Museum.

Lewis Hayden played major roles in planning several attempts to free captured fugitives by force. Fellow Baptist Robert Morris, the first black admitted to the bar in Massachusetts, was active in their legal defense. Dozens of other black church members aided the effort to protect fugitives in the city by contributing time, money, clothing, transportation, and medical services to the work of the Boston Vigilance Committee.[39]

When fugitives could not be hidden from slavecatchers or rescued by legal action, the financial resources of the five black congregations were tapped. Grimes proved to be particularly skilled at raising funds for such purposes. In 1850 he collected $1,300 from his congregation to buy the freedom of four members, including the two exiled deacons who had fled to Canada West. Another $1,800 was solicited to purchase Thomas Sims after he was returned to slavery by federal officials in April 1851, but the amount proved insufficient, and he remained in bondage in Georgia and then Mississippi until the Civil War. When Anthony Burns was returned to bondage in Virginia in 1854, Grimes and lay activist Coffin Pitts spearheaded a successful drive to procure the funds to effect his purchase. Amazingly, all this was done at a time when the Twelfth Baptist Church was also seeking money to complete its building project. The other black congregations in the city raised lesser but significant amounts for the same purpose.[40]

The law's impact on families created other crises for the black churches. Many couples were separated as fugitives fled Boston, leaving free black spouses and children behind. Black congregations attempted to reunite these families by purchasing the freedom of the refugees and returning them to the city. In the meantime, they continued to care for those family members left behind. Determining the marital status of fugitives who had left a partner behind in slavery proved to be a stickier situation. Runaway slave Thomas Teamoh came to Boston in the mid-1850s, abandoning his common-law spouse, Margaret Reddick, in Virginia, and joined Grimes's church. When he wanted to remarry, Grimes refused to perform the ceremony until the fugitive could demonstrate that his slave wife had committed adultery, thus annulling his earlier marriage to her. Determining the outcome of such cases at times created dissension within congregations.[41]

Abolitionism echoed the social teachings of Boston's black churches. Congregations instructed members that slavery was a sin and that resisting the institution was a virtuous act. Black clergy and lay activists alike held that God sanctioned acts of protest and defiance aimed at eradicating social evils. No evil, they argued, was greater than slavery. Writings by David Walker and Maria W. Stewart and the prayers and sermons of ministers such as Leonard Grimes demonstrate that religious motivation lay behind most black antislavery efforts in the city. In fact, Boston's black congregations viewed such work as part of their gospel mandate.[42]

From the perspective of local black ministers, opposition to slavery was an act of holiness and a Christian duty. By word and deed, they encouraged black lay involvement in antislavery activities, convincing parishioners that emancipation was the unfolding of God's plan for black people.[43] The opportunity to view themselves as instruments in this holy struggle inspired black abolitionists with a sense of the righteousness of their work. This helped them to overcome qualms about the morality of particular tactics, including violence. At the same time, the belief that God would ultimately prevail against the sin of slavery kept them from becoming disheartened by the tide of events—even during the critical decade of the 1850s, when the Fugitive Slave Act, the Kansas-Nebraska Act, and the *Dred Scott* decision convinced some blacks that there was no hope for them in the United States.

No individual captured the spiritual quality of black abolitionism in Boston better than David Walker, an active layman in the May Street Church. His famous *Appeal to the Coloured Citizens of the World* was a black abolitionist jeremiad—a warning to whites of the divine judgment to come as a result of the sin of slavery. The 1829 pamphlet bitterly charged white Americans with immorality and hypocrisy and called down God's wrath upon the nation. Despite the *Appeal*'s rhetorical threats of violent black revenge, it ended with the hope that God would change the hearts of white Americans and save them from annihilation. The *Appeal* was first and foremost a call to repentance. Walker did not desire that slaveholders be destroyed, but rather that the institution of slavery be overthrown. Only if whites failed to repent, he warned, would God free the slaves through physical force. Yet, if compulsion was needed, Walker predicted, blacks would be God's willing instruments.[44]

Boston's black pastors and their more articulate lay activists followed David Walker's example, drawing on their faith to chastise white churches for moral blindness on the slavery issue and to defend their own actions against proslavery religious attacks. William Wells Brown, who lectured for the movement at home and abroad, regularly censured American churches for being bulwarks of slavery. In his *Appeal*, Walker openly blamed "the preachers of the religion of Jesus Christ" for the institution's continued existence.

Once his freedom had been purchased by the Twelfth Baptist Church, Anthony Burns challenged the pastor of his former church in Virginia on the subject of slavery. Informed that he had been excommunicated because his earlier flight from bondage had violated both human and divine ordinance, Burns rejected the premise that he had disobeyed God's law by running away. Citing verse after verse of scripture to buttress his argument, he contended that his owner, by enslaving him, was the one who had committed an outrage against divine law. Burns maintained that God had planted a desire for freedom in the human heart, and that the spirit of God had impelled him to seek that freedom no matter what the danger. For this reason, he argued, he was not breaking but obeying God's law by running away. He closed his letter by admonishing the Virginia clergyman to study carefully the theology implicit in the Golden Rule.[45]

Each of Boston's black churches offered a collective witness against the sin of slavery, but none more so than the local AMEZ congregation, which had been founded out of a desire on the part of some members of the May Street Methodist Church to sever all ties with the proslavery Methodists of the South. Even as pastors of varying persuasions came and went, the church continued to adhere to an outspoken antislavery posture. When the AMEZ General Conference met in Boston in June 1859, John J. Smith and Aaron A. Bradley, members of the local body, persuaded delegates to adopt a resolution labeling slavery "the crowning sin of the nation." As William Lloyd Garrison had done earlier, Smith and Bradley condemned all churches that refused to speak out against the institution as "enemies of God and man," stating in no uncertain terms that it was "the highest and most imperative duty of the Church of Christ to 'lift up its voice and spare not' until every yoke is broken and every slave is free."[46]

Religious rituals drawn from the black churches helped to strengthen the antislavery beliefs of Boston's black abolitionists and endowed them with a higher purpose. Most black antislavery gatherings were reminiscent of worship services, complete with prayers, favorite Protestant hymns, and frequent biblical references. This routine especially characterized annual events such as the July 14th observances of the abolition of the African slave trade (through the early 1830s) and the August 1st celebrations of the end of slavery in the British empire (after 1834). On such occasions, blacks assembled in local churches to hear sermons, sing hymns, furnish testimonials, and offer up prayers of thanksgiving. Congregations also proclaimed numerous fast days and prayer meetings designed to hasten the coming of the day of emancipation.[47]

In much the same way, worship services in Boston's black churches were filled with abolitionist sentiment. Sermons often carried an antislavery message. When fugitive slaves such as J. Sella Martin and Elijah Grissom entered the pulpit, they took their experiences as bondsmen with them. On numerous occasions, Grimes postponed his Sunday sermons to allow time for an antislavery speaker. Black abolitionist William Cooper Nell recalled that "Education, Anti-Slavery and Temperance always received . . . deserved attention" in the preaching of John T. Raymond, and that "lecturers on the various reforms were cordially invited to address his church."[48] An invocation by Samuel Snowden, the seamen's minister, illustrates the extent to which thoughts of the horrors of slavery mingled with prayers to the divine in these congregations: "O Lord, bless the good British ship *Buzzard*, that rescued a cargo of slaves the other day on the African coast. Give her a fair wind, Lord, and drive her right into port."[49]

Scholars have long been divided on the temperament of the black churches. Some contend that African-American congregations have fostered an otherworldly preoccupation, diverting attention from the cruel realities of daily existence. Other insist that they have been vigorous agencies of advocacy, resistance, and social change. There can be little doubt, however, about the character of Boston's black churches during the antebellum years. Focusing on this world as well as the next, they provided meeting places, manpower, money, and motivation for the fight against slavery. They brought together blacks of all classes and stations, inspiring them to protect and defend family members who were fugitives from bondage and, more broadly, to battle for the freedom of all slaves. Although the extent and nature of this antislavery activity varied from time to time and congregation to congregation, the church remained the one place where Boston's black abolitionists found the encouragement, the strength of conviction, and the spiritual sustenance to carry on the struggle, no matter what the cost.

NOTES

1. *Liberator*, January 9, 1852.

2. *Pennsylvania Freeman*, August 25, 1853. For an elaborate 1842 estimate, generated before the establishment of the Twelfth Baptist Church, see Martin Moore, *Boston Revival, 1842: A Brief History of the Evangelical Churches of Boston* (Boston, 1842), pp. 95–96, 123–25, 129–31.

3. John Daniels, *In Freedom's Birthplace: A Study of the Boston Negroes* (Boston: Houghton Mifflin, 1914), p. 22; James Oliver Horton and Lois Horton, *Black Bostonians: Family Life and Community Struggle in the Antebellum North* (New York: Holmes and Meier, 1979), p. 39. There is some disagreement among historians about the extent to which white religious racism provoked the formation of Boston's black congregations. For a brief overview of this debate, see George A. Levesque, "Black Boston: Negro Life in Garrison's Boston, 1800–1860" (Ph.D. diss., State University of New York at Binghamton, 1976), p. 274n.

4. See, for example, William Cooper Nell, *Colored Patriots of the American Revolution* (Boston: Robert F. Wallcut, 1855), pp. 33–34; *Liberator*, December 10, 1847.

5. *Liberator*, July 28, 1832.

6. Robert C. Hayden, *Faith, Culture, and Leadership: A History of the Black Church in Boston* (Boston: Boston Branch NAACP, 1983), p. 12.

7. Horton and Horton, *Black Bostonians*, pp. 51–52.

8. Hayden, *Faith, Culture, and Leadership*, p. 3; Robert C. Hayden, *The African Meeting House in Boston: A Celebration of History* (Boston: Boston Public Library, 1987), p. 7.

9. Quoted in Hayden, *Faith, Culture, and Leadership*, p. 4. Horton and Horton, *Black Bostonians*, p. 40.

10. Quoted in George A. Levesque, "Inherent Reformers—Inherited Orthodoxy: Black Baptists in Boston, 1800–1873," *Journal of Negro History* 60 (October 1975): 509; Horton and Horton, *Black Bostonians*, pp. 40–41.

11. Levesque, "Black Boston," pp. 277–94.

12. Hayden, *Faith, Culture, and Leadership*, pp. 12–13; *Sketches and Business Directory of Boston and Vicinity: For 1860 and 1861* (Boston, [1860]), p. 46; James Mudge, *History of the New England Conference of the Methodist Episcopal Church, 1796–1910* (Boston: New England Conference, 1910), pp. 82–83, 255–56.

13. Hayden, *Faith, Culture, and Leadership*, pp. 18–19; Daniel A. Payne, *History of the African Methodist Episcopal Church* (Nashville, 1891), p. 120; *Liberator*, December 17, 1836, January 28, 1837, July 20, 1838; Moore, *Boston Revival*, p. 129.

14. *Liberator*, July 27, 1838; Moore, *Boston Revival*, p. 130; Hayden, *Faith, Culture, and Leadership*, pp. 23–24.

15. William H. Hester, *One Hundred and Five Years by Faith* (Boston: Publication of the Twelfth Baptist Church, 1946), pp. 9–18.

16. Moore, *Boston Revival*, pp. 95–96, 123, 125, 129–31; William L. Andrews, ed., *Sisters of the Spirit: Three Black Women's Autobiographies of the Nineteenth Century* (Bloomington: Indiana University Press, 1986), pp. 205–207.

17. Carol V. R. George makes this point effectively for black churches throughout the North. See her "Widening the Circle: The Black Church and the Abolitionist Crusade, 1830–1860," in Lewis Perry and Michael Fellman, eds., *Antislavery Reconsidered: New Perspectives on the Abolitionists* (Baton Rouge: Louisiana State University Press, 1979), pp. 75–95.

18. Much of the information in this paragraph is based on a review of *The Liberator* for the years 1831 to 1860. Also see Hayden, *African Meeting House*, pp. 19–24; Hester, *One Hundred and Five Years*, p. 18; S. N. Dickinson, *The Boston Almanac for the Year 1843* (Boston, 1843), p. 88; Levesque, "Inherent Reformers," p. 516.

19. Oliver Johnson, *William Lloyd Garrison and His Times* (Boston, 1880), p. 71.

20. Horton and Horton, *Black Bostonians*, p. 28.

21. *Liberator*, March 16, 1838; R. J. M. Blackett, *Beating against the Barriers: The Lives*

of Six Nineteenth-Century Afro-Americans (Baton Rouge: Louisiana State University Press, 1986), pp. 198–99; *Douglass' Monthly*, January 1861.

22. For a comparison to black clergy activists elsewhere in the antebellum North, see David E. Swift, *Black Prophets of Justice: Activist Clergy before the Civil War* (Baton Rouge: Louisiana State University Press, 1989), which studies six ministers in New York and Connecticut.

23. Horton and Horton, *Black Bostonians*, pp. 46–50; Jane H. Pease and William H. Pease, *They Who Would Be Free: Blacks' Search for Freedom, 1830–1861* (New York: Atheneum, 1974), pp. 70–71; Blackett, *Beating against the Barriers*, pp. 189–251.

24. Levesque, "Inherent Reformers," pp. 515–18. Randall Burkett of the W. E. B. DuBois Institute at Harvard University helped convince me that organizational differences between black Baptist and Methodist denominations were an important factor influencing clergy activism.

25. Hayden, *Faith, Culture, and Leadership*, pp. 12–13, 18–19, 23; C. Peter Ripley, Roy E. Finkenbine, Donald Yacovone et al., eds., *The Black Abolitionist Papers*, 5 vols. (Chapel Hill: University of North Carolina Press, 1985–92), vol. 3, pp. 363–64, 455–56; "The Autobiography of Rev. Thomas James," *Rochester History* 37 (October 1975): 10–19; C. C. Burleigh to Samuel J. May, April 3, 1835, Anti-Slavery Collections, Boston Public Library; Eliza A. Gardner, "Historical Sketch of A.M.E. Zion Church, Boston, Mass., U.S.A.," in Jacob W. Powell, *Bird's Eye View of the General Conference of the African Methodist Episcopal Zion Church* (Boston: Lavelle Press, 1918), p. 31.

26. Blackett, *Beating against the Barriers*, pp. 185–88; *Pennsylvania Freeman*, August 25, 1853; William G. Hawkins, *Lunsford Lane: Another Helper from South Carolina* (Boston, 1863), pp. 195–98; Hayden, *Faith, Culture, and Leadership*, p. 34.

27. Boston *Morning Chronicle*, August 15, 1844.

28. Horton and Horton, *Black Bostonians*, pp. 47–48, 106–11.

29. Ibid., p. 48; *Black Abolitionist Papers*, vol. 3, pp. 455–56.

30. Levesque, "Black Boston," pp. 277–94; Blackett, *Beating against the Barriers*, pp. 198–99; *Douglass' Monthly*, January 1861; New York *Anglo-African*, January 31, February 21, 1863.

31. The list of delegates from the First Independent Baptist Church to annual conferences of the Boston Baptist Association is conveniently reprinted in Levesque, "Inherent Reformers," pp. 520–22. For a list of the officers of Boston's AMEZ church, see Gardner, "Historical Sketch," pp. 29–32. A more detailed listing of black Boston abolitionists by congregation has been compiled by the author from dozens of sources.

32. Henry Highland Garnet, *Walker's Appeal, with a Brief Sketch of His Life* (New York, 1848), p. vii.

33. Levesque, "Inherent Reformers," pp. 520–22; *Liberator*, July 27, 1838; Gardner, "Historical Sketch," pp. 29–31. The movement of black abolitionists into Grimes's church during the 1850s is clear from a review of the annual minutes of the American Baptist Missionary Convention from 1849 to 1860.

34. *Liberator*, August 4, 1837, December 16, 1842, August 28, 1846; Thomas H. Jones, *The Experience of Thomas H. Jones, Who Was a Slave for Forty-Three Years* (Worcester, Mass., 1857), pp. 47–48.

35. Will B. Gravely, "The Rise of African Churches in America (1786–1822): Reexamining the Contexts," *Journal of Religious Thought* 41 (Spring-Summer 1984): 73.

36. Levesque, "Black Boston," p. 294n; Leonard P. Curry, *The Free Black in Urban America, 1800–1850: The Shadow of the Dream* (Chicago: University of Chicago Press, 1981), p. 249.

37. Moses Roper, *A Narrative of the Adventures and Escape of Moses Roper, from American Slavery* (Philadelphia, 1838), p. 83n.

38. *Pennsylvania Freeman*, August 25, 1853; George W. Williams, *History of the Twelfth Baptist Church, Boston, Mass., from 1840 to 1874* (Boston, 1874), p. 20.

39. *Liberator*, October 4 and 11, 1850; *Boston Journal*, August 17, 1883; Hayden, *Faith, Culture, and Leadership*, p. 29; Horton and Horton, *Black Bostonians*, pp. 101, 106–108; Blackett, *Beating against the Barriers*, pp. 91–92.

40. *Pennsylvania Freeman*, August 25, 1853; Horton and Horton, *Black Bostonians*, pp. 107, 111; Stanley W. Campbell, *The Slave Catchers: Enforcement of the Fugitive Slave Law, 1850–1860* (Chapel Hill: University of North Carolina Press, 1968), p. 120; Hester, *One Hundred and Five Years*, pp. 17–18.

41. *Pennsylvania Freeman*, August 25, 1853; William H. Mulligan, Jr., ed., "The Pressure of Uncertain Freedom: A Documentary Note on the Antebellum Black Family," *Negro History Bulletin* 42 (October–December 1979): 107; Thomas R. Watson, *A Sketch of the Past and Present Condition of the Twelfth Baptist Church* (Boston, 1880), pt. 2, pp. 1–16.

42. This was true of black churches throughout the antebellum North, a point well made in Monroe Fordham, *Major Themes in Northern Black Religious Thought, 1800–1860* (Hicksville, N.Y.: Exposition Press, 1975), pp. 111–34. For an instructive Boston example, see Marilyn Richardson, ed., *Maria W. Stewart, America's First Black Woman Political Writer: Essays and Speeches* (Bloomington: Indiana University Press, 1987), pp. 3–74.

43. This was most evident in the careers of Paul, Snowden, Beman, Raymond, Grimes, and Martin.

44. Charles M. Wiltse, ed., *David Walker's Appeal to the Coloured Citizens of the World* (New York: Hill and Wang, 1965), pp. 1–78. For the characteristics and history of antebellum black jeremiads, see David Howard Pitney, *The Afro-American Jeremiad: Appeals for Justice in America* (Philadelphia: Temple University Press, 1990), pp. 3–34.

45. *Black Abolitionist Papers*, vol. 1, pp. 312, 350–51; Wiltse, *David Walker's Appeal*, pp. 35–43; Fordham, *Major Themes*, p. 124.

46. *Liberator*, June 24, 1859.

47. This paragraph is based on a review of *The Liberator* from 1831 to 1860 and the New York *Anglo-African* from 1859 to 1863. Also see William B. Gravely, "The Dialectic of Double-Consciousness in Black American Freedom Celebrations, 1808–1863," *Journal of Negro History* 67 (Winter 1982): 302–17.

48. Nell, *Colored Patriots*, p. 364.

49. Johnson, *William Lloyd Garrison and His Times*, p. 72.

CHAPTER NINE

Marilyn Richardson

"What If I Am a Woman?"

Maria W. Stewart's Defense of Black Women's Political Activism

In spite of the fact that society dictated that nineteenth-century women should maintain their lives within carefully circumscribed boundaries according to standards set by the notion of the "Cult of True Womanhood," some women, in the cause of freedom, heroically fought to break through these barriers. One of the earliest of these, Marilyn Richardson reminds us, was Maria Stewart, a black abolitionist and feminist who, nurtured by the climate of Boston abolitionism, became during the 1830s "the first American-born woman of any race to lecture in public on political themes."

Influenced politically by David Walker and given strong support by William Lloyd Garrison, himself a strong champion of women's rights, Maria Stewart, in spite of a relatively brief stay in Boston, nonetheless made her mark, particularly in a remarkable series of essays and speeches (some delivered to audiences comprising both men and women). Attacking colonization, black slavery, and the continuing subjugation of women, Stewart would continually remind her audiences that "all the nations of the earth are crying out for liberty and equality. Away, away with tyranny and oppression."

According to Richardson, Maria Stewart's most important contribution was her continuing effort to redefine black women's lives through economic cooperation, education, and a strong organizationally based social commitment. Militant activism and a striving for unity were the keystones of her creed during her Boston years, a time when she was able to create a unique and pathbreaking brand of abolitionist and feminist thought for others to emulate.

Maria W. Stewart (1803–1879), a black woman, is recognized as the first American-born woman of any race to lecture in public on political themes and leave published copies of her texts. Active in Boston, Massachusetts, as early as 1831, she preceded the Grimké sisters, Sarah and Angelina, often cited as the earliest American women political writers and activists, by almost five years. Stewart's Boston essays and speeches were gathered in a single volume, *Productions of Mrs. Maria W. Stewart,* first published in 1835.[1]

Stewart was also a forerunner of many of the most influential nineteenth-century African American abolitionists and women's-rights activists. These included Sojourner Truth, who in 1843 began her mission of traveling and speaking for freedom and human rights; Frederick Douglass, who escaped slavery in 1838 and soon began his career as one of history's leading abolitionists and champions of human rights, establishing himself at the famous Nantucket meeting of 1841; and Frances Ellen Watkins Harper, who delivered her first public lecture, "The Elevation and Education of Our People," in New Bedford, Massachusetts, in 1854.

Stewart was born Maria Miller. Little is known of her origins or her early life. Orphaned, childless, and widowed, in a brief autobiographical note accompanying an 1833 essay she wrote:

> I was born in Hartford, Connecticut, in 1803; was left an orphan at five years of age; was bound out to a clergyman's family; had the seeds of piety and virtue early sown in my mind, but was deprived of the advantages of education, though my soul thirsted for knowledge. Left them at fifteen years of age; attended Sabbath schools until I was twenty; in 1826 was married to James W. Stewart; was left a widow in 1829.[2]

No artist's or photographer's likeness has yet emerged of this enigmatic woman. We must settle, for the moment, for a brief, gallant description of Stewart as a young woman. In a delightful reminiscence written following their 1879 reunion in Boston, in what was to be the final year of both their lives, Stewart's friend, abolitionist editor and publisher William Lloyd Garrison, wrote to her in Washington, D.C., where she then lived:

> It is seldom, indeed, that two persons, after a separation of forty-six years, are permitted to see each other again in the flesh . . . . The sight of you at once carried me back in memory to the very commencement of the anti-slavery movement in this city. You had not long been married, and were in the flush and promise of a ripening womanhood, with a graceful form and pleasing countenance.[3]

Garrison goes on to describe Stewart coming to the recently opened *Liberator* office with a manuscript which they discussed. "I not only gave you words of encouragement," he wrote, "but in my printing office put your manuscript into type, an edition of which was struck off in tract form."[4]

During a public career in Boston of barely three years' duration, Stewart's first publication was that essay, a religious and political pamphlet called *Reli-*

Angelina Grimké, age about 39. From a daguerreotype printed in *William Lloyd Garrison: The Story of His Life* (1885). The Boston Athenæum.

gion and the Pure Principles of Morality, the Sure Foundation on Which We Must Build. It was advertised in *The Liberator* of October 8, 1831, as "For sale at this office, a tract addressed to the people of color, by Mrs. Maria W. Steward [*sic*], a respectable colored lady of this city." A collection of religious essays appeared the following year, *Meditations from the Pen of Mrs. Maria W. Stewart* (Boston: Garrison and Knapp, 1832).

Stewart's affiliation with Garrison was to develop into a lifelong friendship. An early supporter of her public lectures, Garrison printed notices of her speaking engagements in *The Liberator,* and often followed up with accounts of those occasions including lengthy excerpts from her remarks. For a crusading editor such as Garrison, Stewart's essays and lectures were not only strong statements in support of his publication's stands, they were also, given her race and gender, news in and of themselves.

On September 21, 1832, Maria Stewart mounted the platform at Boston's Franklin Hall and delivered a lecture before what in that day was known as a "promiscuous" audience, that is to say, one composed of both men and women. On that particular occasion Stewart spoke out against the colonization movement, a controversial scheme to expatriate certain black Americans to West Africa. "Why sit ye here and die?" she demanded, in her characteristically

The Liberator, second masthead, first used March 23, 1838. The Boston Athenæum.

challenging style. "If we say we will go to a foreign land, the famine and pestilence are there, and we shall die. If we sit here, we shall die."[5] Hers was a call to action, urging blacks to stay the course here in America and demand their rights from their white oppressors. "And now that we have enriched their soil and filled their coffers," she declared, "they would drive us to a strange land. But before I go, the bayonet shall pierce me through."[6] At the same time, Stewart called upon blacks to plan wisely for the future in this country by establishing strong, self-sufficient educational and economic institutions within their own communities.

By the early nineteenth century there was already a recognized, if not universally approved-of, community of American women evangelists, preachers, and missionaries, black and white, of various creeds, denominations, and professions of faith. Still, at the time it was considered highly irregular for a woman to put herself forward, as did Stewart, to speak on primarily political matters.

Stewart was a woman of profound religious faith, a pioneer black abolitionist, and a defiant champion of women's rights, and her message was unsparing and urgent. It was intended as a goad to her people to organize against the tyranny of slavery in the South and to resist and defy the restrictions of bigotry in the North.

In her other speeches as well—"An Address, Delivered before the Afric-American Female Intelligence Society of America" (1832); "An Address Delivered at the African Masonic Hall" (1833); and "Farewell Address to Her Friends in the City of Boston" (1833)—Stewart constructed a spirited series of arguments citing feminist precedents drawn from biblical, classical, and historical sources. Likely the first African American to lecture in defense of women's rights, she called on black women to develop their highest intellectual capacities, to enter, without apology, into all spheres of the life of the mind, and to participate in all constructive activities within their communities, from religion and education to politics and business.

A Female Missionary Instructing a Native African. Engraved by J. H. Hills after a painting by Henry Meyer. Used as a frontispiece in volume 1, number 1 of *The Abolitionist* (1833). The Boston Athenæum.

Stewart's earliest intellectual influence was the Bible. It served in great measure to define her public voice, and also to shape her literary style. Affiliated with the First African Baptist Church at the African Meeting House on what was then Belknap Street and is today Smith Court off Joy Street on Beacon Hill, Stewart and her husband were married, in 1826, by the founding minister, the Reverend Thomas Paul. It was following her husband's death, however, that Stewart underwent a conversion experience which led to the assumption of what might be called her secular ministry. Throughout her lectures and her essays, her political analysis is informed by a pervasive religious consciousness, and her intense piety shaped her decidedly evangelical style, on paper or before an audience.

Stewart frequently incorporated biblical passages, occasional stanzas from hymns, and even invocations to prayer into her texts. Her belief was that God and humanity must work in concert toward the day when "knowledge would begin to flow and the chains of slavery and ignorance would melt like wax before the flames."[7] From the start, her religious vision and her sociopolitical agenda were intrinsically bound together, defined one by the other:

> I felt a strong desire . . . to devote the remainder of my days to piety and virtue and now possess that spirit of independence that were I called upon, I would willingly sacrifice my life for the cause of God and my brethren. All the nations of the earth are crying out for liberty and equality. Away, away with tyranny and oppression.[8]

With the publication of her first political pamphlet, Stewart moved into the proscribed realm of masculine authority. The authoritative word, written or spoken, was a longstanding male prerogative in every context in which she existed, social, religious, and political. And it was a prerogative not willingly relinquished. If in the beginning was the Word, Stewart had been taught that it was the patriarchal word of a God who had created Eve as Adam's helpmeet. Stewart, distinct from the vast majority of women of her day, black or white, was a reader, a writer, and a student of texts. Her intellectual hunger led her to a social activism whereby she attempted to reconcile those contradictions, perceived by her as well as by her critics as between her gender and her public, political persona.

Stewart defended her public stance by declaring herself to be a passive instrument in God's hands: "The spirit of God came before me and I spake before many."[9] With such an assertion, she struck a balance between the demands of passivity before divine will and the active role she would urge her sisters to assume in taking ever greater responsibility for their lives and their communities. Her appeal to divine intervention was all the more a protective justification for her views, given that Stewart was a devoted follower of the writings and activities of her contemporary David Walker.

Walker's *Appeal . . . to the Coloured Citizens of the World, but in Particular . . . to Those of the United States of America* (1829) was his manifesto. It was a

The African Meeting House, Smith Court, Boston (about 1832). The Boston Athenæum.

learned, impassioned, and incendiary document advocating the armed uprising of blacks as one option to hasten the end of slavery. There was soon a price on Walker's head, and, following the publication of subsequent editions of his *Appeal,* in 1830 he was found dead under circumstances such that the cause of his death remains a mystery to this day.

Proclaiming her willingness to follow her political mentor in death for the cause of emancipation and human rights, Stewart declared, "Many will suffer for pleading the cause of oppressed Africa . . . and I shall glory in being one of her martyrs. . . . [God] is able to take me to himself, as he did the most noble, fearless and undaunted David Walker."[10]

Endorsing Walker's strategic analysis, Stewart declared in a speech at Boston's African Masonic Hall:

> America has become like the great city of Babylon . . . . She has put [Africans] beneath her feet and she means to keep them there; her right hand supports the reins of government and her left hand the wheel of power, and she is determined not to let go her grasp. But many powerful sons and daughters of Africa will shortly arise, who will put down vice and immorality among us, and declare . . . that they will have their rights; and if refused, I am afraid that they will spread horror and devastation around. I believe that the oppression of injured Africa has come up before the majesty of heaven.[11]

It is against this background of religious, militant activism that Stewart developed her analysis of the role and potential of women in the African American context. From the earliest formulation of her views in the essay "Religion and the Pure Principles of Morality," Stewart singled out the women in her audience by citing what she considered their special responsibilities within the black community. "Ye daughters of Africa, Awake! Arise! . . . distinguish yourselves," she exhorted. "Show forth to the world that ye are endowed with noble and exalted faculties."[12]

Early in her career, Stewart encouraged black women to devote themselves to the advancement of opportunities for their children. She followed the conventional pattern of favoring male offspring over female, and of seeing in young men the hope for the future of the race. She called upon mothers to cultivate their daughters' finer sensibilities such that young men would "fall in love with their virtues." In this she was generally in accord with the professed nineteenth-century American ideal of "True Womanhood," whereby a woman was measured in terms of her "piety, purity, submissiveness and domesticity."[13] Both her personal experience as a servant and her observation of life in Boston's black community (where women's labor as laundresses, seamstresses, domestic workers, and proprietors of boardinghouses, among other occupations, was crucial to keeping their households intact) made clear to Stewart the inherent insult to black women embodied in such definitions of womanhood. Furthermore, Stewart pointed out, no matter how hard-working or virtuous they might be, black women were, by white definition, considered subject to sexual compromise. The

Sculptor Edmonia Lewis (b. 1844), active in Boston during the early 1860s, was among the artists who turned their talents to the cause of abolition. The Boston Athenæum.

pillars of the temple of "True Womanhood" were upheld, as historian Barbara Welter succinctly comments, by the American woman's "frail, white hand."[14]

While testifying to firsthand knowledge through "bitter experience . . . that continual hard labor deadens the energies of the soul, and benumbs the faculties of the mind," Stewart asked her sisters to "strive to excel in good housewifery, knowing that prudence and economy are the road to wealth." This was clearly a position consistent with the traditional sphere of influence allotted to women.

In almost the same breath, however, she boldly redefined black women's domestic situation—as homemakers and as servants—as a status to be transcended. "How long," she asked with incisive eloquence, "shall the fair daughters of Africa be compelled to bury their minds and talents beneath a load of iron pots and kettles?" Calling on black women to pool their economic resources, Stewart conjured the vision of a time not far off when they might "be able to lay the corner stone for the building of a High School, that the higher branches of knowledge might be enjoyed by us."[15]

Such an emphasis on black women's formal education was not rooted solely in concepts of feminine cultural refinement; it was a matter of the greatest political urgency. For Maria Stewart, the pursuit of literacy was a sacred quest at a time when laws passed in the South made it a crime to teach blacks, slave or free, to read or write. Hers is the earliest recorded call to black women to take up what would become one of the greatest traditions of their social and political history, their pioneering works as teachers, founders of schools, and innovators in many areas of black education. Freedom, literacy, and religion were, as Loewenberg and Bogin remark in their study of nineteenth-century African American women, "a trinity of interlacing values." The achievement of literacy was for blacks, slave or free, "a move toward freedom of mind and spirit."[16]

While the building of an institution such as Stewart envisioned was an enterprise greater than Boston's African American women were prepared to undertake at that period, there was established in that city an organization which embraced many of the ideals of unity and self-help which Stewart advocated. The Afric-American Female Intelligence Society of Boston, organized in September of 1831 (some four months prior to the first formal organizational meeting of the New England Anti-Slavery Society in January of 1832), stated its purpose and goals in the preamble to the group's constitution:

> Whereas the subscribers, women of color of the Commonwealth of Massachusetts, actuated by a natural feeling for the welfare of our friends, have thought it fit to associate for the diffusion of knowledge, the suppression of vice and immorality, and for cherishing such virtues as will render us happy and useful to society, sensible of the gross ignorances under which we have too long labored, but trusting by the blessing of God, we shall be able to accomplish the object of our union—we have therefore associated ourselves.[17]

This society, along with others organized throughout the country, drew black women together in mutual assistance associations. By the end of the century they had become an affiliated network of African American women's groups united under the motto "Lifting As We Climb." In an address to the Boston Society, Maria Stewart reiterated her emphasis on unity and radical action as the key to African American advancement. She saw the organized activity of black women in particular as crucial to that achievement:

> The suffering Greeks, their proud souls revolted at the idea of serving a tyrannical nation . . . made a mighty effort and arose; their souls were knit together in the holy bonds of love and union; they were united and came off victorious. Look at the French in the late revolution! . . . "Liberty or Death!" was their cry.[18]

Stewart goes on to cite the Haitians, the Poles, and the Russians as willing to fight, succeed or fail, for their own liberation, and makes a striking comment on the relationship among African Americans, white Americans, and Native Americans: "And even the wild Indians of the forest are more united than our-

Maria Weston Chapman. From a daguerreotype taken about 1847. The Boston Athenæum.

selves. Insult one of them and you insult a thousand. They also have contended for their rights and privileges, and are held in higher repute than are we."[19] She concludes by calling upon her sisters to exert such influence as they possess:

> O woman, woman! Upon you I call; for upon your exertions almost entirely depends whether the rising generation shall be anything more than we have been or not. O woman, woman! your example is powerful, your influence great; it extends over your husbands and your children.[20]

We know that Stewart read the Bible, *The Liberator,* and the works of David Walker. Another source which was to have profound influence on her thought is identified in her writings only as "Sketches of the Fair Sex." This book, the full title of which is *Woman, Sketches of the History, Genius, Disposition, Accomplishments, Employments, Customs, and Importance of the Fair Sex in All Parts of the World Interspersed with Many Singular and Entertaining Anecdotes by a*

Friend of the Sex, was published by one John Adams (1750–1814) in London in 1790. It was likely known to Stewart in an 1807 American edition.

This compendium of fact ("Laws and Customs respecting the Roman Women"), fancy ("Of the First Woman and Her Antediluvian Descendants"), and eccentric inquiry ("A Comparison between the Mahometans and Dutch with Regard to Their Women") was a volume likely to open new horizons for a reader such as Stewart. Adams's evocation of an international sisterhood, diverse, influential, and equally valid in the context of their cultural relativity, would provide an array of potential role models unavailable to most black women in slaveholding America.

Many of the women Stewart spoke of most approvingly early in her career were those wives and mothers who exercised influence upon their husbands and children, and through them perhaps upon the world beyond the home. Over time, presumably inspired in significant measure by her wider reading, those women are replaced in her later work by examples of biblical and historical figures who wield genuine power and authority.

It is in her "Farewell Address to Her Friends in the City of Boston," delivered in September of 1833, that Stewart most provocatively propounds her synthesis of religious, abolitionist, and feminist analyses. In that speech, delivered in the schoolroom of the African Meeting House on Beacon Hill, a building well known as a center of community activity and protest in antebellum black Boston, she set forth her most detailed discussion of black women's rights and responsibilities. In a brilliant rhetorical ploy which curiously portends Sojourner Truth's famous cry, both question and declaration, "Ain't I a Woman?" Stewart forthrightly challenged her audience:

> What if I am a woman; is not the God of ancient times the God of these modern days? Did he not raise up Deborah, to be a mother and a judge in Israel? Did not Queen Esther save the lives of the Jews?[21]

She attacked head-on the oft-quoted biblical prohibition against women making themselves heard. "St. Paul declared that it was a shame for a woman to speak in public. . . . Did St. Paul but know of our wrongs and deprivations, I presume he would make no objections to our pleading in public for our rights."[22]

In the course of developing a commentary upon biblical texts familiar to her audience, albeit from a distinctly female perspective, Stewart introduced her secular agenda, "holy women ministered unto Christ and the apostles; and women of refinement in all ages, more or less, have had a voice in moral, religious and political subjects."[23]

Citing Adams's *Sketches of the Fair Sex,* she speaks generally:

> Among the Greeks, women delivered the Oracles; and the respect the Romans paid to the Sibyls is well known . . . . The prediction of the Egyptian women obtained

much credit at Rome, even under the emperors . . . . The religious spirit which has animated women in all ages . . . has made them by turns martyrs, apostles, warriors, and concluded in making them divines and scholars.[24]

She then elaborates in greater detail as she warms to her theme:

In the 13th century, a young lady of Bologne devoted herself to the study of the Latin language, and of the laws . . . . And to be admitted as an orator she had neither need of indulgence on account of her youth or of her sex. At the age of twenty-six, she took the degree of Doctor of Laws, and began publicly to expound the Institutions of Justinian. At the age of thirty, her great reputation raised her to a chair, where she taught the law to a prodigious concourse of scholars from all nations . . . . And such was the power of her eloquence, that her beauty was only admired when her tongue was silent.[25]

We can only imagine the reaction of those who listened to this show of learning as Stewart proclaimed the lives of those women and offered them up to her audience as models to emulate. In a cascade of rhetorical questions, she insisted upon the possibility of her contemporaries' rising to heights of achievement similar to those attained by the women she discussed. "Why cannot a religious spirit animate us now?" "Why cannot we become divines and scholars?" "What if such women as are here described should rise among our sable race?" All of this was possible, she declared, for

if such women as are here described have once existed, be no longer astonished . . . that God at this eventful period should raise up your own females to strive, by their example, both in public and private, to assist those who are endeavoring to stop the strong current of prejudice that flows against us so profusely at present. No longer ridicule their efforts, it will be counted for sin . . . . For it is not the color of the skin that makes the man or woman, but the principle formed in the soul. Brilliant wit will shine, and come from whence it will; and genius and talent will not hide the brightness of its lustre.[26]

The ridicule about which Stewart speaks was a part of what she frequently described in her essays and speeches as the harsh and often censorious response to her outspokenness emanating even from many of those she hoped would be her allies. Her observations were affirmed in a letter written almost two decades later by the African American historian and integrationist William Cooper Nell to his friend William Lloyd Garrison. "In the perilous years of '33–'35," he recalled, "a colored woman—Mrs. Maria W. Stewart—fired with a holy zeal to speak her sentiments on the improvement of colored Americans, encountered an opposition even from her Boston circle of friends, that would have dampened the ardor of most women."[27]

Feeling herself to be a prophet with little honor in her own land, following her speech at the African Meeting House, Stewart bade farewell to Boston. She moved to New York City, where she continued her political activities and

Sarah Grimké, age about 50. From a daguerreotype printed in *William Lloyd Garrison: The Story of His Life* (1885). The Boston Athenæum.

taught school to earn her living. She joined women's organizations, attended the Women's Anti-Slavery Convention of 1837, and was an active participant in a black women's literary society.

The volume of her collected works, *Productions of Mrs. Maria W. Stewart,* appeared in 1835 and was advertised in Boston and elsewhere for sale along with the major antislavery and human rights publications of the abolitionist movement. Within a year of its appearance, other women, black and white, following the dictates of intellect and conscience, began to emerge from the shadows of reticence and convention and, taking the path she had opened, walked up the steps to the platforms of churches and meeting halls throughout the land to proclaim the social gospel of liberation and justice for all.

NOTES

Sections of this essay appeared in slightly different form in the Introduction to Marilyn Richardson, ed., *Maria W. Stewart, America's First Black Woman Political Writer: Essays and Speeches* (Bloomington: Indiana University Press, 1987).

Original editions of Maria W. Stewart's essays, speeches and religious meditations are virtually all to be found in a few rare book collections, including items at the Boston Athenæum. The work treated in this essay is gathered for the first time in this century in Marilyn Richardson, ed., *Maria W. Stewart, America's First Black Woman Political Writer: Essays and Speeches* (Bloomington: Indiana University Press, 1987). To give the reader practical access to this material, notes citing quotations from Stewart are cross-referenced to page numbers in Richardson. Readers wishing to see the original documents—all of which are printed; there are to date no known manuscript sources of Stewart's work—may wish to consult the "Textual Note" in Richardson, as well as the National Union Catalog.

1. Maria W. Stewart is named as a "regular contributor" in the African Methodist Episcopal Church publication *Repository of Religion and Literature, and of Science and Art,* published in Baltimore, Maryland, from the late 1850s to the mid-1860s. She is listed as Mariah W. Stewart, probably an indication of the proper pronunciation of her given name. Stewart was a resident of Baltimore during much of that period.

2. Maria W. Stewart, "Religion and the Pure Principles of Morality, the Sure Foundation on Which We Must Build" (Boston: Garrison and Knapp, 1831), in Marilyn Richardson, ed., *Maria W. Stewart, America's First Black Woman Political Writer: Essays and Speeches* (Bloomington: Indiana University Press, 1987), pp. 28–29.

3. William Lloyd Garrison to Maria W. Stewart, April 4, 1879. Published in *Meditations from the Pen of Mrs. Maria W. Stewart* (Washington, D.C., 1879). Richardson, p. 89. Garrison was mistaken in his recollection of her marriage. She had been, in fact, recently widowed.

4. Ibid., p. 89.

5. "Lecture Delivered at the Franklin Hall" (1832), in *Productions of Mrs. Maria W. Stewart* (Boston: Friends of Freedom and Virtue, 1835). Richardson, p. 45. Franklin Hall, at 16 Franklin Street in Boston, was the site of regular monthly meetings of the New England Anti-Slavery Society.

6. Ibid., p. 45.

7. Stewart, "Religion and the Pure Principles of Morality." Richardson, p. 31.

8. Ibid., p. 29.

9. "Mrs. Stewart's Farewell Address to Her Friends in the City of Boston" (1833), Richardson, p. 67.

10. Stewart, "Religion and the Pure Principles of Morality," Richardson, p. 30.

11. Stewart, "An Address Delivered at the African Masonic Hall" (1832), in *Productions.* Richardson, p. 63.

12. Stewart, "Religion and the Pure Principles of Morality." Richardson, p. 30.

13. Barbara Welter, *Dimity Convictions: The American Woman in the Nineteenth Century* (Athens: Ohio University Press, 1976), ch. 2, "The Cult of True Womanhood," p. 21.

14. Ibid.

15. Stewart, "Religion and the Pure Principles of Morality." Richardson, p. 37.

16. Bert James Loewenberg and Ruth Bogin, eds., *Black Women in Nineteenth-Century*

American Life: Their Words, Their Thoughts, Their Feelings (University Park: Pennsylvania State University Press, 1976), p. 282.

17. *The Liberator,* January 7, 1832.

18. Stewart, "An Address Delivered before the Afric-American Female Intelligence Society of America," n.d., probably Spring 1832. Richardson, pp. 53–54.

19. Ibid., p. 54.

20. Ibid., p. 55.

21. Stewart, "Mrs. Stewart's Farewell Address to Her Friends in the City of Boston." Richardson, p. 68.

22. Ibid.

23. Ibid.

24. Ibid., p. 69.

25. Ibid., p. 70.

26. Ibid., p. 69–70.

27. William Cooper Nell to William Lloyd Garrison, published in *The Liberator,* March 5, 1852.

CHAPTER TEN

Dorothy Porter Wesley

Integration versus Separatism

William Cooper Nell's Role in the Struggle for Equality

*W*hile Maria Stewart's close ties to Boston and to William Lloyd Garrison were of short duration, William Cooper Nell's remained strong and continued through most of his lifetime. Here Dorothy Porter Wesley reminds us of the great historical significance not only locally, but also statewide and nationally, of the Boston black community's successful struggle to integrate the city's schools.

At the center of this struggle was William Cooper Nell, perhaps the most strident supporter of integration in the nation. Not only did Nell actively battle for integrated classrooms, railway cars, militia companies, and places of public entertainment, Wesley explains, but he also moved one giant step beyond most of his fellow blacks when he made clear his opposition to separate black churches, a view that placed him well outside the black mainstream.

Yet Nell maintained the courage of his convictions, earning the respect of black and white abolitionists alike, most notably William Lloyd Garrison, with whom Nell maintained a close friendship until Nell's death in 1874. But in addition to his strong support for abolition and integration, Nell was an able historian, becoming the first black in the United States to chronicle his people's past, in books such as Services of Colored Americans, in the Wars of 1776 and 1812 *and* The Colored Patriots of the American Revolution. *He was also a talented journalist, his writings appearing in both William Lloyd Garrison's* The Liberator *and Frederick Douglass's* North Star. *As Wesley illustrates, Nell was a man for all seasons whose passionate love for freedom and justice epitomized the antebellum struggle for equality of Boston's black community. If Boston's blacks were unique in terms of what they were able to achieve prior to the Civil War, much of that uniqueness stems from the contributions made by figures such as William Cooper Nell.*

Young Frederick Lewis, a student in the Boston schools, was extremely nervous as he rose to speak at the Southac Street Church before a large gathering organized by Boston's adult black community. There was a festive air about the place that he could feel. Everyone there had come to celebrate the successful culmination of a fifteen-year struggle to integrate the city's schools and to honor the driving force behind that struggle, William Cooper Nell. It was a cold mid-December evening, and there were already signs that winter was coming. But the happy warmth inside the church was felt by everyone, and that warmth helped relax Frederick Lewis a bit as, no longer groping for words, he began to speak.

William Cooper Nell. Courtesy of The Massachusetts Historical Society.

"Long live William C. Nell, the noble champion of Equal School Rights! We hail thee! . . . Our youthful hearts bless thee for thy incessant labors and untiring zeal in our behalf."[1] As Nell listened to these glowing words of praise and looked at the young man before him reciting them, he could not help but recall events just a little more than twenty-five years earlier, when he was thirteen years old and a pupil at the segregated Smith School located in the basement of the Belknap Street Baptist church, events that would shape the rest of his life.

He had been notified during a visit to the school by the mayor of Boston, Harrison Gray Otis, and the chairman of the School Committee, Samuel T. Armstrong, that he was to receive an award for excellence in scholarship. Two

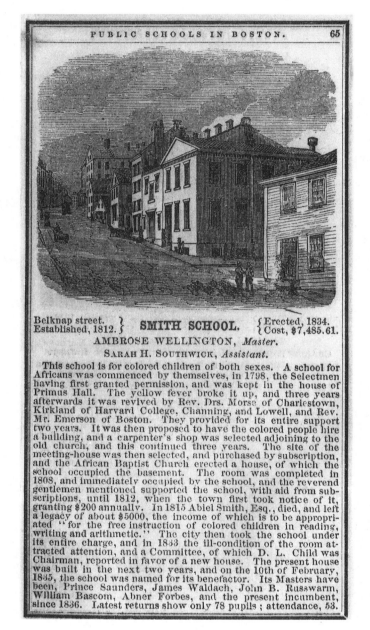

The Abiel Smith School for black students, Beacon Hill, Boston (1849). The Boston Athenæum.

other black students, Nancy Woodson and Charles A. Battiste, were to be given similar prizes. But instead of receiving a silver medal bearing the likeness of Benjamin Franklin, the award given to the best white students in the Boston school system (an award "legitimately our due," Nell recalled), Armstrong presented each of the three black students only with a letter which would allow them to go to James Loring's bookstore, where they would receive a book on Franklin's life.[2]

Moreover, while the white students who won Franklin medals were also invited to a dinner, held at Faneuil Hall, the colored students were excluded. Nell, however, was present at the dinner, having persuaded one of the waiters

The Franklin Medals. Named for Benjamin Franklin, these medals were presented by the Boston School Committee to encourage scholarship in the free schools of Boston. The Boston Athenæum.

FRANKLIN MEDALS.

who was helping serve the meal to allow him to come and help wait on some of the guests. Armstrong was also present, and when he saw Nell he called him over and whispered, "You ought to be here with the other boys." Nell vowed that night "that God helping me, I would do my best to hasten the day when the color of the skin would be no barrier to equal school rights."[3]

William Cooper Nell was born in Boston on December 20, 1816, to William Guion Nell, a tailor by trade from Charleston, South Carolina, and Louisa Nell, a native of Brookline, a town bordering Boston. Early in life he learned about his people's struggle for freedom, particularly from a close friend and associate of his father, David Walker. Nell's father was a charter member of the Massachusetts

General Colored Association, an organization founded in 1826 for the purpose of racial betterment and the abolition of slavery. Almost from birth Nell was instilled with notions of the importance of freedom and racial equality.

However, it was not until 1840 that he, together with William Lloyd Garrison, Wendell Phillips, Francis Jackson, and Henry W. Williams, signed a petition requesting that the city government grant "equal school rights" to Boston's black children. Although it was rejected, in the coming years many similar petitions would be submitted to various authorities in the city and eventually across the state, bearing thousands of signatures demanding the elimination of segregation. Nell was the moving force behind nearly every one of these petition efforts.

But each of these efforts ended in failure, thanks in large part to the intransigence of the Boston School Committee. Nell recalled how all of these defeats had convinced many members of the city's black community that they must now take the logical next step and move their struggle into the courts, leading to one of the most important battles in the history of the Massachusetts judicial system, *Roberts v. the City of Boston* (1849). Benjamin Roberts, a printer, with the seeming support of most of the black community, decided to bring suit against the city in behalf of his five-year-old daughter Sarah, who had been unceremoniously denied the right to attend any of the neighboring schools because she was black, and the public schools of Boston admitted only white pupils. Acting for the plaintiff, Sarah Roberts, and presenting the opening arguments, was Charles Sumner, already a renowned lawyer in Boston, who believed strongly in race equality. He pointed out that there was nothing in the Massachusetts Constitution that permitted segregation in the schools, also noting that Boston was the last place in the Commonwealth that clung to the idea. While these arguments would largely fall on deaf ears, they would have a significant impact on the state legislature when it eventually determined in 1855 to grant equal school rights.

Robert Morris, who in 1847 had become the first black in Massachusetts (and the second in the nation) to pass the bar, was associated with Sumner all through the court proceedings. His very presence, Nell believed, "was a living protest against all exclusive color institutions."[4] But much to their surprise and chagrin, Boston's blacks lost the case, largely as a result of the state supreme court's support for both the total authority of the School Committee in all matters pertaining to education, and the notion of "separate but equal," the idea that separation of the races was acceptable as long as the facilities available to the two races were of equal quality. Ironically, less than half a century later, the United States Supreme Court, in the landmark case of *Plessy v. Ferguson* (1896), would cite the Roberts case as the key precedent in favor of "separate but equal."

Disheartened, but refusing to give up, Boston's blacks now began to turn to statewide petition efforts in order to broaden their base of support. The result was a document with 1,469 signatures, more than 300 collected from every part of Boston by Nell. Lewis Hayden, probably the wealthiest black in Boston and certainly the city's most renowned conductor for the Underground Railroad, collected 87 additional signatures.

Nell's network of support extended into Nantucket and Salem, where school integration battles had been successfully fought during the early 1840s. In Salem Mrs. Charles Lenox Remond, Mrs. George Putnam, and Charlotte Forten, then a student at the Salem Normal School, all joined in the drive for signatures. Friends of the cause from all across the Commonwealth, many of them white, secured some 300 additional names.

The turning point in the struggle came in 1854 when George F. Wiliams, a white lawyer speaking for the Committee on Public Instruction in Boston, submitted a "report . . . recommending equal rights and equal privileges to colored children."[5] Echoing Charles Sumner's earlier arguments, the report stated that "in no other city or town in the Commonwealth is any distinction made in admitting children to the public schools on the ground of color." And while it might surprise the members of the City Council, the body to which the Committee on Public Instruction was answerable, "they shall be informed that no rule or regulation excluding colored children from our schools exists."[6]

In spite of this, the School Committee refused to budge, leading the state legislature to decide that it had to take action. Ironically, legislation calling for the integration of Boston's schools was passed at a time when the Know-Nothings were in control politically in the Commonwealth, a party that professed to despise immigrants, especially Irish Catholics who were settling by the thousands all across the Northeast. Nonetheless, it was the Native American or Know-Nothing party that successfully pushed for passage of the legislation in March 1855 that finally integrated Boston's schools. The bill was signed into law the following month by the Know-Nothing governor of Massachusetts, Henry Gardner.

All of these events were quickly moving through William Cooper Nell's mind as he rose to accept the thanks of his fellow black Bostonians for what he, more than anyone else, had brought to fruition. Most of all Nell emphasized the help he had gotten through the many years of struggle. He praised William Lloyd Garrison and Wendell Phillips, who time and time again had raised their voices before legislative and other committees in support of equal school rights. But Nell also recalled how, at times when the battle was not going well and he felt most frustrated, he was angry that more support was not forthcoming from broader segments of the free black community.

"Would that the nominally free colored Americans were generally active in this great struggle; for then a chord would be struck, which, vibrating through this pro-slavery nation, would hasten the long looked for day of full emancipation." But victory had finally come, and in Boston there had been so many heroes in the struggle for school integration. But "the highest praise . . . must go to the mothers of the boys and girls" who had accompanied him to "various school-houses, to the residences of teachers and committeemen" to be certain that the "laws of the Old Bay State were actually applied in good faith."[7]

It is not surprising that Nell chose to champion the cause of Boston's black children, given the unpleasant memories of his own boyhood experiences in a segregated school and the negative impact this must have had upon so many young black boys and girls. Clearly it was their hopes and aspirations that had inspired and encouraged him in his fight for equal school rights and integration. Finally, when he came to the end of his speech, he told his listeners how on the day before school began, when integration was at last to become a reality, he happened to be looking out his window (he lived on Beacon Hill across the street from the segregated Smith School) when he noticed a young boy jubilantly raise his hand as he passed the school and gleefully say to his friends, "Good bye for ever, colored school! Tomorrow we are like other Boston boys."[8]

Certainly no other person in the city of Boston was as worthy of such a testimonial. At the conclusion of his remarks, the colored citizens of Boston presented Nell with a gold watch, a token of their regard, their esteem, and their thanks. Black abolitionist, novelist, and playwright William Wells Brown perhaps echoed their feelings best when he said, "No man in New England has performed more uncompensated labor for humanity, and especially for his own race than William C. Nell."

Earlier in the evening Wendell Phillips had drawn a laugh from the audience when he explained how pleased he was over the recent victory because through it all "he was tired of having Mr. Nell come to him with his petitions. Mr. Nell could never be found without them. He was glad that he had got rid of him, and was quite willing to take free schools instead." But on a more somber note, Phillips warned that this was no time for feelings of euphoria or self-satisfaction. A battle had been won, but the war was still being fought.

> The best thing learned by these struggles is, how to prepare for another. I should never think of Massachusetts a state fit to live in, until I see one man, at least as black as the ace of spades, a graduate of Harvard. . . . When they have high schools and colleges to which all classes and colors are admitted on equal terms, then I should think Massachusetts was indeed the noblest representative of the principles that planted her. We are greatly indebted to the young man whom we have met to honor; if Nell had not been the nucleus there would have been no cause, if he had not gone up to the legislature, no body would have gone . . . he had been true to his race, true to his idea. . . . [He] invested his capital in the children of his fellow citizens, in the ideas which will prevail hereafter, and when he goes down to the grave, those whom he has benefitted will remember and honour him, as one who trusted in the honesty of Massachusetts, and waited to prove she could be just.[9]

William Lloyd Garrison, who could always count on Nell as one of his staunchest supporters, was enthusiastically applauded when he rose to come to the platform to honor Nell. He told how he had been "familiar with the history of Mr. Nell from an early period in the anti-slavery movement; and he had ever found him true to principle and duty." At last victory had been achieved, "in a good degree through Mr. Nell's indefatigable efforts."[10]

When the legislature put an end to separation in education in 1855, Boston became the first major American city to integrate its school system. The struggle had finally ended. William Cooper Nell had again made it clear to the world that he would never accept segregated institutions of any kind for his people.[11] Nell's early association with Garrison had played a key role in his becoming perhaps America's most strident integrationist. One of his first jobs had been as an errand boy for *The Liberator*. Garrison quickly recognized Nell's abilities and appointed him as apprentice in the newspaper's offices, at a time when "no colored boy could be apprenticed to any trade in any shop where white men worked."[12] During his lifetime Nell worked side by side with many dedicated white persons. He studied in the law office of William I. Bowditch, a prominent attorney and abolitionist, although in the end he decided not to enter the legal profession. When Nell left Boston to go to Rochester to become the publisher of Frederick Douglass's *North Star* in 1847, he lived in the home of abolitionist Amy Kirby Post. And it is not surprising that Nell, the integrationist who refused even to support the idea of separate churches for blacks, frequently attended the Reverend Theodore Parker's Memorial Meeting House in West Roxbury.

Again and again Nell strongly urged blacks to abandon "all separate action," in spite of the fact that his father had been one of the founders of the all-black Massachusetts General Colored Association. Then when Garrison established the New England Anti-Slavery Society in 1831, the black organization decided not to remain a separate racial group, becoming instead an auxiliary of the Garrisonian organization.

During the 1830s Nell helped establish many organizations designed to bring racial self-improvement. These included the Juvenile Garrison Independent Society, the Boston Minor's Exhibition Society, the Young Men's Literary Society, the Boston Mutual Lyceum, the Histrionic Club, and the Adelphic Union Library Association. Membership in these organizations was open to all regardless of race. Regular meetings were held and programs planned to stimulate the mind, develop able public speakers, and build among Boston's black community a broader knowledge of history and literature.

Nell went out of his way to secure the most talented and distinguished lecturers, especially for the Adelphic Union Library Association. Although founded by blacks in 1838, the organization was colorblind. The group purposely moved their meetings from Beacon Hill and rented a hall in a more central location in Boston, inviting all who wanted to attend. Nell was quick to point out with pride how "our lecture room was visited by representatives from all classes of the community."[13]

Nell sensed that if the young blacks of his generation were to bring about full integration, they must first do all they could to attain a high standard of intellectual excellence. It is not surprising, then, that in 1840, the year Nell spearheaded the first petition drive for equal school rights, one of the topics discussed at the Adelphic Union lecture series was the question, "Do separate churches and schools for colored people tend to foster prejudice?"[14]

Nell certainly knew the value of black organizations, particularly in the early days, but he did not believe they should remain exclusively black. In fact, as a representative from Boston, he attended the National Negro Convention held in Buffalo in 1843, but despite seeing only black faces before him, he spoke out against all exclusively black organizations. He could not agree with those delegates who advocated "distinctly separate Negro action," always urging instead that blacks "become part and parcel of the general community."[15]

Nell also strongly opposed the idea of a Colored National Council. From his perspective such a group represented "a step backward in the uphill struggle for equality, and thus hindered rather than advanced the progress of the Negro." As a result Nell labored endlessly "for a union . . . not based on complexional considerations."[16] He even went so far as to encourage the abolition of black churches. Wherever and whenever he could, he advocated integration. Yet he never allowed his strong support for integration to isolate him from participation in efforts to improve the lot of all black people.

When the Freedom Association, a black group, was organized in Boston in 1842 to help protect fugitive slaves, Nell became an active member. But in 1846, when the biracial Vigilance Committee was established for the same purpose, he quickly threw his support to that group because of his longstanding belief that integrated action was always the most effective.

Eventually Nell and Frederick Douglass would cross swords over the issue of integration versus separation. For some time, however, the two remained very close, especially as long as Douglass continued to demonstrate strong support for Garrisonian principles. Nell had even moved from Boston to Rochester in 1847 to serve as publisher of Douglass's *North Star*. But eventually, as a politicized Frederick Douglass began to turn away from the Garrisonian emphasis on moral suasion as the best means to end slavery, and also began to cast doubt upon the Garrisonian view that the Constitution was a proslavery document, the break between Nell and Douglass began to build, and in a very real sense served as a reflection of the growing Garrison-Douglass schism.

As a result, the two men often found themselves in opposition to one another at national convention meetings. They particularly disagreed over the value and viability of all-black schools of manual labor. While Nell tended to doubt the value of separate institutions, no matter what the argument for their existence, Douglass was more willing to accept such institutions if they were the only constructive alternative available at the time. According to Douglass, it was better to have an all-black school than to have no school at all. Nell did not quite agree. "If colored organizations can best promote the cause of Freedom and Humanity," he said, "let them try; fallacious though I deem the theory to be."[17]

Naturally Nell also opposed "Jim Crow" in public transportation. During the early 1840s, as the battle heated up to stop the railroads of Massachusetts from running separate cars for blacks and whites, Nell often made clear his own feelings, in one instance riding with Wendell Phillips on an Eastern Railroad car reserved for whites. Under a great deal of pressure, especially from Boston's

The young Frederick Douglass. Engraving by J. C. Buttre in *Autographs for Freedom* (1854). The Boston Athenæum.

black community, this railroad eliminated its policy of separate cars for blacks in 1843.

Always the activist, Nell frequently showed his anger and frustration at the way segregation was forced upon blacks in places offering entertainment. Nell especially loved the theater. He wrote and directed plays performed by members of the Histrionic Club, one of the many organizations which he had founded. But he was infuriated at the way many of the Boston theaters discriminated against persons of color. Even when they were admitted, and they often were not, it was only to the seats in a segregated section of the hall or auditorium.

On one occasion, in May 1853, Nell's friend Sarah Parker Remond, Charles

HOWARD ATHENÆUM THEATRE, HOWARD STREET.

The *Howard Athenæum Theater*, on Howard street, was built in 1846, on the site of the Miller Tabernacle, and was opened for public performances in the fall of that year: this, at particular times, has been a pet establishment with the public, and with judicious management will maintain its elevated value with the admirers of good histrionic exhibitions.   Messrs, Baker & Eng-

The Howard Athenæum Theatre, Boston, built in 1846. The Boston Athenæum.

sons, and changed its name to that of NATIONAL THEATER; he continued proprietor and manager, until his decease in 1849, and since that time it has been under the control of his talented widow.

Lenox Remond's sister, invited Nell and her sister Caroline to attend a performance of the opera *Don Giovanni* which was being presented at the Howard Athenæum. Sarah had sent a Salem expressman to purchase three tickets for the dress circle. The three arrived at the theater, presented their tickets at the door, and quietly proceeded to their seats. But an usher stopped them. He told them that they could not be admitted to the dress circle, and that either they could have their money returned to them or they had to be seated in the special gallery set aside for people of their color. They rejected both propositions, and after angry words were exchanged, a police officer was called and they were forcibly ejected from the theater.

At one point during the altercation, Sarah Remond was pushed down the stairs and fell. As a result she brought a civil suit for damages amounting to five hundred dollars. Henry Palmer, an agent for the opera company, and Charles Philbrick, the police officer, were charged with assaulting Miss Remond and were found guilty, but they were fined only one dollar by the police court. Before the civil suit was decided, Sarah Remond agreed to accept a small sum on the condition that she, her sister, and Nell be given tickets to the opera for the seats they had originally purchased. Since their object was not to make money from a lawsuit but to assert their rights, Sarah Remond withdrew the suit. A few weeks later, in a letter to a friend, Nell noted triumphantly how "we attended operas afterwards in as good shape as anybody."[18]

But in November of that same year, Nell again had cause for complaint, this time over the poor treatment received by blacks who wanted to attend concerts held at the Music Hall. Apparently blacks had frequently been excluded from these concerts, leading one of them to send a strong letter of complaint. The person in charge of the musical program replied that he had never authorized the exclusion of persons from his concerts on the basis of their color. He then promised the injured parties that they and their friends would have the same facilities as other ticket holders. Still caught up in the struggle to integrate the city's schools, and always intent upon publicizing such incidents, Nell pointedly remarked how he "cherished the hope that Boston may soon conquer her prejudices against an injured and patient race."[19]

Yet even after the school integration victory in 1855, conditions were slow to change. In 1862, at the height of the Civil War, John Swett Rock, a black abolitionist and lawyer, complained that

> no where in the United States is the colored man of talent appreciated. Even in Boston, which has a . . . reputation for being anti-slavery, he has no field for his talents. We are colonized in Boston. . . . We are proscribed in some of the eating houses, many of the hotels, and all the theatres but one. Boston . . . supports . . . two places of amusement, the sole object of which is to caricature us, and to perpetuate the existing prejudices against us. . . . [And] do not our liberal anti-slavery politicians dine . . . at the Parker House. . . . The colored man is proscribed in some of the churches, and . . . this proscription is carried even to the grave-yards. This is Boston—by far the best, or at least the most liberal large city in the United States.[20]

Unfortunately, Nell would have had to agree. Even the earlier victories in the effort to integrate Boston's theaters had seemingly come to nothing.

In April 1866, a year after the Civil War had ended and four months after the Thirteenth Amendment to the Constitution abolishing slavery had been ratified, William Cooper Nell's name headed a list of nine prominent black Bostonians who forwarded a petition to the Senate and House of Representatives complaining that "the Boston Theatre, the Continental Theatre, and the Howard Athenæum . . . are daily excluding proper persons from their exhibitions

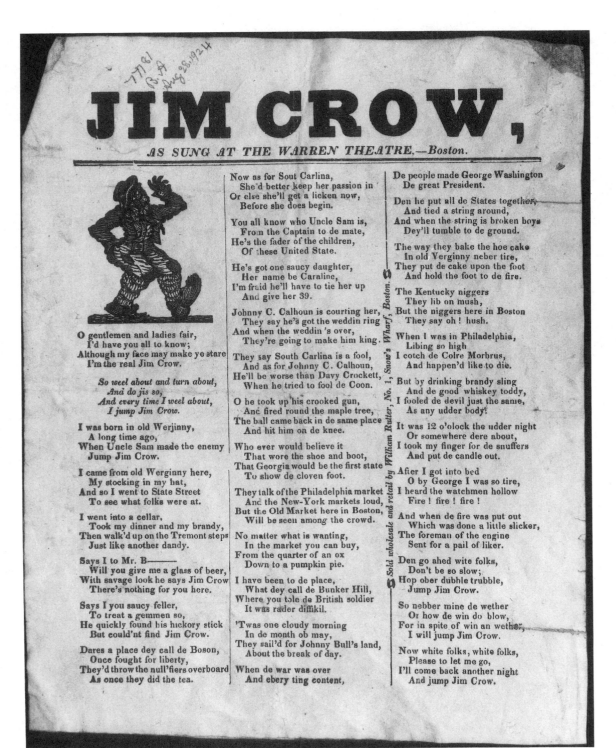

JIM CROW,

AS SUNG AT THE WARREN THEATRE.—Boston.

O gentlemen and ladies fair,
  I'd have you all to know;
Although my face may make ye stare
  I'm the real Jim Crow.

  So weel about and turn about,
    And do jis so,
  And every time I weel about,
    I jump Jim Crow.

I was born in old Werjinny,
  A long time ago,
When Uncle Sam made the enemy
  Jump Jim Crow.

I came from old Werginny here,
  My stocking in my hat,
And so I went to State Street
  To see what folks were at.

I went into a cellar,
  Took my dinner and my brandy,
Then walk'd up on the Tremont steps
  Just like another dandy.

Says I to Mr. B——
  Will you give me a glass of beer,
With savage look he says Jim Crow
  There's nothing for you here.

Says I you saucy feller,
  To treat a gemmen so,
He quickly found his hickory stick
  But could'nt find Jim Crow.

Dares a place dey call de Boson,
  Once fought for liberty,
They'd throw the null'fiers overboard
  As once they did the tea.

Now as for Sout Carlina,
  She'd better keep her passion in
Or else she'll get a licken now,
  Before she does begin.

You all know who Uncle Sam is,
  From the Captain to de mate,
He's the fader of the children,
  Of these United State.

He's got one saucy daughter,
  Her name be Caraline,
I'm fraid he'll have to tie her up
  And give her 39.

Johnny C. Calhoun is courting her,
  They say he's got the weddin ring
And when the weddin 's over,
  They're going to make him king.

They say South Carlina is a fool,
  And as for Johnny C. Calhoun,
He'll be worse than Davy Crockett,
  When he tried to fool de Coon.

O he took up his crooked gun,
  And fired round the maple tree,
The ball came back in de same place
  And hit him on de knee.

Who ever would believe it
  That wore the shoe and boot,
That Georgia would be the first state
  To show de cloven foot.

They talk of the Philadelphia market
  And the New-York markets loud,
But the Old Market here in Boston,
  Will be seen among the crowd.

No matter what is wanting,
  In the market you can buy,
From the quarter of an ox
  Down to a pumpkin pie.

I have been to de place,
  What dey call de Bunker Hill,
Where you tole de British soldier
  It was rader diffikil.

'Twas one cloudy morning
  In de month ob may,
They sail'd for Johnny Bull's land,
  About the break of day.

When de war was over
  And ebery ting content,

De people made George Washington
  De great President.

Den he put all de States together,
  And tied a string around,
And when the string is broken boys
  Dey'll tumble to de ground.

The way they bake the hoe cake
  In old Verginny neber tire,
They put de cake upon the foot
  And hold the foot to de fire.

The Kentucky niggers
  They lib on mush,
But the niggers here in Boston
  They say oh ! hush.

When I was in Philadelphia,
  Libing so high
I cotch de Colre Morbrus,
  And happen'd like to die.

But by drinking brandy sling
  And de good whiskey toddy,
I fooled de devil just the same,
  As any udder body.

It was 12 o'olock the udder night
  Or somewhere dere about,
I took my finger for de snuffers
  And put de candle out.

After I got into bed
  O by George I was so tire,
I heard the watchmen hollow
  Fire ! fire ! fire !

And when de fire was put out
  Which was done a little slicker,
The foreman of the engine
  Sent for a pail of liker.

Den go ahed wite folks,
  Don't be so slow;
Hop ober dubble trubble,
  Jump Jim Crow.

So nebber mine de wether
  Or how de win do blow,
For in spite of win an wether,
  I will jump Jim Crow.

Now white folks, white folks,
  Please to let me go,
I'll come back another night
  And jump Jim Crow.

Sold wholesale and retail by William Rutter, No. 1, Snow's Wharf, Boston.

"Jim Crow," a song sheet broadside from the Warren Theatre, Boston. The Boston Athenæum.

and invidiously discriminating against them solely on account of their color." The petitioners demanded that "any theatre or place of public amusement that shall exclude colored persons or discriminate against them" be required to forfeit its license.[21] Clearly little had changed.

John Rock's 1862 attack had included a vehement complaint that blacks still had not been allowed to participate on the Union side in the Civil War. Rock, together with Robert Morris, William Watkins, and Nell, had for many years been fighting against the Massachusetts Militia Law that allowed only whites to serve. As early as 1853, Nell had drafted two petitions to the state legislature arguing for black participation. "Just erase the word white," he had written, so that blacks might finally be enrolled.[22]

In 1851 Nell had published his *Services of Colored Americans, in the Wars of 1776 and 1812.* Simultaneously, Nell sent the first of several petitions to the Massachusetts legislature requesting an appropriation of one hundred dollars for the erection of a monument to Crispus Attucks, the only black among the five men killed in the 1770 Boston Massacre, and who some felt had been the first martyr of the American Revolution. But the committee to which the petition had been referred reported that it could see nothing in the circumstances attending Attucks's death that would justify the legislature's appropriating money to erect a monument in his memory.[23]

"The rejection of this petition," said Nell, "was to be expected if we accept the axiom that a colored man never gets justice in the United States, except by mistake."[24] It was not until 1888, thirty-seven years later, that a memorial statue to Crispus Attucks was finally completed. Although Nell did not live to see this, he was present on March 5, 1858, when another of his goals became a reality, the institution by the city of a Crispus Attucks Day celebration. The event was held in Faneuil Hall and included speeches, music, and an exhibition of relics, documents, and emblems, a few "living mementos of Revolutionary historic interest."[25] Nell was able to continue these annual celebrations for several years.

At the same time that Nell was initiating his unsuccessful petition drive in behalf of a monument to Attucks, he was also beginning to raise the issue of the injustice inherent in the fact that only free white persons were eligible for positions in the federal government. This policy did not change until 1861, when John Gorham Palfrey, an abolitionist, was appointed postmaster of Boston. Palfrey courageously chose to ignore the racial restrictions that were prevalent at the time by appointing Nell as one of the clerks in the postal department. As a result, Nell became the first black to hold a post in the federal government.[26]

On April 30, 1867, Nell and five other past and present employees in the Boston Post Office "who by complexion are identified with the class so long proscribed in the United States" wrote to John Palfrey to thank him for granting them appointments in the post office. "This act of justice on your part," they wrote, "was in glorious keeping with your manumission of a number of slaves—yours by inheritance. . . . The gratitude inspired by your noble record will live perennially in the hearts of your obedient servants."[27]

Nell continued to hold his position in the post office until his death on May 25, 1874. He was survived by his wife and two sons. Funeral services were held in Parker Memorial Church three days later. William Wells Brown, Wendell Phillips, and William Lloyd Garrison were among the prominent individuals who presented eulogies, as did poet Elijah William Smith, who had written the following for the occasion:

> Another soldier gone!
> One of the Spartan band
> Who fought the fight
> With weapons bright
> When slavery ruled the land. . . .
>
> Dear, faithful friend, farewell!
> Our gratitude is there
> The prayers we breathe
> Thy name shall wreathe
> With memory's flowers divine.[28]

Nell was buried in the Forest Hills Cemetery, not far from where his close friend William Lloyd Garrison, who died May 24, 1879, would also be interred, nearly five years to the day later. But it was not until September 18, 1989, that a monument was finally placed at Nell's gravesite.[29]

Throughout his life, Nell fought segregation. No other man of his time served on so many committees or circulated so many petitions in the cause of freedom. In addition, he lectured on issues related to antislavery and equal rights while carrying on the business of the Anti-Slavery Office at 21 Cornhill. A capable journalist, he contributed many articles, announcements, and letters to Garrison's *Liberator,* Douglass's *North Star,* and other newspapers.

Nell was also the person, no matter what his position in the organization, who always took pains to notify the public regularly about where and when meetings were to be held. He also submitted important information about the progress being made by blacks in the various apprenticeships that prepared them for careers, the opening of new business ventures, and regarding scholastic attainments. Throughout his lifetime, Nell continually did all he possibly could to prove that "prejudice against color is not invincible."[30]

Many would argue that no person in Boston is more worthy of a tribute for service to humanity than William Cooper Nell, and many also continue to wonder why the city of Boston that he served so well in the cause of racial justice, especially during the struggle for "equal school rights," has never named a school building in his honor. By the time of his death, Nell had made his mark—as abolitionist, as historian, as integrationist, and as humanitarian. He as much as anyone continually drove Boston's antebellum black community forward.

William Lloyd Garrison had driven the point home during the early years of

Arms of the United States of North America. From *The Legion of Liberty and Force of Truth* (1857). The Boston Athenæum.

the struggle when he had urged Boston's blacks "to cooperate like a band of brothers and depend upon themselves to raise their own character."[31] That sentiment became a creed for Nell and for so many other members of the black community during the years prior to the Civil War, as they propelled themselves rapidly and hopefully along a path that would lead to a full realization of the long-sought goals of freedom and equality.

NOTES

1. *Triumph of Equal School Rights in Boston: Proceedings of the Presentation Meeting of Colored Citizens of Boston, Dec. 17, 1855* . . . (Boston: R. F. Wallcut, 1856), pp. 2, 3; "Meeting of Colored Citizens of Boston," *National Anti-Slavery Standard,* January 5, 1856, p. 1.

2. "Address of Mr. Nell," in *Triumph of Equal School Rights in Boston,* p. 5.

3. William C. Nell, "Equal School Rights," *The Liberator*, April 7, 1854, p. 55.

4. *Triumph of Equal School Rights in Boston*, p. 7.

5. Ibid., p. 6; John Daniels, *In Freedom's Birthplace: A Study of the Boston Negroes* (Boston: Houghton Mifflin, 1914), p. 448.

6. *The Liberator*, August 18, 1854, p. 132.

7. *Triumph of Equal School Rights in Boston*, p. 9.

8. *The Liberator*, December 28, 1855, p. 207.

9. William Wells Brown, *The Black Man, His Antecedents, His Genius and His Achievements* (New York: Thomas Hamilton, 1863), p. 238.

10. *Triumph of Equal School Rights in Boston*, p. 16.

11. Ibid., pp. 18, 19, 20.

12. James Oliver Horton and Lois E. Horton, *Black Bostonians: Family Life and Community Struggle in the Antebellum North* (New York: Holmes and Meier, 1979), p. 58.

13. William C. Nell, "Adelphic Lectures," *The Liberator*, February 5, 1847; William C. Nell, "Adelphic Lecture, Delivered by Wendell Phillips" *The Liberator*, March 19, 1847, p. 47; "The Adelphic Union in Boston," *National Anti-Slavery Standard* 5 (November 28, 1844): 103; William C. Nell, *Colored Patriots of the American Revolution* (Boston: Robert F. Wallcut, 1855), pp. 113–14.

14. "Do Separate Churches and Schools for Colored People Tend to Foster Prejudices?" *The Liberator*, January 8, 1841, p. 7; Nell, *Colored Patriots of the American Revolution*, pp. 359–60.

15. William C. Nell, "Letter to Wendell Phillips, August 4, 1843"; National Negro Convention, 1843, *Minutes of the National Convention of Colored Citizens; Held at Buffalo, on the 15th, 16th, 17th, 18th and 19th of August 1843, For the Purpose of Considering Their Moral and Political Condition as American Citizens* (New York: Piercy and Reed Printers, 1843), pp. 30–36; William C. Nell, "State Council," *The Liberator*, January 25, 1854, p. 15.

16. William C. Nell, "Colored National Council," *The Liberator*, July 27, 1855, p. 120.

17. William C. Nell to George Downing, September 12, 1854.

18. *Salem Gazette*, May 17, 1853; *Frederick Douglass' Paper* 6 (June 10, 1853): 3; William C. Nell to Amy Post, May 25, 1853; the playbill for *Don Giovanni* included the notice "No Colored People Admitted to Any Part of the House, Except Gallery." The Howard Athenæum, located on the south side of Howard Street, opened as a theater on October 13, 1845. A serious fire occurred on February 25, 1846. The rebuilt building was reopened October 5, 1846. Playbills for performances as late as 1858 contained the special notice admitting colored persons only to the gallery.

19. William C. Nell, "Monsieur Jullien's Concerts," *The Liberator*, December 16, 1853, p. 197. On November 23, 1854, Nell wrote to Amy Post: "I flatter myself as having been somewhat instrumental in breaking down the proscription of colour at the New Boston Theatre—a beautiful, spacious and costly temple of the drama." Nell wrote a letter to the manager of the theater before the season commenced. The manager then decided to admit parties of blacks to seats of their choice. Several cases against segregation in Boston halls of entertainment occurred. See "Has a Negro the Right to Sit in the Family Circle of a Theatre?" (*The Plaintiff McCrea*), *National Anti-Slavery Standard* 17 (March 21, 1857): 2; "Justice vs. Colorphobia" (*Burton vs. Shoff*), *The Liberator*, November 16, 1860; Case of Molyneau Hewlett, *Commonwealth of Massachusetts House of Representatives, Doc. 356, April 1866*.

20. *The Liberator*, August 15, 1862, p. 131.

21. *Petition of William C. Nell and Others to the Honorable Senate and House of Representatives of the Commonwealth of Massachusetts*, no. 356, 1866 (Boston, 1866), pp. 2–3.

22. Robert P. Smith, "William Cooper Nell: Crusading Black Abolitionist," *Journal of Negro History* 55 (July 1970): 189; *The Liberator*, August 5, 1853; Nell, *Colored Patriots of the American Revolution*, pp. 103, 107–11; William C. Nell, "Letter from Boston, March 31, 1860," *Weekly Anglo-African*, April 14, 1860; William C. Nell, "Equal

Rights of Colored Citizens," *The Liberator*, May 24, 1861; William C. Nell, "Equal Militia Rights," *The Liberator*, June 14, 1861.

23. *Petition of William C. Nell and Others to the House of Representatives, March 1851, Commonwealth of Massachusetts, House of Representatives, Bill No. 100* (Boston, 1851), pp. 1–5.

24. Smith, "William Cooper Nell," p. 188.

25. William C. Nell, "Commemorative Meeting in Faneuil Hall," *The Liberator*, February 26, 1858, p. 35; "The Boston Massacre, March 5, 1770. Commemorative Festival in Faneuil Hall, March 6, 1858," pp. 42–43.

26. Smith, "William Cooper Nell," p. 194; William C. Nell and James Monroe Trotter to Charles Sumner, February 14, 1869.

27. William C. Nell and others to John G. Palfrey, April 10, 1867.

28. Pauline E. Hopkins, "Elijah William Smith: A Colored Poet of Early Days," *The Colored American Magazine* 6 (December 1902): 100.

29. *The Boston Daily Globe*, May 26, 1874, p. 8; *San Francisco Elevator*, June 27, 1874, p. 3; *Harvard Gazette*, October 20, 1989.

30. William C. Nell, "Improvement of Colored People," *The Liberator*, August 24, 1855, p. 134.

31. *The Liberator*, May 19, 1832, p. 77.

✧ APPENDIXES

APPENDIX A

Black Women in Boston Who Were Known Heads of
Households Prior to the Civil War

Nancy Alexander, 25 Belknap St. (rear)
Mrs. Allen, 5 Belknap St.
Mary Armstead, Belknap St.
Sarah Arnable, 92 Cambridge St.
Catherine Barbadoes, 28 Belknap St.
Chloe Barbadoes, Belknap St.
Rebecca Barbadoes, 15 West Centre St.
Mary Bates (address unknown)
Betsey Beckit, 29 Belknap St.
Phebe Bradshaw, 21 Garden St.
Mary Ann Brooks, Southac St.
Lucy Brown, Belknap St.
Mary Brown, Botolph St.
Sarah Burr, 16 Belknap St.
Susan Burrick, Southac St.
Eliza Burrows, 6 May St.
Alice Bush, 31 South Russell St.
Elizabeth Camel, Belknap St.
Mrs. D. L. Carteaux, 110 Cambridge St.
Harriet Clark, West Centre St.
Jane Clark, Southac St.
Anna Clary, 1 Wilberforce
Hannah Cosey, 10 May St. (rear)
Sarah Crouse, Botolph St.
Ruth Curtis, Southac St.
Sarah Cutler, South May St.
Chloe Dalton, Belknap St.
Grace Anne Dean, West Centre St.
Nancy Dorsey, Southac St.
Mrs. Thomas T. Duffee, 7 West Centre
  St.
Mary A. Eastman, 15 West Centre St.
Mary Elisburg, 25 Belknap St. (rear)
Elizabeth Fisher, Botolph St.
Mary Fowler, Belknap St.
Tamer Francis, West Cedar St. (rear)
Polly Furgson, May St.
Nancy Gambo, 12 West Centre St.
Eliza A. Gardner, 20 N. Anderson St.
Nancy Gardner (address unknown)
Sylvia Garish, May St.
Susan Garrison, 26 Belknap St.
Judy George, 14 Belknap St.

Emma Gray, 24 Phillips St.
Lucy Gray, Southac St.
Mrs. Gray, Alley
Lucy Green, Southac St.
Sylvia Hall, May St.
Betsey E. Hallem, 10 May St.
Lucy Heminway, 12 West Centre St.
Catherine Henson, 17 Belknap St.
Mary Henson, 9 West Centre St.
Nancy Herrick, Botolph St.
Frances Hicks, Southac St.
Affice Hondless, Southac St.
Phoebe Hoyt, Smith Place
Anne Jackson, May St.
Chloe Jackson, 15 Belknap St.
Hannah Jackson, West Centre St.
Eunice Jefferson, Belknap St.
Jane Jefferson, Belknap St.
Elizabeth Johnson, 15 West Centre St.
Mrs. Phoebe Johnson, 9 West Centre St.
Sylvia Jonas, Belknap St.
Hannah Jones, Belknap St.
Mrs. Aaron Joseph, Wilberforce Place
Dolly Kelson, West Centre St.
Margaret Key, Botolph St.
Sarah Krouse, Botolph St.
Margaret Lamnos, 21 Belknap St.
Diana Lewis, 11 Belknap St.
Catherine Lindsey, 12 West Centre St.
Mrs. Maldny, Belknap St.
Lucy Montgomery, George St.
Patience Morey, May St.
Esther Murray, 12 West Centre St.
Catherine Paul, 26 George St.
Margaret Pennington, 2 Smith Court
Lydia Porter, Belknap St.
Lydia Potter, 4 Grove St.
Paschal Randolph, 18 Irving St.
Mary Rice, Southac St.
Chloe Russell, Belknap St.
Sarah Russell, Southac St.
Betsey St. Pierre, May St.
Margaret Scarlett, 11 S. May St.

Letecia Scott, Grove St. near Southac
Mrs. Benjamin Shepherd, 10 West Cedar St.
Lucy Sherod, Alley
Mrs. A. Skeen, 6 May St.
Chloe Smith, Belknap St.
Phoebe Smith, 27 Belknap St.
Lenea Stewart, South Russell St.

Mary Stockbridge, 92 Cambridge St.
Theresa Turner, 17 Belknap St.
Maria Weeks, Southac St.
Mary Williams, Southac St.
Sarah Williams, 10 May St.
Mrs. William Wright, 2 Botolph St.
Hannah Young, Southac St.

APPENDIX B

Black Persons of Prominence Who Resided in Boston's West End
Section Prior to the Civil War

Solomon Alexander, 2 Belknap St.
John B. Bailey, 16 Blossom Court
Edward B. Bannister, 18 Grove St.
James G. Barbadoes
Andrew T. Bell, 24 May St.
Rev. Jehiel C. Beman, 13 N. Grove St.
Aaron A. Bradley, 88 Southac St.
Lemuel Burr, 3 Southac St.
Eli Caesar, 1 Botolph St.
Amos Clark, 90 Cambridge St.
Anthony Clark, 82 Southac St.
George Clark, 27 Belknap St. (rear)
Jonas W. Clark, 20 Grove St.
Joseph F. Clark, 4 Southac St.
James P. Clary, 11 Southac St.
John P. Coburn, 2 Southac St.
Thomas Cole, Southac Court
Henry Cook, 36 Southac St.
Samuel Cook, 53 Myrtle St.
John B. Cutler, Southac Court
Stephen Dalton, 20 Belknap St.
Thomas Dalton, 29 S. Russell St.
John Davis, 54 Charles St.
Dr. John V. De Grasse, 31 Charles St.
Mark R. DeMortie, 136 Myrtle St.
Robert Fallen, 6 Southac St.
John J. Fatal, 16 N. Grove St.
Joseph J. Fatal, 2 Southac St.
Rev. Thomas Freeman, 86 Southac St.
Peter Gambol, 14 Belknap St.
Caesar Gardner, 9 Belknap St.
Joseph H. Glover, 57 West Cedar St.
Rev. Leonard A. Grimes, 28 Grove St.
Primus Hall, George and May Sts.
Lewis Hayden, 66 Southac St.
William Henry, 29 Belknap St. (rear)
Thomas Henson, 72 Middlesex St.
John T. Hilton, 12 Belknap St.
Peter Howard, 82 Cambridge St. (shop)
Henry Johnson, 15 West Centre St.
William Johnson, 13 Southac St.

William Junier, 6 Southac St.
Edward B. Lawton, 48 Bridge St.
Barzillai Lew, 2 Holden Place
Joel W. Lewis, 4 Southac St.
John H. Lewis, 52 Southac St.
Joseph Lewis, 25 Belknap St. (rear)
Julian McCrae, Botolph and Southac Sts.
John Marshall, 25 Belknap St. (rear)
Rev. John Sella Martin, 170 Cambridge St.
William C. Nell, Smith Court
William G. Nell, Bridge St.
Rev. Thomas Paul, 26 George St.
William T. Powell, 62 Joy St.
George Putnam, 16 Belknap St.
Peter Randolph, 20 Botolph St.
Benjamin F. Roberts, 2 Barton St.
Charles H. Roberts, 36 Southac St.
John E. Scarlett, Smith Court
John J. Smith, 11 Anderson St.
Peter Smith, 9 West Cedar St.
Isaac Snowden, 5 Belknap St.
Rev. Samuel Snowden, 5 Southac St.
George S. Spywood, 4 Southac St.
James Stewart, 25 Belknap St.
Patent Stewart, 156 Cambridge St.
John R. Taylor, 5 Southac St.
George Teamoh, 8 Grove St.
Thomas Teamoh, 5 Southac St.
John Thompson, 19 May St.
George Tolliver, 71 Cambridge St.
David Walker, Bridge St.
George Washington, 5 Smith Court
Henry Watson, 2 Wilberforce Place
Benjamin Weeden, 5 Smith Court
Henry Weeden, Belknap St. (rear)
Henry H. White, 9 Garden St.
Henry Wilson, 23 Belknap St. (rear)
John Wright, 6 Southac St.
William Wright, 9 Southac St. (rear)

APPENDIX C

Partial List of Boston's Black Voters, Election of 1864

George I. Albert, 65 Southac St.
John Anderson, 2 Joy St.
John Anderson, 4 James Place
John Austin, 13 Garden St.
John Bailey, 50 Southac St. (rear)
G. F. Bamdien, 168 Cambridge St.
Archie Barlow, 6 Southac St.
Wesley Bishop, 52 Southac St.
Alfred R. D. Blain, 36 Southac St.
Louis H. Blair, 73 Joy St.
William H. Blair, 73 Joy St.
Daniel Blue, 88 Southac St.
Felix Boss, 2 Sears Place
Jacob Bracey, 19 Garden St.
Charles O. Brady, 81 Joy St.
Martin W. Brooks, 10 Anderson St.
David Brown, 5 Anderson St.
John Brown, 44 Southac St.
John S. Brown, 8 Anderson Place
Daniel Butcher, 3 Revere St.
Joseph N. Butler, 8 Southac St.
Isaac Cannon, 3 Southac St.
Henry Carney, 72 Joy St.
Samuel Carroll, 1 James Place
Titus Church, 6 Southac St.
Richard Churwell, 136 Myrtle St.
Roderick Cooley, 64 Southac St.
Charles Copeland, 18 Grove St.
John E. Cotton, 61 Joy St.
James Cox, 10 Southac Place
Milton Crew, 4 Belknap Place
Milton H. Dandridge, 22 Southac St.
Daniel Davis, 60 Southac St.
Jacob Davis, Wilberforce Place
James Davis, 30 Southac St.
Tobey G. Davis, 3 Belknap St.
Edward C. Day, 154 Cambridge St.
George De Coker, 40 Southac St.
William H. Derby, 94 Revere St.
Henry DeShields, 65 Southac St.
John Dorsey, 48 Southac St.
Henry C. Duffin, 6 Southac St.
David Easton, 80 Southac St.
William Elisha, 42 Southac St.
George Ellis, 4 Belknap St.
John W. Ellis, 40 Irving St.
Frederick Fatal, 88 Southac St.
James W. Flint, 53 Revere St.
Cyrus Foster, 4 Southac St.
Charles Fountaine, 8 Southac St.
Edward Francis, 43 Garden St.
Edward Franklin, 43 Garden St.
Isaac Franklin, 19 Rochester St.

John G. Franklin, 7 Sears Place
Barzillai Freeman, 71 Joy St.
Frank Freeman, 9 Southac St.
Osmone Freeman, 71 Joy St.
Peter L. Freeman, 71 Joy St.
Rufus Freeman, 36 Southac St.
Richard Gardner, 42 Grove St.
George Garnett, 15 Southac St.
Lewis Gaul, 8 Anderson St.
Rufus Gilbert, 72 Joy St.
William Gilbert, Wilberforce Place
Benjamin H. Glover, 11 Anderson St.
John Grant, 63 Revere St.
Francis P. Gray, 24 Southac St.
Charles H. Greeland, 24 Southac St.
John A. Grimes, 28 Grove St.
James Hamilton, 29 Anderson St.
A. T. Hardy, 7 Anderson St.
William Hare, 18 Grove St.
Henry Harris, 59 Joy St.
Prince Harris, 22 Southac St.
William Harvey, 15 Southac St.
George W. Hawkins, 28 Southac St.
Joseph Hayden, 66 Southac St.
Lewis Hayden, 66 Southac St.
John I. Hector, 4 Stanhope Place
Caleb Henry, 2 Garden St.
Moses Hillman, 2 Southac St.
Aaron Hogan, 3 Southac St.
Peter Holmes, 2 Smith Court
Edward Hopson, 1 Wilberforce
Lawrence Hosea, 8 Grove St.
William H. Hughes, 110 Cambridge St.
Charles Jackson, 52 Southac St.
William Jackson, 3 Sears Place
William Jackson, 6 Belknap St.
William H. Jackson, 2 Southac St.
Stephen Jacobs, 6 Southac St.
John H. Jenkins, 29 Southac St.
Archelaus Johnson, 8 Southac St.
David Johnson, 52 Joy St.
Gabriel Johnson, 52 Joy St.
John H. Johnson, 1 Belknap St.
Stephen Johnson, 63 Southac St.
Edmund Jones, 65 Southac St.
William Jones, 8 Southac St.
Jacob Lew, 61 Joy St.
Jimiri Lew, 3 James Place
Nathaniel Lew, 3 James Place
Henry Livingston, 3 Derne St.
John Logan, 13 Garden St.
William Logan, 6 Grove St.
Marcus McBridge, 2 Garden St.

James McKenzie, 5 Cambridge St.

Henry Madden, 52 Southac St.

William Marick, 62 Southac St.

George Mason, 2 Garden St.

Richard Miles, 63 Southac St.

Henry Mitchell, 53 Joy St.

Francis Moore, 7 Smith Court

Jacob I. Moore, 7 Smith Court

Henry Morris, 40 Southac St. (rear)

Edwin Nahar, 18 Grove St.

Samuel Napier, 1 Strong Place

William C. Nell, 20 Grove St.

Henry Nichols, 73 Southac St.

Benjamin Northrup, 150 Russell St.

Hosea Peters, 2 Belknap St.

Coffin Pitts, 67 Joy St.

Edward Posey, 2 Joy St.

George W. Potter, 69 Joy St.

William T. Powell, 62 Joy St.

James W. Prittow, 10 Sears Place

William H. Purnell, 73 Joy St.

John Read, 1 Wilberforce Place

Macy Riggs, 6 Wilberforce Place

William Riley, 70 Southac St.

Ralph Roberts, 5 Lawrence Place

John Robertson, 8 Derne St.

Burrill Robinson, 8 Southac St.

John A. Robinson, 11 Anderson St.

William Robinson, 8 Southac St.

John S. Rock, 83 Southac St.

George A. Rue, 22 Southac St.

George L. Ruffin, 18 Grove St.

James L. Ruffin, 18 Grove St.

John L. Ruffin, 18 Grove St.

Edward C. Ruhler, 9 Sears Place

William Rumsley, Smith Court

James Saunders, 11 Southac St.

James Scott, 3 Smith Court

James Scott, 86 Southac St.

R. T. Scott, 3 Anderson St.

Carter Selden, 1 Southac Place

Samuel H. Shipley, 6 Sears Place

William H. Simpson, 66 Southac St.

Stephen Small, 172 Cambridge St.

William Small, 2 Garden St.

Burrill Smith, 169 Cambridge St.

Charles Smith, 2 Grove St.

Elijah W. Smith, Jr., 1 Southac St.

Frank Smith, 8 Grove St.

James Smith, 32 Garden St.

John Smith, 2 Thompson St.

John H. Smith, 62 Southac St.

Robert Stevens, 28 Southac St. (rear)

James T. Sydney, 61 Southac St.

Thomas Taylor, 3 Smith Court

John W. Teamoh, 5 Southac St.

Henry L. W. Thacker, 5 Southac St.

Forrister Thompson, 40 Southac St.

Peter Thompson, 28 Southac St.

Dudley Tidd, 78 Southac St.

James Titus, 31 Anderson St.

George H. Turner, 48 Southac St.

✧ BIBLIOGRAPHY

Selected Material Related to the Abolition Movement in Boston,
on Exhibit at the Boston Athenæum

The Abolitionist; or, Record of the New England Anti-Slavery Society. Boston: Garrison and
    Knapp, 1833.

Anti-Slavery Alphabet. Philadelphia: Printed for the Anti-Slavery Fair, 1847.

Anti-Slavery Record. Vol. 1. New York: Published for the American Anti-Slavery Society,
    1835.

The Association of Franklin Medal Scholars. Boston: George C. Rand and Avery, 1858.

Austin, James T. *Remarks on Dr. Channing's "Slavery."* Boston: Russell, Shattuck and
    Co. [etc.], 1835.

Bassett, William. *Letter to a Member of the Society of Friends, in Reply to Objections against
    Joining Anti-Slavery Societies.* Boston: Isaac Knapp, 1837.

Bearse, Austin. *Reminiscences of Fugitive Slave Law Days in Boston.* Boston: Warren Rich-
    ardson, 1880.

Beck, John. *The Doctrine of Perpetual Bondage, Reconciled with the Infinite Justice of God.*
    Savannah, Ga.: Published for the Author, 1800.

Beecher, Catherine E. *An Essay on Slavery and Abolitionism.* Philadelphia: Henry Perkins
    [etc.], 1837.

Boston Female Anti-Slavery Society. *Annual Report for 1835.* Boston, 1836.

Boston Mob of "Gentlemen of Property and Standing." *Proceedings of the Anti-Slavery
    Society Meeting . . . on the Twentieth Anniversary of the Mob of October 21, 1835.*
    Boston: R. F. Wallcut, 1855.

The Boston Slave Riot and the Trial of Anthony Burns. Boston, 1854.

Bourne, George. *Picture of Slavery in the United States of America.* Middleton, Conn.:
    Edwin Hunt, 1834.

Bowditch, William Ingersoll. *The Rendition of Anthony Burns.* Boston: Robert F.
    Wallcut, 1854.

Brown, Henry "Box." *Narrative of Henry Box Brown, Who Escaped from Slavery Enclosed
    in a Box.* Boston: Brown and Stearns, 1849.

Brown, William Wells. *The Anti-Slavery Harp, for Anti-Slavery Meetings.* Boston: Bela
    Marsh, 1851.

———. *A Description of . . . Original Panoramic Views of the Scenes in the Life of an Amer-
    ican Slave.* London: Charles Gilpin [1849].

———. *Memoir.* Boston: At the Anti-Slavery Office, 1859.

———. *Narrative of William Wells Brown, Fugitive Slave.* Boston: At the Anti-Slavery
    Office, 1847.

Case of the Slave Child Med. Boston: Isaac Knapp, 1836.

Channing, William Ellery. *The Duty of the Free States.* Boston: William Crosby, 1842.

———. *Emancipation.* Boston: E. P. Peabody, 1840.

———. *A Letter to the Abolitionists.* Boston: Isaac Knapp, 1837.

———. *Slavery.* Boston: James Munroe, 1835.

Chapman, Maria Weston. *How Can I Help Abolish Slavery? or, Counsels to the Newly
    Converted.* New York: American Anti-Slavery Society, 1855.

———. *Songs of the Free and Hymns of Christian Freedom.* Boston: Isaac Knapp, 1836.

———. *Ten Years of Experience: The 9th Annual Report of the Boston Female Anti-Slavery
    Society.* Boston: Oliver Johnson, 1842.

Child, Lydia Maria. *Anti-Slavery Catechism.* Newburyport, Mass.: Charles Whipple,
    1839.

————. *An Appeal in Favor of That Class of Americans Called Africans.* Boston: Allen and Ticknor, 1833.

————. *The Evils of Slavery and the Cure of Slavery.* Newburyport, Mass.: Charles Whipple, 1839.

————. *The Oasis.* Boston: Allen and Ticknor, 1834.

————. *The Patriarchical Institution, As Described by Members of Its Own Family.* New York: American Anti-Slavery Society, 1860.

The Colonizationist and Journal of Freedom (May 1833). American Colonization Society, 1833.

Constitution of a Society for Abolishing the Slave Trade. With Several Acts of the Legislatures of the States of Massachusetts [etc.]. Providence, R.I.: John Carter, 1789.

Craft, William. *Running a Thousand Miles for Freedom; or, The Escape of William and Ellen Craft from Slavery.* London: W. Tweedie, 1860.

Douglass, Frederick. *My Bondage and My Freedom.* Auburn: Miller, Orton and Mulligan, 1855.

————. *Narrative of the Life of Frederick Douglass.* Boston: The Anti-Slavery Office, 1845.

Eldridge, Eleanor. *Eleanor's Second Book.* Providence, R.I.: B. T. Albro, 1839.

————. *Memoirs.* Providence, R.I.: B. T. Albro, 1842.

A Few Facts respecting the American Colonization Society and the Colony at Liberia. Boston: Perkins and Marvin, 1832.

Garrison, William Lloyd. *An Address Delivered before the Free People of Color.* Boston: Stephen Foster, 1831.

————. *Thoughts on African Colonization.* Boston: Garrison and Knapp, 1832.

Griffiths, Julia, ed. *Autographs for Freedom.* Auburn: Alden, Beardsley [etc.], 1854.

Grimké, Angelina E. "Appeal to the Christian Women of the South" [New York]. From the *Anti-Slavery Examiner* 1, no. 2 (September 1836).

Hatfield, Edwin F. *Freedom's Lyre; or, Psalms, Hymns, and Sacred Songs for the Slave and His Friends.* New York: S. W. Benedict, 1840.

Henson, Josiah. *The Life of Josiah Henson, Formerly a Slave.* Boston: Arthur D. Phelps, 1849.

Higginson, Thomas Wentworth. *The New Revolution: A Speech before the American Anti-Slavery Association.* Boston: R. F. Wallcut, 1857.

Hill, Thomas. *Christmas, and Poems on Slavery.* Cambridge, Mass.: Printed for the Author, 1847.

Jacobs, Harriett. *Incidents in the Life of a Slave Girl.* Edited by L. Maria Child. Boston: Printed for the Author, 1861.

Jones, Thomas H. *The Experience of Thomas H. Jones, Who Was a Slave for Forty-Three Years.* Worcester, Mass.: Henry J. Howland, 1857.

Kemble, Frances Anne. *Journal of a Residence on a Georgian Plantation in 1838–1839.* London: Longman, Green [etc.], 1863.

The Legion of Liberty! and Force of Truth. New York: Published for the American Anti-Slavery Society, 1857.

Lewis, R. B. *Light and Truth . . . Containing the Universal History of the Colored and the Indian Race . . . by a Colored Man.* Boston: Published for a Committee of Colored Gentlemen, 1844.

The Liberator 1, no. 1 (January 1, 1831). William Lloyd Garrison, ed. Boston.

Mann, Horace. *New Dangers to Freedom, and New Duties for Its Defenders.* Boston: Redding and Co., 1850.

May, Samuel. *The Fugitive Slave Law and Its Victims.* New York: American Anti-Slavery Society, 1856.

Memorial to the Congress of the United States on the Subject of Restraining the Increase of Slavery in the New States. . . . Prepared in Pursuance of a Vote of the Inhabitants of Boston. Boston: Sewell Phelps, 1819.

Morse, Jedidiah. *A Discourse Delivered at the African Meeting House in Boston, July 14, 1808, in Grateful Celebration of the Abolition of the African Slave Trade.* Boston: Lincoln and Edmands, 1808.

New England Anti-Slavery Society. *Annual Report.* No. 1. Boston: Garrison and Knapp, 1833.

———. *Constitution.* Boston: Garrison and Knapp, 1832.

Parker, Theodore. *The New Crime against Humanity.* Boston: B. B. Mussey, 1854.

Phillips, Wendell. *Argument . . . in Support of the Petitions for the Removal of Edward Greely Loring from the Office of Judge of Probate.* Boston: J. B. Yerrinton, 1855.

———. "The Murder of Lovejoy." In *Speeches and Lectures.* Boston: James Redpath, 1863.

———. *Review of Webster's Speech on Slavery.* Boston: American Anti-Slavery Society, 1850.

Randolph, Peter. *Sketches of Slave Life.* Boston: Printed for the Author, 1855.

Report of the Proceedings at the Examination of Charles G. Davis, Esq., on a Charge of Aiding and Abetting in the Rescue of a Fugitive Slave. Boston: White and Potter, 1851.

Report of the Twentieth National Anti-Slavery Bazaar. Boston: J. B. Yerrinton, 1854.

Report to the Primary School Committee . . . on the Petition of Sundry Colored Persons for the Abolition of the Schools for Colored Children. Boston: J. H. Eastburn, 1846.

Sons of Africans: An Essay on Freedom . . . by a Member of the African Society in Boston. Boston: For Members of the Society, 1808.

Southwick, Sarah H. *Reminiscences of Early Anti-Slavery Days.* Cambridge, Mass.: Privately Printed, 1893.

Spooner, Lysander. *A Defence for Fugitive Slaves.* Boston: Bela Marsh, 1850.

———. *The Unconstitutionality of Slavery.* Boston: Bela Marsh, 1847.

Stewart, Maria W. *Productions of Mrs. Maria W. Stewart, Presented to the First African Baptist Church & Society.* Boston: Friends of Freedom and Virtue, 1835.

Stowe, Harriet Beecher. *Uncle Tom's Cabin.* Boston: John P. Jewett, 1851.

Stuart, Moses. *Conscience and the Constitution: With Remarks on the Recent Speech of the Hon. Daniel Webster . . . on the Subject of Slavery.* Boston: Crocker and Brewster, 1850.

Sumner, Charles. *The Barbarism of Slavery: A Speech on the Bill for the Admission of Kansas as a Free State.* Washington, D.C.: Thaddeus Hyatt, 1860.

———. *The Crime against Kansas. Speech . . . in the Senate of the United States, May 19, 1856.* New York, 1856.

———. *The Slave Oligarchy and Its Usurpations.* Speech, November 2, 1855, in Faneuil Hall, Boston.

The Suppressed Book about Slavery! New York: Carleton, 1864.

The Trial of Thomas Sims on an Issue of Personal Liberty, on the Claim of James Potter of Georgia. Boston: Wm. S. Damrell, 1851.

Vassa, Gustavus. *The Life of Olaudah Equiano, or Gustavus Vassa, the African.* Boston: Isaac Knapp, 1837.

Walker, David. *Appeal . . . to the Coloured Citizens of the World.* Boston: Printed for the Author, 1829.

Webster, Daniel. *Daniel Webster on Slavery: Extracts from Some of the Speeches . . . Together with the Great Compromise Speech of March 7, 1850.* Boston: William Carter, 1861.

Weld, Theodore, Angelina Grimké Weld, and Sarah Grimké, comps. *American Slavery As It Is: Testimony of a Thousand Witnesses.* New York: American Anti-Slavery Society, 1839.

Weld, Theodore. *The Bible against Slavery.* New York: American Anti-Slavery Society, 1838.

Whittier, John Greenleaf. *Justice and Expediency; or, Slavery Considered with a View to Its Rightful and Effectual Remedy, Abolition.* Haverhill, Mass.: C. P. Thayer, 1833.

———. "Massachusetts to Virginia." In *Lays of My Home, and Other Poems.* Boston: William D. Ticknor, 1843.

[Whittier, John Greenleaf]. *Narrative of James Williams, an American Slave.* New York: Published for the American Anti-Slavery Society, 1838.

✦ CONTRIBUTORS

ADELAIDE M. CROMWELL is Professor Emerita at Boston University and has long been interested in the history of the black community, a subject to which she was first introduced while a Teaching Fellow at Harvard. At Boston University she became the first Director of the African-American Studies Program. She has coedited *Apropos of Africa: Sentiments of American Negro Leaders towards Africa from the 1800s to the 1950s* (1969), and edited *Dynamics of the African/Afro-American Connection from Dependency to Self-Reliance* (1987). She is the author of *An African Victorian Feminist: The Life and Times of Adelaide Smith Casely Hayford, 1868–1960* (1986), and her dissertation, "The Negro Upper Class in Boston: Its Development and Present Social Structure," is soon to be published by the University of Arkansas Press.

ROY E. FINKENBINE is Assistant Professor of History at Hampton University in Virginia. A specialist on the African-American experience before the Civil War, he coedited *The Black Abolitionist Papers, 1830–1865* (1985–92). He is currently working on a book-length study of black abolitionism in antebellum Boston.

WILLIAM E. GIENAPP was educated at Yale University and the University of California, Berkeley, where he received his Ph.D. in 1980. After teaching at the University of California, Berkeley, and the University of Wyoming, he joined the History Department at Harvard University in 1989. He has published a number of essays on antebellum society and politics in books and scholarly journals. He is the author of *The Origins of the Republican Party, 1852–1856* (1987), which was awarded the Avery O. Craven Prize, and is coauthor of a textbook in United States history, *Nation of Nations* (1990). Most recently he has written an essay on "The Antebellum Era" for the *Encyclopedia of American Social History* (1992).

ROBERT L. HALL, Associate Professor of African-American Studies and History at Northeastern University, has held several fellowships, including a Whitney M. Young, Jr., Memorial Fellowship and a Smithsonian Institution postdoctoral fellowship. His articles and essays have appeared in several anthologies, journals, and reference volumes. He is coeditor (with Carol B. Stack) of *Holding on to the Land and the Lord: Kinship, Ritual, Land Tenure and Social Policy in the Rural South* (1982), and has recently completed *"Do, Lord, Remember Me": Religion and the Forging of Afro-American Culture in Florida, 1565–1940*.

JAMES OLIVER HORTON is Professor of History and American Studies at George Washington University and Director of the Afro-American Communities Project of the National Museum of American History at the Smithsonian Institution. He is the coauthor (with Lois E. Horton) of *Black Bostonians: Family Life and Community Struggle in the Antebellum North* (1979). His most recent book is *Free People of Color*, recently published by the Smithsonian Press.

LOIS E. HORTON is Associate Professor of Sociology and American Studies at George Mason University. She is the coauthor of *Black Bostonians: Family Life and Community Struggle in the Antebellum North* (1979) and of *City of Magnificent Intentions: A History of the District of Columbia* (1983).

DONALD M. JACOBS is Professor of History at Northeastern University, where he has taught various courses in African-American history since 1969. He has edited *Antebellum Black Newspapers* (1976), an index to four newspapers published in New York City, and *Index to the American Slave* (1981), a topical index to forty volumes of interviews with ex-slaves initially compiled under the sponsorship of the W.P.A. Federal Writer's Project. Professor Jacobs has lectured frequently and published widely on Boston's antebellum black community. His *While the Cabots Talked to God: Racial Conflict in Antebellum Boston—The Black Struggle, 1825–1861* is forthcoming.

BERNARD F. REILLY, JR., is currently Head of the Curatorial Section of the Library of Congress' Prints and Photographs Division. He received his Master's Degree in Art History from Bryn Mawr College, and has been for several years the Library's specialist in political art and propaganda. His most recent publication is *American Political Prints, 1766 to 1876: A Catalogue of the Collections in the Library of Congress* (1991).

MARILYN RICHARDSON is the author of *Black Women and Religion: An Annotated Bibliography* (1980) and *Maria W. Stewart, America's First Black Woman Political Writer* (1987), as well as numerous essays and articles. She has taught and lectured widely, in this country and abroad, on African-American women's intellectual and cultural history, and is currently at work on a study of the life and career of nineteenth-century African-American sculptor Edmonia Lewis.

JAMES BREWER STEWART is James Wallace Professor of History at Macalester College, St. Paul, Minnesota. In addition to biographies of Joshua Giddings (1970) and Wendell Phillips (1986), he is the author of *Holy Warriors: The Abolitionists and American Slavery* (1976) and, most recently, *William Lloyd Garrison and the Challenge of Emancipation* (1991).

DOROTHY PORTER WESLEY helped build what is today one of the world's largest archives of black history and culture, Howard University's renowned Moorland Spingarn Research Center. The first black to receive a Master's degree in Library Science from Columbia University, she has written or edited many works, including *Early Negro Writings, 1760–1837* (1971) and *Afro-Braziliana: A Working Bibliography* (1978). She is currently editing the writings and speeches of William Cooper Nell, and is also working on a biography of the Remond family of nineteenth-century Salem, Massachusetts.

✧ INDEX